Ancient Hindu Refugees

Studies in Anthropology 6

MOUTON PUBLISHERS
THE HAGUE · PARIS · NEW YORK

Ancient Hindu Refugees

Badaga Social History 1550–1975

PAUL HOCKINGS

University of Illinois, Chicago

MOUTON PUBLISHERS

THE HAGUE · PARIS · NEW YORK

ISBN: 90-279-7798-4

For M.N. SRINIVAS

Men that undertake only one district are much more likely to advance natural knowledge than those who grasp at more than they can possibly be acquainted with; every kingdom, every province should have its own monographer.

GILBERT WHITE
The Natural History of Selborne

Contents

Maps

Diagrams

Tables

Acknowledgements

A work of this size calls forth the assistance of numerous friends and colleagues. First and foremost I have to thank over 700 Badagas who have been interviewed. M. N. Thesingh, an Adikiri, and K. Lakshmanan, B.A., a Gauda, have been my constant guides and companions during the four years (1962–1963, 1969–1970, 1972, 1976–1977) that I have spent with the Badagas. It is a pleasure to record my gratitude to them for their valuable assistance.

Several university colleagues have lent their advice and encouragement over the years, notably Murray B. Emeneau, David G. Mandelbaum, Wilbur Schramm and Anthony Walker. Robert W. Gage was of great assistance with the statistical procedures, and Nina M. Richardson did some of the initial research for Chapter 9. K. Lakshmanan, Reiner Protsch, Alice Streckeisen and Elizabeth Traugott have all helped me with a welter of translation. Br. R. Bächtold and Paul Jenkins, Archivists of the Basel Mission, and the many nameless librarians at the University of California, Berkeley, the British Museum, the Bodleian, la Bibliothèque nationale de France, the Regenstein Library, the Connemara Library in Madras, the Government Epigraphist's Office, Mysore, and the Collector's Office, Ootacamund, have rendered sterling service in the hunt for obscure but relevant publications.

This research has been supported by several different agencies, among them the American Institute of Indian Studies, the Social Science Research Council, the Ford Foundation, the University of

Illinois, Chicago, the Council for Scientific and Industrial Research and the Institute for Communication Research at Stanford University. To each and all, my thanks for the sinews of war.

Lastly I wish to record my gratitude to Mary F. Hockings and Amelia Fessler for their patient typing, editing, retyping and re-editing, and to Arthur Hockings for preparing the diagrams and maps.

University of Illinois, Chicago PAUL HOCKINGS
January, 1979

Introduction

Documentation of Badaga culture spans a period from 1800 to the present, one-and-three-quarter centuries of changing conditions described by several dozen Western observers, none of them trained anthropologists. The Badagas of modern times are also observers, sometimes very astute ones, of their own changing culture; but they too know little about the way of life pursued by their ancestors before 1800.

In the present work I have tried to answer certain questions about change in this South Indian community, drawing on three sources of data: namely what modern Badagas believe about their society, what outside observers have written, and what I have myself seen and heard while living among the Badagas during the past sixteen years. It must be stressed that these sources are distinct and cannot be expected to yield precisely the same conclusions; in part therefore the answers to my questions may vary depending on the source of the evidence.[1]

Structural-functional anthropology is ill-equipped to explain cultural, or for that matter social change. In 1926 Malinowski (p. 132) stated that functional theory 'aims at the explanation of anthropological facts at all levels of development by the part which they play within the integral system of culture, by the manner in which they are related to each other within the system, and by the manner in which this system is related to the physical surroundings.' But what if an anthropological 'fact', such as the conversion of some members of the community to Christianity, does not appear to play any part whatsoever in the integral system of the culture and bears no clear relationship to those other 'facts' which are integral to that culture? How did the Badaga millenarian movement of the 1860s, for instance, contribute to the integration of their culture?—the Badagas got the idea that a god was coming to them to consume the German missionary and perform the miracles of Jesus Christ. He did not come, the sick were not cured, and they were extremely dejected. Yet, important though it then seemed to Badagas, this cult movement neither perceptibly integrated their society nor as it happened disintegrated it; nor did it persist. What then was its function, and how do we explain the movement in structural-functional terms? In fact these and other aspects of cultural change during the period we are to examine cannot be adequately explained by reference to universal hypotheses about the working of society. Instead we must attempt to show how the local problems of the Badagas have given rise to local changes, local compromises, explanations and solutions, all of which have been worked out by the Badagas in their own terms of reference, to suit their special needs. Cultural changes have perhaps been induced by outsiders, but not introduced; the Badagas themselves were responsible for modifications in their way of life since their first contact with aliens.

Only when we have determined the nature of cultural change among Badagas and have essayed some explanation for it will we be ready to make any comparisons with the way other societies have operated and changed. We cannot and should not try to explain their specific case by introducing some extraneous model of society, be it structural-functional or evolutionary, and expecting it to fit the Badaga facts in such a way as to explain them. The present study is therefore a contribution to the ethnography and history of a well-known Indian region rather than an essay in comparative sociology.

The Badagas are clearly aware of how they differ from other communities in this region. Thus only people of their community have Baḍagu as their mother-tongue: only Badaga men and women wear the distinctive dress and carry a characteristic mark on the forehead; only Badagas live in their recognized villages which bear distinctively Badaga place-names; and only Badagas can marry Badaga women and thus belong in a widespread network of kin. As the community is a grouping where potential membership is the same as actual membership, no problem arises in practice over who is a Badaga and who is not.

The coherence of Badaga society was already a *fait accompli* by 1800, and we know of scarcely any villages founded much after that date. In effect their colonization of the Nilgiris and the consolidation of various refugee groups into a unity were events of what we must academically call prehistory. From the Badagas' point of view, however, the advent of a few foreign literati did not nudge their community from the darkness of prehistory into the gloomy light of historicity. Until today nobody, Badaga or otherwise, has published a history of the community: are they therefore still prehistoric?

Be that as it may, their past is of extreme importance to them, and is still vividly recalled in an oral history of legends that are taken for fact and in most cases probably *are* based on actual events. Badaga legends are highly consistent from one part of the district to another and are sufficiently precise about the more insignificant details to convince me that, like the Maori genealogists of old, Badagas have long maintained a fairly accurate interest in their past and in teaching the young about it. Some of these unwritten legends take the form of epic ballads that are sung throughout the night while waiting for someone to die and in other situations where time has to be killed. This should not deceive us into considering the legends mere entertainment: it is true that they are delightfully entertaining to Badagas, but legends are also crucial to their convictions about how the social system should operate. It is these highly credible tales about who settled which village that explain to all the 120,000 Badagas the regulations governing village exogamy and other aspects of the relation between a kinship system, a pattern of settlement and a social hierarchy.

Instead of relegating Badaga legend to the 'folklore' pigeon-hole in the hope that a content analysis will later be made of it, I propose to examine briefly what the legends do and do not cover in Badaga prehistory. Most of them are tales of supposed events, often mysterious, often tragic, events in the lives of personages who lived on the Nilgiri Hills. Stories of love and magic belong to this group. A second group are the political tales, legends of chieftains and East India Company officials who came to the hills for conquest, plunder or sport. A third group are the local legends of Badaga colonization. These three groups deal with varying aspects of Badaga origins. The tales of personal exploits, often amorous in nature, are cited to explain the beginning of particular lineages or villages. The political tales explain the origin of villages and the emergence of various village officials. The accounts of who settled which place now explain the pattern of exogamy within the community. A fourth group of legends embrace all sorts of events and arrangements resulting from Badagas' contact with the Toda, Kota and Kurumba tribes indigenous to the area. These legends validate the whole system of economic interdependence which has held these groups rigidly together for so long and has led to a minimum division of labour within the Badaga community.

Here are the quasi-historical events Badagas have chosen to remember. Yet the one great event of their past not clearly recalled now is the actual flight from Mysore. They are explicit that their ancestors did not all come to the Nilgiris at the same time, and yet many nowadays claim they had been refugees fleeing from Tippu Sultan. So vague are people about their ancestors' flight that the only legend I have located on the subject is obviously coloured by a nineteenth-century borrowing from the Book of Exodus. It tells how the Badagas, hotly pursued by Moslem soldiers, came to the Moyar River, the northern limit of the district, at which point the waters opened up and enabled them to pass. As one might guess the pursuers were all drowned when the river closed up again behind the Badagas.

While it may be true that the latest arrivals were fleeing from Tippu or the four Mysore Wars, the great bulk of the people were refugees from earlier scourges or were purposely brought to settle the hills. The 370 villages in which they now live were virtually all in existence when the British first settled there a mere twenty years after Tippu's death. By the start of the nineteenth century the Badagas were consolidated as a Nilgiri society and their work of colonization completed.

For the early days of their settlement we fortunately have the independent record of an Italian priest who visited the Nilgiris in 1603 and met both Badagas and Todas there. When we couple this fact with the linguistic evidence that Badagas speak an archaic dialect of Kannada, it becomes most likely that the first major wave of refugees arrived as the Moslem hordes were destroying the great Hindu empire of Vijayanagar in Karnataka in 1565. There is no doubt that this was the direction from which the Badagas came. Aside from speaking a dialect of Kannada, their very name means 'northerner', and their adherence to the

Lingayat faith is equally telling, for the sect is almost confined to Karnataka State.

Nor are Badaga legends more informative about the period *before* they left Mysore (i.e., Karnataka). The names of a few ancestral villages there are still recalled, but little else. The Ha:ruva clan are reputed (chiefly by themselves) to have been Brahmins; the Wodea phratry bears the same name as a high-ranking Lingayat subcaste in Mysore. But beyond these sparse ideas and the general impression that the refugees had not been urban we can really say nothing about 'Badaga' social organization prior to their migration from the core area. Perhaps that is the way they would have it, for there is nothing very relevant to their present organization in a pattern of hierarchically organized, multicaste villages—which is what recent Mysore society has been and presumably was in medieval times.

Once settled on the Nilgiri Hills the immigrants encountered challenges that were new to them. Life in Mysore during the Vijayanagar Empire and after its collapse had undoubtedly not been calm; indeed many during those troubled years were induced to desert their native villages. Yet the regulation of their lives had until this exodus been certain: the demands of the religious calendar, of caste regulations, of client and patron, and of the ruling families were well known and omnipresent. One could only escape from that society, if need be, by embracing nature in the guise of an ascetic.

In the Nilgiris the separation of society and nature was perhaps more severe, a stark contrast which would not brook the ambivalence of ascetics wandering beyond the pale of society into the comforting embrace of nature. Here asceticism was unknown and nature anything but warm: she flaunted a dismal climate in which men could easily die from exposure and cold when cut off from their fellows. The jungles surrounding every hamlet were infested with all the dangerous animals known to Mysore, but here they were more proximate, seemingly more numerous and minatory. The small community of Badagas collaborated comfortably with their neighbours, the Todas and Kotas. But around this plural society they all drew a rigid boundary: everything beyond it was the terrifying realm of the wild. It contained not only the obvious terrors, the tigers, panthers, elephants, hyenas, buffaloes, wolves and bears, but the even more frightening and mysterious Kurumba sorcerers, who could turn into any one of these animals. This sharp division between nature and society was expressed in a variety of ways. Clearest perhaps was the ethical prescription that while it is evil for a Badaga to kill people he does good in the eyes of the community *and of God* if he kills Kurumbas or tigers, 'since these are both murderers' (as the matter was once explained to me). The Badagas have always been what would popularly be termed a most superstitious people: they suspect the sorcerer's artifice behind every noise in the jungle, every unexplained malady, every strange event; and they glean a multitude of tidings, both good and bad, from the everyday behaviour of snakes, crows, jackals, cattle and dozens of other creatures and conditions that surround them. A further indication of the gulf between nature and society is perhaps that in their pre-British law the severest Badaga punishment short of hanging was ostracism—expulsion from the village; and this was reserved for the enormity of incest.[2]

For an Indian peasant society the Badagas have some quite extraordinary features, fit to provide enough exotica for any undergraduate anthropology course. This fact has not been duly appreciated by the dozens of ethnologists who have come to the Nilgiris and attached themselves with passion to the colourful Todas or the shy jungle tribes. The Badagas may outwardly appear a much more 'typical' Indian farming community, and yet they do not have true subcastes or multicaste villages; they practise hypergamy *and* hypogamy even across the vegetarian boundary; several forms of polygamy are acceptable; they have a sort of young men's house; marriage is permitted across generation levels to the point where a man may in theory marry a woman *and* her daughter *and* her mother simultaneously, and villages hold a memorial ceremony once in fifty years when every member of a generation has died. Add to these features the frequent ghost exorcisms, fire-walking and occasional massacres, and the anthropologist has much to explain.

THE TERRAIN

The Nilgiri Hills, also known as the Blue Mountains, constitute a massif some 1500 sq. km. in area, situated in southern India at the juncture of the three linguistic and cultural areas of Karnatak, Malabar and Tamilnad. In the British period it was an administrative unit of the Madras Presidency. Today the Nilgiris form one small district of Tamil Nadu, altogether covering 2543 sq. km. This is the homeland of the Badaga, Toda, Kota and Kurumba communities; nowadays numerous other peoples also live there.

The plateau is generally in the elevation of 2000–2500 m., and one peak, Doḍḍabeṭṭa, among the highest in peninsular India, reaches 2633 m. In contrast to this the western quarter of the district averages around 1000 m. in elevation and forms a major portion of the Wainad Plateau. The main indigenous communities there are the Panias, Kurumbas, Nayakas and Chettis, but there are also a few Badagas (Wainad Gaudas) and Kotas.

The escarpment of the Nilgiri Plateau falls away very steeply, and on the eastern edge actually drops some 2000 m. in about 3 km. These slopes always have been covered in dense subtropical jungle which harbours tigers, leopards, buffaloes, elephants, snakes and malarial mosquitoes, and formerly dangerous hunting tribes still feared for their sorcery. Until the advent of the British early in the nineteenth century the three communities living on the summit of these hills—Badagas, Kotas and Todas—were therefore extremely isolated.

The undulating, unevenly wooded downland making up the entire plateau experiences considerable variation in rainfall. The Nilgiris receive from 60 to 160 inches of rain annually, depending on the topographical aspect. Western parts of the plateau rely mainly on the southwest monsoon in July and August; the eastern parts derive much of their rain from the northeastern monsoon in October-December. The average mean daily temperature in the centre of the plateau is around 15°C, while in the Wainad the climate is much hotter and wetter.

For the mildly invigorating qualities of its climate the plateau is therefore scarcely rivalled anywhere in the Asian tropics, and from 1819 British residents began to take advantage of this healthful region. Soon the towns of Coonoor, Kotagiri and Ootacamund (the district headquarters), and the military station at Wellington, took shape and expanded. More recently the town of Gudalur (Gudalu:ru) has grown up in the Wainad, at the foot of the western escarpment. Ootacamund, Coonoor and Gudalur are now the headquarters of the three administrative divisions or *taluks* into which the district was divided by the British.

THE NILGIRI POPULATION

When the British began to settle on the plateau they brought with them a great variety of Tamilian, Mysorean, Malabari and other dependents, including a few Eurasians. With this contact people of southern India began to learn about the strange men, scarcely Hindus, who already inhabited these hills. Immigrants began to find labouring jobs on the tea and coffee plantations from the 1840s; and as they took up this new occupation they brought the indigenous Nilgiri tribes into closer contact with the traditions and practices of South Indian Hinduism. Today the plantations are the main source of the district income, and they attract an ever-increasing number of migrant labourers from elsewhere in South India. In 1971 there were some 370,000 immigrants living in the Nilgiris, three-quarters of the total population (see Appendix 1).

These immigrants belong to a wide range of castes. Normally, while maintaining occupational roles in Nilgiri society, they also attempt to continue the behaviour that distinguishes their own castes and try to keep up social ties with their places of origin. From the point of view of the indigenous communities, however, these caste distinctions are of little importance: immigrants are classified under seven rough headings—Tamilians, Kanarese, Andhras, Malayalis, Christians, Moslems and Europeans (lit. 'Kings'). The indigenous people are aware that there are caste divisions within these categories but are unconcerned with them; and as the immigrants are classed according to mother-tongue or religious creed, they are not even organized by the local residents into a simple caste hierarchy. It is true that Andhras, for example, are thought to have an inferior status; but this is because they are nearly always day-labourers for the Nilgiri farmers. Their low status, like that of other labourers, is determined by their poverty and poor education rather than by their caste affiliations. There *is* a status hierarchy in the Nilgiris, but it has economic and educational determinants that should not be confused with the ritual determinants of caste ranking elsewhere in India.

Except among Todas, Kotas and Europeans, the rate of population growth in this district has been remarkably high: for the decade 1961–1971 it was a staggering 38%, attributable to continuing immigration as well as to the increase of births over deaths. This greatly surpasses the State average of 22.3% and the all-India figure of 24.8%. This demographic factor, together with a high rate of literacy and the fact that plantations make this one of the wealthier districts in southern India, indicates that the Nilgiris are by no means typical of rural India. Indeed they tend towards the upper extreme for the nation in population growth, volume of immigration, natural wealth, and—most important—rural literacy, education, and knowledge of the outside world.

NOTES

1. I have not adopted the popular but chauvinistic approach of seeking out the Aryan, Dravidian or autochthonous elements in Badaga culture—in my view, a sterile and simplistic exercise.
2. An ostracized person would not live in the jungle, but would look for a distant hamlet where he might be accepted; see below, p. 171, 198.

1

The Migration from Mysore

There is no doubt that before they settled in the Nilgiris the homeland of the Badagas lay in the Mysore Plain. Their own legends as well as those of the Kotas are quite explicit on this point, and some of the clans are even able to identify places in Mysore whence their ancestors came. (The most northerly village they now inhabit is still within Karnataka State.)

One need look no further than their language for confirmation of the legend. There are six discernible dialects of Baḍagu that we identify as Standard, Wodea, Kumba:ra-Be:da, Kundena:ḍu, Wainad and Ha:sanu:ru. The dialects are differentiated as much by vocabulary as by phonology and are demonstrably variant forms of Kannada speech. No linguist has ever claimed anything other than this for Baḍagu, since it and the Kannada of Mysore are, with some effort. mutually intelligible.

The very name *Baḍaga* is usually cited as prime evidence of their origin to the north of the Nilgiris: [1] the Kannada word *baḍaga* means 'northerner'. It also has the meaning 'servant'. If we postulate that the name derives from Kannada *baḍaka* instead, then we have the additional meanings 'lean, thin, feeble man' or 'a man who beats and bangs' (Kittel, 1894, 1068–1073). There are thus four possible etymologies for the name. The last two meanings verge on the scurrilous, however, and would hardly have been used by the immigrants in self-identification. One would expect such epithets to be applied to immigrants only by some other group, perhaps the Todas had they known Kannada; yet Todas now call them *ma:v.* But were any of the Badagas ever servants?

There are two small phratries living on the northern edge of the plateau near Si:gu:ru. These are the Kumba:ras ('potters') and the Be:das ('hunters'), both of whom report they came initially to this locality while in the service of the chieftain of Ummattu:r (southern Mysore district). The title of 'servant' might have been applied to both these groups but that would not explain how the entire immigrant community came to be called *Baḍaga.* In this context it is particularly worth noting that most of the immigrants arrived before the Be:das and Kumba:ras, who reached the hills in the seventeenth century; yet in 1603 Finicio was already calling the whole community Badega.[2]

We are thus left with the presumption that Badagas are so called because of their northern origin.[3] The case of the Be:das and Kumba:ras, phratries with the same material culture and social organization as other Badagas and a demonstrable tie with Karnataka, merely bears out the connexion with that state.

The fact that a sizeable minority (over 10,000) of the community is Lingayat further underlines the tie with Mysore, for this religious sect finds nearly all of its followers within Karnataka State, virtually none being in Tamil Nadu apart from these in the Nilgiri region. Some Lingayat Badagas are even able to relate how their ancestors left two now-deserted villages in Mysore and that they were then already converts to Lingayatism (or Virashaivism).

DATING THE MIGRATION

Legends are always inaccurate over dates, if only because they pass from generation to generation without modification of reference to times past. There are, however, various other kinds of evidence which also shed some light on the dating of the migration.

Published Estimates

Several writers well versed in Badaga culture have hazarded guesses as to the dating, based in part on legends they heard. Serious attention should be paid, I feel, to the earlier publications:

Author	*Date of publication*	*Estimate*
John Sullivan	1819 (p. liv)	'about 300 years ago'
Benjamin Ward	1821 (p. lxx)	'about four centuries ago'
Thomas Baber	1830 (p. 315)	'about three centuries ago'
Henry Harkness	1832 (pp. 105–106)	'about six generations ago, during the anarchy which succeeded upon the downfall of the Vijayanagara empire,' i.e., 1565
Harry Congreve	1847 (p. 122)	'six generations ago'
John Ouchterlony	1848 (p. 81)	'3 or 4 centuries ago'
John Dulles	1855 (pp. 458–459)	'six generations since'
George Pope	1879 (p. 346, note)	"Many fled . . . in 1603"
William Stokes	1883b (p. 288)	'about 322 years ago'
Harold Stuart	1893 (p. 243)	'about three centuries ago'
Hanna Rhiem	1900 (p. 498, trans.)	'about three hundred years ago'
Edmond Périé	1933 (p. 97, trans.)	'some 350 years . . . when the Vijayanagar Empire collapsed'
M.K. Belli Gowder	1938–41 (pp. 5–8)	'seven hundred years back', or 'from 1300 to 1600'
N. Kariabettan	1958b (p. 2, trans)	'in the 11th Century'

It will be seen that nearly all of these authorities place the migration in the sixteenth century, which was when the Vijayanagar Empire (covering roughly Karnataka) broke up. M.K. Belli Gowder correctly dismisses the oft-mentioned ravages of Tippu Sultan in the late eighteenth century as a cause of the migration and instead suggests that the Moslem invasion responsible was that of Malik Kafur, the Sultan Ala-ud-din's favourite slave, who laid waste the Hoysala kingdom in 1311.[5] Kariabettan, another modern Badaga writer, presents no evidence whatever for his eleventh century dating and is not to be relied upon.

Linguistic Evidence

No competent study of Badagu has yet been completed, but

Dravidian scholars have noted its similarity to medieval Kannada; in particular the two forms of *r* in Baḍagu phonology reportedly 'had dropped out of use [i.e., in Kannada literature] prior to the time of the grammarian Késirája, who lived in the thirteenth century'.[6]

Other Historical Evidence

Here a small digression on mining is pertinent. Finds of Roman coinage in burials on the Wainad and Nilgiri Plateaux and in numerous hordes on the Coimbatore Plain suggest that traders with Rome were actively exploiting the gold mines of this area. We find no mention of gold from this region, however, in the (A.D. 100) *Periplus of the Erythraean Sea.* That there was indeed a native population in the Nilgiris and Wainad in the first millennium A.D. is indicated by the many cinerary burials of this period on the hilltops; several of these contained Roman coins. There is also a reference in the Tamil classic *Silappadikāram* to the Chera king Seṅguṭṭuvaṉ attending a dance performance at Nīlagiri with his army. (*Silappadikāram:* Vañjikaṇḍam, Kālkōṭ Kadai, xxvi, verses 85, 105, 120. See also Breeks, 1973; Grigg, 1880; Das, 1957; Naik, 1966; Hockings, 1975; Noble, 1976.)

Gold workings in the Nilgiri Wainad undoubtedly date back over many centuries:

> There are miles of country where almost every stone has been turned over, hillsides entirely sluiced away, mountain slopes simply honey-combed with shafts, remains of old aqueducts, adits, and bunds. . . . The existing caste of gold workers are the Korumbars, but they confine themselves entirely to alluvial washings. When questioned they tell you of a tradition . . . of hillmen called Vehdahs, . . . by whose hands all these wonderful quarryings were carried out (Sewell, 1882, 224).

The cinerary burials and Wainad gold mines have nothing to do with Badaga history, aside from a possibility that the chieftains of Ummattu:r fortified Nelliala before coming to the Nilgiri Plateau because they were engaged in gold mining thereabouts.

More relevant perhaps are accounts of old workings on the Nilgiris around Ootacamund and Nañjana:ḍu. Midway between the two places, on One Cairn Hill, there was apparently a medieval town of gold or iron miners, whose mines were protected by a now-disappeared mud fortress. Traces of their town stretch for nearly a kilometer.[7] Badaga traditions do not mention this mining activity, and there is no basis for supposing Badagas initially occupied the hills as prospectors or mine-slaves. If such old quarries (which might even be Roman) have any relevance at all to Badaga history, it can only be because the Ummattu:r chieftains may have turned their eyes towards the Nilgiris in search of the gold that it was rumoured could be found there. In recent times there has been no gold mining in the district, except in the Wainad during the feverish speculation of 1879–1882. (Francis, 1908, 16–19; for other references, see Hockings, 1975, 49–50; 1978, 43–47).

While archaeology is of no assistance, kinship provides a rough guide to the antiquity of the Badaga community. The Gauda headman of Tu:ne:ri, paramount chief of the Badagas, can name nineteen generations of forefathers. His was probably the first village founded (Francis, 1908, 364), and as seventeen of the headmen were resident there the antiquity of Tu:ne:ri must go back to the early seventeenth century if we allow twenty years per generation.[8]

Another line of argument is that all Hindu Badagas are Shaivites (including those who are Virashaivas), whereas in southern Mysore there is now a large minority of Vaishnavites. That sect had its inception there with the conversion of the Mysore kings to Vaishnavism around 1610, which suggests that the Badagas were already in the Nilgiris by that date and so not affected in the way that lowland communities were (Grigg, 1880, 218; Macleane, 1893, 64; Wilks, 1930, vol. I, 52). That some if not all were indeed in the hills was confirmed by Finicio (1603).[9]

It has been argued that the respect shown to Badagas by the Todas and Kotas, for example in customary salutations, indicates that they had entered the Nilgiris while the Mysore kings were still in the ascendancy and had some territorial claims over the Nilgiris (Grigg, 1880, 218; see below, 112). The Be:da phratry, who arrived rather more recently as huntsmen and tax collectors in the retinue of the chieftain of Ummattu:r, 'still call the Mysore chiefs . . . their Kartas or lords' (Grigg, 1880, 268–269, quoting Metz, 1864). Such an argument does not accord with the widespread tale of flight from Moslem oppressors, which depicts some Badagas initially coming to the Nilgiri tribes with caps in hand:

'Because of the trouble that the Mohammedan made for us . . . we have come, making ourselves to escape. This country is yours . . . We are helpless. You must help us.' Such is the Kota version. In response a council of Todas, Kotas and Kurumbas allowed the Badagas to settle provided they paid the now-customary tribute to these tribes (Harkness, 1832, 106–107; Natesa Sastri, 1892, 735–754; Rhiem, 1900, 498; Emeneau, 1946, 257; see below, 113–116). Not all Badagas migrated within a generation or two, and while some may have been fleeing from Moslem soldiers other bands came later for other reasons.

Clearly there were several waves of immigrants brought sometimes by famine conditions, sometimes by Moslem attempts at forcible conversion, sometimes perhaps by a Mysorean policy to colonize the hills. The Kotas are explicit that once a few Badagas had arrived more came over the succeeding years (Belli Gowder, 1938–1941, 3; Emeneau, 1946, 259). The early explorers Ward (1821) and Harkness (1832) both recorded that the people had settled over many years, and Ward added that some had been 'invited' there by the chieftains of Ummattu:r, under whose suzerainty the Nilgiris had rested for a period. This story suggests that some Badagaṣ, refugees from famine rather than Islam, had settled in the hills as part of a pacification programme aimed at increasing the revenue there.[10] Others, it is popularly believed, fled from Moslem rulers who wanted to marry or seduce good-looking Hindu girls. In search of refuge from this threat they travelled up to 150 km. On reaching the hills the women were given facial tattoos and dressed in white cloths (as they still are) to resemble Kota women, while men adopted the Toda shawl for greater warmth: in effect a conscious and lasting attempt was made to resemble the hill tribes and to adopt a tribal model of social organization.[11]

The early pattern of occupancy was one of scattered homesteads in widely separated parts of the plateau. These clusters of small wooden huts grew into lineage centres and so into villages, usually maintaining strict exogamy. Until the advent of *Pax Britannica* in the early nineteenth century, the houses were built around three sides of a plaza, with its open side facing downhill for defensive purposes. Today only De:na:ḍu preserves that plan; the other villages, of which there are about 370, are made up of several parallel lines of houses running along a hillside. Traditionally the senior brother among the patrilineal descendants of the founder was the village headman. Neighbouring villages (*haṭṭi*), though of different lineages and even of different phratries, grouped themselves together for protective purposes under the headmanship of one prominent village into what I have called communes (*u:r*).[12] Thus Ke:ti, for example, is the leading village in Ke:ti commune, which embraces fifteen other contiguous villages, most of them belonging to one maximal lineage *(kuḍumbu)*. The village headman of Ke:ti is also headmen of the commune.

We shall now examine legends of how the various clans and phratries became established on the hills to clarify the history of this intermittent migration. The recently formed Christian phratry will not be considered at this point, as it is more relevant to my discussion of modern cultural change.[13] The Christians, whether Protestant or Catholic, are distributed among fourteen intermarrying clans which trace their descent from six of the Hindu phratries.

The categories in what follows are treated roughly in order of social superiority. This hierarchy is not accepted, however, by Ha:ruvas and their supporters. Since Ha:ruvas come from the Brahma sept they have recently laid claim to an origin as Brahmins and therefore see themselves as superior to Wodeas and all other Badagas. At the other extremity they consider the Kumba:ras and Be:das to rank below Toreas, since the traditional occupations of the former—potters and huntsmen—could place them below Torea servants in the caste ideology of the Indian plains. The great majority of Badagas, in contrast, place Wodeas at the top and Toreas at the bottom of their social hierarchy.

WODEAS

The Badaga Lingayats are generally acknowledged to have been among the later groups to arrive. The contention that they were already Lingayat at that time (Macleane, 1893, 64) provides a meagre clue to the date of their migration, for their sect was founded in the mid-twelfth century and this constitutes a *terminus post quem*. Within sixty years of the founder's death (traditionally A.D. 1168) this egalitarian Hindu faith had spread throughout the Kannada-speaking region. It became the state religion when King Vijaya Wodeyar came to the throne in 1399 and remained so until 1610. However a descendant of his, Raja Wodeyar (who ruled from 1578 to 1617), drove the eponymous Wodeya chieftain Udaiya Raya of Ummattu:r up into the Nilgiris and captured his

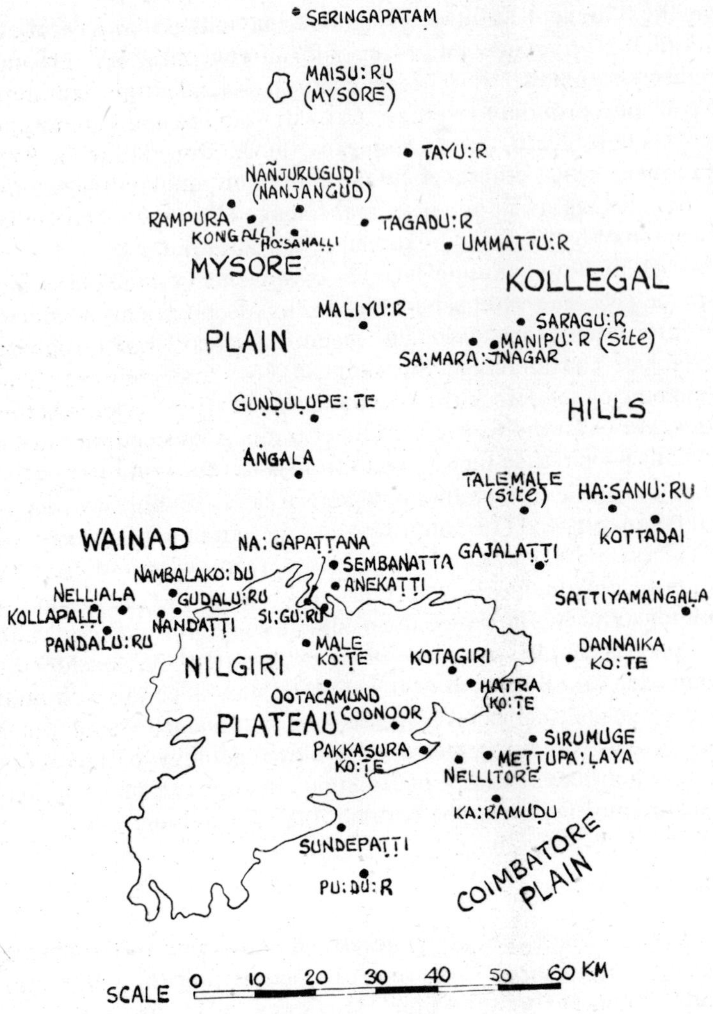

Map 1. Map to illustrate the migrations of the Badagas.

realm in 1613. Badaga Wodeas now claim to have come with this man and to be descended through him from the royal house of Mysore (Grigg, 1880, 218, 220, 225; Natesa Sastri, 1892, 754–755; Rice 1897, vol. II, 296, 364; Hayavadana Rao, 1930, vol. V, 862). Some came from the Lingayat monastery at Aṅgala and first settled at a subsequently deserted village called Ukkupalle, near

Cinna Kunnu:r (on the northern edge of the Nilgiris). Traditionally these were the Wodeas of Maduve clan, who had previously been *Jaṅgama* priests. When other Wodeas arrived from Tagadu:r they formed a separate clan called Ko:ve:ru, as they were of that sept. Yet other Wodeas came to the Nilgiris from a monastery at Saragu:r, and since that was a village in the former Hindu kingdom of Koṅgu this particular clan of Wodeas have ever since been nicknamed Koṅgaru ('Koṅgu people') by other Badagas. Later on, when Tippu's troops seized the Nilgiri fortress of Male Ko:ṭe, an Ummattu:r outpost, the Wodeas who were dependent on its chiefs were reportedly left destitute, but they remained in the hills.[14]

The relative recency of this Wodea migration derives some support from Badagu dialectology. As I have mentioned, there are six dialects of the language, three of these seemingly distinctive by reason of geography: speakers living in the Kundena:ḍu, Ha:sanu:ru and Wainad areas used to be quite isolated from the rest of the community, a situation that would encourage the growth of separate dialects in the course of several centuries. The distinction of Wodea and of Kumba:ra-Be:da from Standard Badagu cannot, however, be explained in geographic terms, for the Wodeas, Kumba:ras and Be:das live in and beside villages where Standard Badagu is spoken. Only by postulating that these three groups arrived speaking a more modern form of Kannada than the earlier immigrants who spoke a medieval variety can we account for this disparity. Their own legend fully bears out this hypothesis: they claim to have all come to the hills together in the service of an Ummattu:r chieftain when the Gaudas had already arrived, the Wodeas as Lingayat priests, the Kumba:ras as palace servants, the Be:das as huntsmen and tribute collectors. Not only do the Wodeas claim descent from the royal house, however (Metz, 1864, 48–49; Grigg, 1880, 220; Natesa Sastri, 1892, 754–755): the Kumba:ras also maintain they 'belonged to' the ruling family of Chamaraj Wodeya, though they probably had a servile rather than a kin relationship, particularly as this phratry is Shaivite (not Lingayat), while the royal family has been Vaishnavite since 1610. The fact that the Wodeas have a dialect distinct from Kumba:ra-Be:da is to be explained by class distinctions. As in many parts of India the orthodox, vegetarian, high-status Woderu priests spoke differently from the low status, meat-eating servants of the chieftain for the two did not intermarry or mix socially.

KOṄGARU

Although this name is applied to many Wodeas and is also an epithet for a stupid fellow, *Koṅgaru* literally means 'people from the plains', i.e., from the medieval kingdom of Koṅgu.

There are several villages of Badagas called Koṅgaru; for this is also the name of a high-ranking clan, aside from other usages of the word. Reputedly the Koṅgaru of Ha:llaṭṭi were descended from concubines in the service of the chieftain of Male Ko:ṭe. Other Koṅgaru were Lingayats who, like the Adikiris, came from Saragu:r in southern Mysore. Their traditional occupation, up to 1900, was said to have been temple custodians and priests (Rhiem, 1900, 499–500). They are usually considered descendants of a Wodea man and a Gauda woman. Again we encounter the tale of some Koṅgaru having fallen away from their principles and been denied *liṅgas* because one of their youths ate meat to please a low-caste girl whom he loved (Metz, 1864, 49–50; Grigg, 1880, 221; Tignous, 1911, 117).

HA:RUVAS

This clan's name is the Kannada word for Brahmin (Kittel, 1894, 1650; Burrow and Emeneau, 1961, 273). Thurston's (1909, vol. I, 73) alternative suggestion that it means 'jumper' and refers to their method of fire-walking is unconvincing. Most phratries walk ceremonially on fire. Now a distinct clan, Ha:ruvas press the claim to Brahmin origin although local legend does not entirely support this. Instead it is generally believed that Ha:ruvas were a group of priests (of a sept called Brahma) who accompanied some Gaudas, though not the earliest group, when they entered the hills.[16] They came from Ho:sahaḷḷi-Girubeṭṭa (or perhaps Haććini Na:ga-paṭṭana), and as they brought no women with them were unable to maintain the endogamy that is so typical of Brahmins.[17] At first they intermarried with the Gaudas of Kasturi clan—itself believed descended from fallen-away Brahmins—and in later years Ha:ru-vas also married Koṅgaru, Adikiris and Kanakkas. Up till the eighteenth century the shortage of marriageable women, which had prompted fraternal polyandry, was somewhat aggravated by the practice of *sati* among Ha:ruva, Gauda and perhaps Torea widows. This custom came to an end, probably under Moslem influence, before the British reached the hills, and Badaga widows have remarried freely ever since, while polyandry has disappeared.[18]

Although Ha:ruvas may marry Gaudas there is a legend that the two groups were originally 'brothers' and thus agnates. When these people first came to the hills, the tale goes, they were wandering through a forest in search of food. At last they found some flesh and many ate it; those abstaining became Ha:ruvas, priests to the rest (Belli Gowder, 1923–1941, 45; Benbow, 1930, 9, 11). Another legend on the same theme relates that the founders of Me:lu:ru Hosa:ṭṭi, the first Ha:ruva village, were two brothers named Uliajjan and Guruajjan. The elder of the pair chose at one time to eat flesh, and when Guruajjan discovered this he went away to found the villages of Taṅga:ḍu and Ha:lakore. Uliajjan became an outcast whose descendants have been absorbed into various Gauda villages (Jogi Gowder, no date, 1–2). The sequence in which the Ha:ruva villages were founded is shown in Diagram 1.

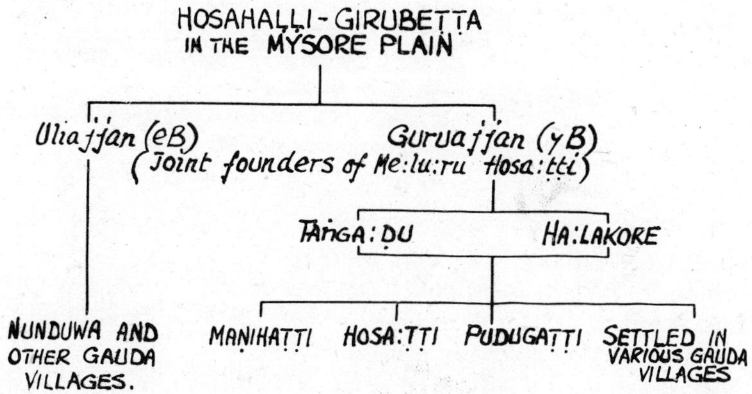

Diagram 1. The descent of the Ha:ruvas.

ADIKIRIS

This clan recall that their Virashaiva ancestors came in a large group from Mallikaḷḷi via Saragu:r (southern Mysore) and settled at Nellitore, a place sacred to them on the plains directly below

Pakkasu:ra Ko:ṭe. It was here that the Virashaiva saint Kariabeṭṭa Raya had earlier drowned himself. Until recently the ruins of their houses were visible; the pool where he drowned still is. After half a century there the community was nearly exterminated by malaria, and six surviving men moved onto the plateau. After staying for a while at Tu:du:ru and Tadasimarahaṭṭi they founded the first five of the sixteen villages which Adikiris still inhabit (Francis, 1908, 316). The sequence of their foundation is shown in Diagram 2. The founder of Adigaraṭṭi was then made a magistrate (*adikari*) by a power nominally ruling over the Nilgiris.

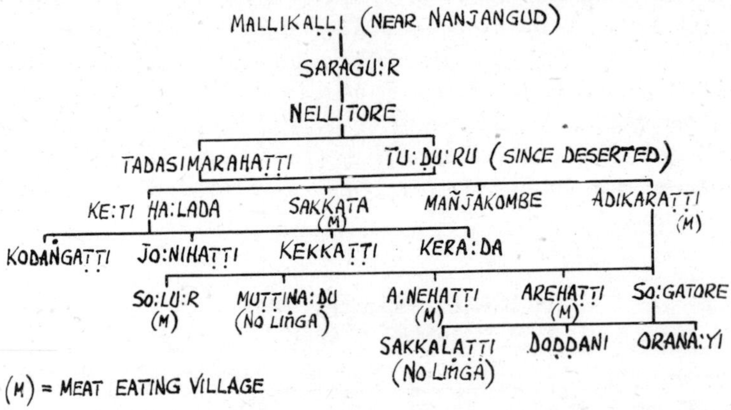

Diagram 2. The descent of the Adikiris.

The Wodea families already living there could not believe that the Adikiris were truly Lingayats (perhaps because they were of an ancient Virashaiva sect) and therefore refused marriage with them. It was this exclusiveness which drove the Adikiris, Kaṇakkas and Kaggusis into marrying non-Lingayats.

Certain of the villages (marked by *M* in the diagram) are now non-vegetarian. There are legendary explanations for this phenomenon. Just as in the story of the founding of Me:lu:ru Hosa:ṭṭi, it is said that Saṅga, the founder and headman of Adigaraṭṭi, was starving and hence began to shoot birds and eat them.[19] His younger brother Liṅga was so incensed that he went away and founded another village, So:gatore. In Adigaraṭṭi and several other villages the founding Adikiris were obliged to marry Gauda women who retained their own customs, including the eating of meat. The descendants of one who married a Sholaga tribeswoman at So:lu:ru became Gaudas too. In Sakkata the Adikiri was obliged to marry a Torea woman, who also could not become a vegetarian.[20] Their offspring married Gaudas and followed Gauda customs, it is said, but their recent descendants in that village are Toreas.

Since that time there has been a clan of meat-eating Adikiris who are not permitted to wear the *liṅga* and who only intermarry with Gaudas. To all intents and purposes their four villages are now Gauda. More recently two villages, Muttina:ḍu and Sakkalaṭṭi, have stopped wearing the *liṅga* but retained vegetarianism, and they are still treated as Adikiris for marriage purposes.

KAṆAKKAS

Prior to 1819 Kaṇakkas were the only literate people in the hills. They were brought there more recently than all other Badagas by the commander of Hatra Ko:ṭe to keep the village accounts; but they also acquired a reputation as therapists and exorcists. While they speak Badagu today, their early writings, still preserved on about 500 palm leaves in Ka:ṭe:ri and Hajju:r, are in an antiquated script of Tamil. Some of the texts are devotional in character, but many are the exercises of tyro scribes. It is rumoured that in origin Kaṇakkas were Gaundans from the Coimbatore Plain who had been converted to Lingayatism before coming to the Nilgiris. *Kaṇakkan* is in fact the name of a Tamilian accounting caste, a few of whom are Lingayats (Thurston, 1909, vol. III, 150). These in the Nilgiris would seem to have been for a while under Tamilian superiors stationed at Dannaika Ko:ṭe or nearby Kallantore.[21]

The first Kaṅakka village to be founded was Ka:ṭe:ri. The man

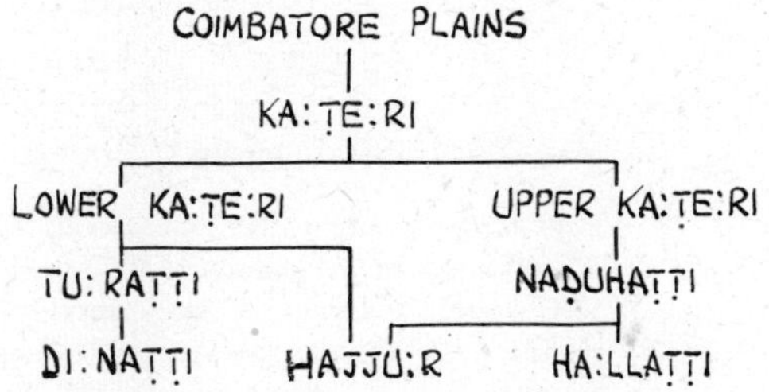

Diagram 3. The descent of the Kanakkas.

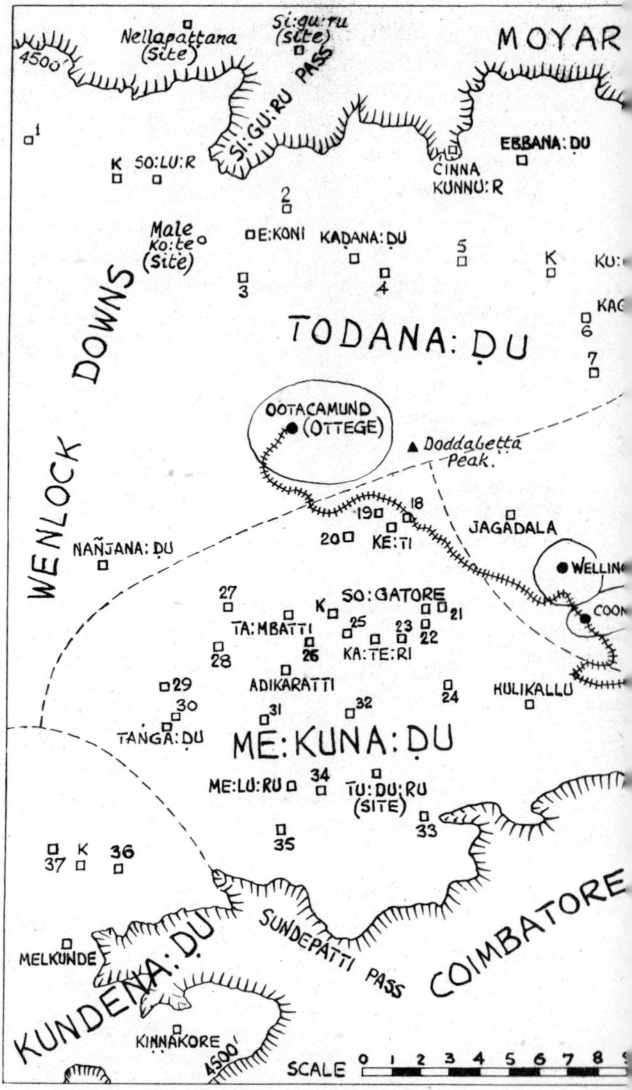

Map 2. The Nilgiri Plateau

Key: K Kota villages; 19 Aććanakal; 28 Ba:kola; 10 Beragan 37 Bikkaṭṭi; 15 Da:bakambe; 31 De:vaso:le (bazaar); 8 Dimbaṭṭ 17 Eḍapaḷḷi; 6 Hajju:r; 30 Ha:lakore; 4 Ha:laṭṭi; 7 Honatale; 1 Hulla:ḍa; 2 Hullaṭi; 3 Kallaṭṭi; 9 Kappaṭṭi; 20 Kereha:da; 3 Koḍe:ru; 33 Kolekombe (bazaar); 29 Manihaṭṭi; 35 Manja kombe; 36 Manju:ru; 34 Me:lu:ru Hosa:ṭṭi; 26 Muttina:ḍu; 1

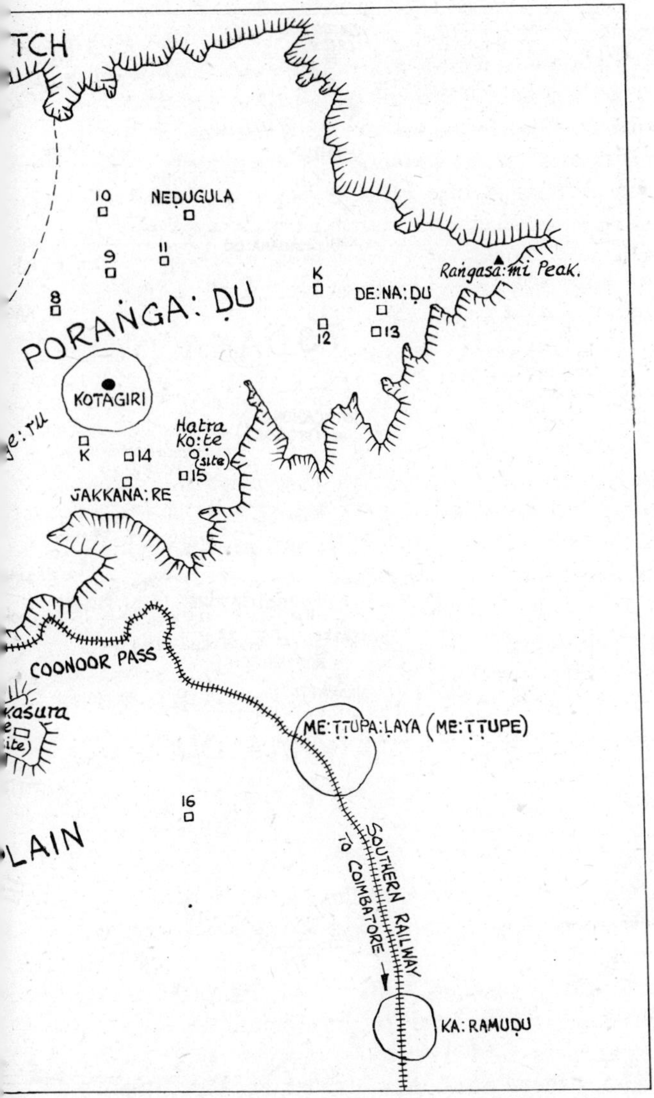

Nellitore; 21 Ne:rikambe; 27 Nunduwa; 1 O:nṯöw (Toda temple); 25 O:ranayi; 22 Sakkalaṭṭi: 14 Sakkata; 24 Se:las (bazaar); 13 So:lu:rmaṭṭa (bazaar); 11 Suḷḷigu:ḍu; 12 Tumbimale; 5 Tu:ne:ri; 23 Tu:raṭṭi; Villages that head COMMUNES are marked on the map by name; as also are modern TOWNS. Old *fortresses* are indicated in italics.

who started it was Jambuliṅgayya, secretary of the chieftain Bijjanarasu. He had two wives whose descendants occupied upper and lower Ka:ṭe:ri; and later generations from each of these areas founded other Kaṇakka villages, as indicated in Diagram 3.

Both the Kaṇakkas and the Adikiris began to intermarry with Ha:ruvas soon after settling in the hills; Adikiris also married Gauda women, while Kaṇakkas intermarried with Kaggusis and Koṅgaru. This step was forced on these Lingayat clans by a shortage of girls in their own community at that time: properly they should only have married other Lingayats.

KAGGUSIS

These people originated in Tagadu:r, from whose monastery they left as a band of refugee *Jaṅgamas* or monks; one clan of Wodeas had an identical origin. They first settled at the village of Kaggusi, and there left off wearing *liṅgas* because of the necessity to marry with Gauda women and the pollution of their *liṅgas* that would follow as a consequence. Later they spread out to establish or occupy another six villages; but on the occasion of a severe drought some retreated from Kaggusi to the lowlands and founded a village near Ha:sanu:ru, where they still live.

GAUDAS

Not only are there ten times as many Gaudas as members of any other phratry: their legendary history is proportionately more complex than any other.

Three facts are relevant to a dating of their arrival. The Gaudas themselves claim to have reached the Nilgiris before any other group, and the Lingayats and Ha:ruvas confirm that their ancestors found Gaudas there when they arrived. Secondly, their paramount chief, living at Tu:ne:ri, can number nineteen generations of ancestors, which would put their arrival back to the sixteenth if not the fifteenth century. Thirdly, we may recall that Finicio saw Badagas at the village of Melcuntaõ in 1603. Assuming this was the Gauda village of Me:lkunda—and no other village offers a closer identification than this—we deduce that at least a part of the Gauda population had immigrated a century or two before the Kumba:ra, Be:da and various Lingayat groupings.

This accords with a Badaga tradition that the very first group of migrants were three brothers of the Kasturi sept or clan, who came from Ka:rahaḷḷi and settled in the Ke:ti Valley, Kundena:ḍu and Ćinna Kunnu:r.[22] Later the eastern half of the plateau was settled by seven brothers, their sister and her husband. Later still yet other Gaudas went to Todana:ḍu and Me:kuna:ḍu divisions.

It is not impossible that the Kasturi Gaudas had the same Virashaiva origins as the Adikiris or Wodeas. Some hold the belief that they were at first vegetarians and Lingayats. As so often happened in legendary times a Kasturi tasted meat, for which his daughter made him give up his *liṅga* to her husband, a Lingayat Adikiri. Thereafter the Kasturis intermarried mainly with other Gaudas.[23] A comparable story maintains that some Gaudas of Neḍugula are descended from 'Koṅgaru', Wodeas of Selandi clan, after some fell away from their phratry's principles and were denied *liṅgas* when one of their youths ate meat to please a Gauda girl whom he loved.[24]

Kasturi ('musk'), we may note, is also the name of a sept among the Kanarese Okkaligas. (Thurston, 1909, Vol, 1, 75, and Vol, III, 256; see below, p. 79). This too reflects the Gaudas' origin, (especially as many Badagas at the 1891 census enumeration gave their caste as Okkaliga).[25] Today, few Badagas agree to a connexion with the Okkaliga community, conceivably because there are now hundreds of poor Okkaligas on the Nilgiri Plateau, recent immigrants who work as labourers and with whom Badagas do not associate except as employers and landlords. A more likely explanation, however, is that enumerators in 1891 failed to discover that *okkaliga* merely means 'permanent resident' in Baḍagu and is not a clan or caste designation among them. Nonetheless there are informants in the Nilgiris and Ha:sanu:ru who agree to an origin among the Okkaligas of Mysore; and both communities share the same rather distinctive personal names.

There is an ancient settlement of Okkaligas in the Coimbatore Plain, for example at the village of Nellitore from which the Adikiris ascended the Nilgiri slopes. The legend of how they got to Nellitore is worth recounting.

> ...Tippu Sultan wanted to marry an Okkaliga bride. The Okkaligas consented to it at first due to fear of the fanatic king, but subsequently decided to run away. So they dressed up a dog

> like a bride, left it in the house and then ran away towards the south by the night. They were, it seems, chased by the Muslim troops but luckily there were floods in the river as soon as the Okkaligas crossed it. The Muslim troops finding it not possible to cross the river, returned to Mysore and the Okkaligas peacefully settled in the forest marginal areas (Nambiar & Bharathi, 1965, 3).

What is remarkable is that precisely the same legend, admittedly embellished with details from the Book of Exodus (xiv. 21–30), has been offered by Badagas both from the Nilgiris and Ha:sanu:ru to account for their flight from Mysore:

> About three hundred years ago one of the Moslem kings desired one of their daughters, and when she refused marriage he threatened to burn and plunder their villages. But the pride of the people was greater than their fear. To find one of their daughters in the harem of a Moslem dog was something that could not be tolerated. . . ; and so, incited by their priests, they decided to escape. . . . With women, children, livestock, and all their cherished possessions, they swiftly escaped to the bank of a river which divided the wild tribes of the Nilgiris from the province of the sultan. . . a part of the army was hastily sent after the fleeing people, who were by that time near the banks of the Mayar, which formed the boundary. But how could they cross over? Strange to say, . . . the river parted and the followers reached the bank on the other side, while the disciples of the Prophet were suddenly swallowed up by the closing waters (trans. from Rhiem, 1900, 498).

As Nellitore is at the foot of the Nilgiri escarpment one is again led to suppose that some Badaga Gaudas derived from this Okkaliga caste. The probability is indeed high, for most Gaudas admit that they came from farming communities in the plains of Southern Mysore, where Okkaligas are today the dominant farming castes.

Another important Gauda clan is called Maduve ('marriage') (also the name of a sept; see Diagram 4. Thurston, 1909, Vol. IV, 292). It was founded by a family of seven brothers led by one Aććini, who fled from Talemale with a sister who was in danger of being ravished by a Moslem chieftain there (Belli Gowder, 1923–1941, 1; Miles, 1951, 69). 'Each of these brothers is said to

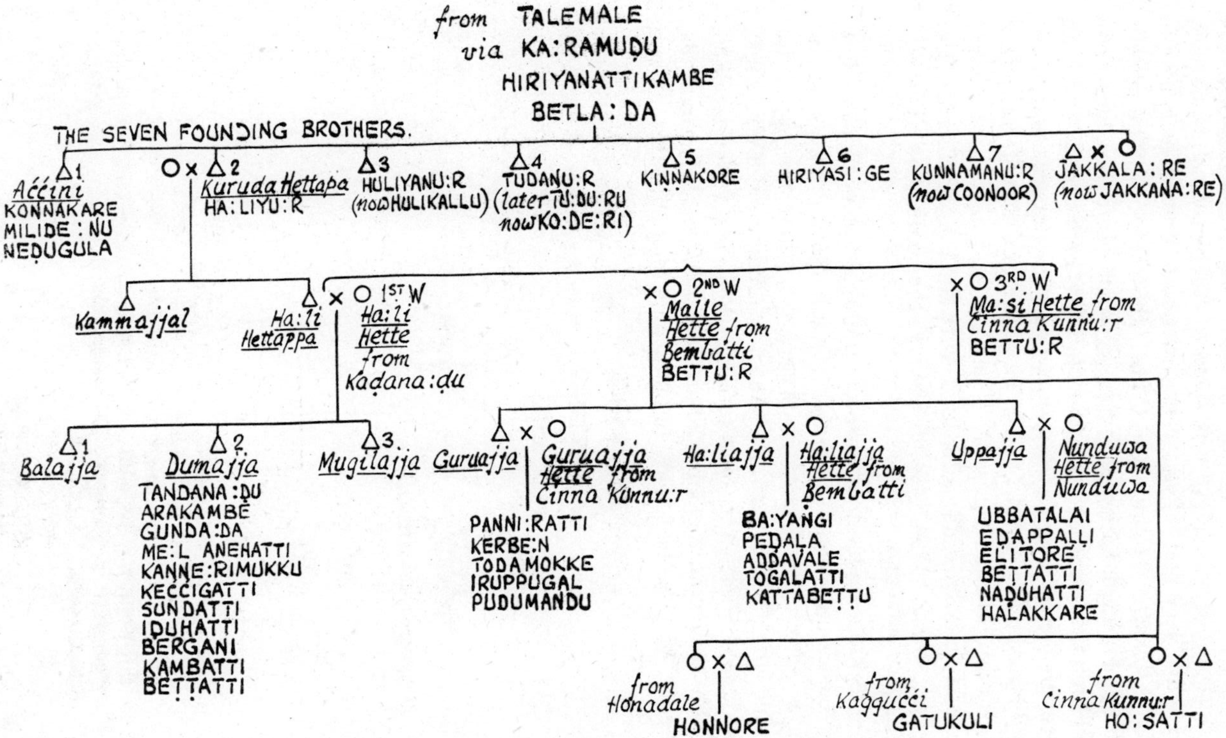

Diagram 4. The descent of the Maduve clan of Gaudas. (Ancestors indicated in italics, villages in capital letters).

have built a house for himself and his family in different parts of the hills, and new villages were constructed by their descendants; so that the Badagas of this class are now scattered over all the tract...' (except Todana:ḍu) (Metz, 1864, 56–57). The sister's husband founded Jakkane:ri village, which thereafter had close affinal relations with the Maduve clan. As these people had been subject to the chieftain of Hatra Ko:ṭe, the clan was sometimes called Hatra (Metz, 1864, 56–57). That chieftain also maintained a palace north of the Nilgiris, at Talemale, and in the last century people of that area still interdined with these particular Badaga Gaudas (Metz, 1864, 47–48. Today the palace is in ruins; Nicholson, 1892, 426).

Nineteenth century literature on Badagas refers to numerous other 'castes' and 'sects', but some of these are in reality clans or lineages within the Gauda phratry, and others are septs; for example, the Duma, Kunaja, Ma:ri, Ma:nika and Beḷḷi (Metz, 1864, 57–60; Shortt and Ouchterlony, 1868, 58–59; Grigg, 1880, 221–222; Macleane, 1893, 64; Thurston, 1909, Vol. 1, 75; on septs, see below, 78–80). The total number of named lineages among

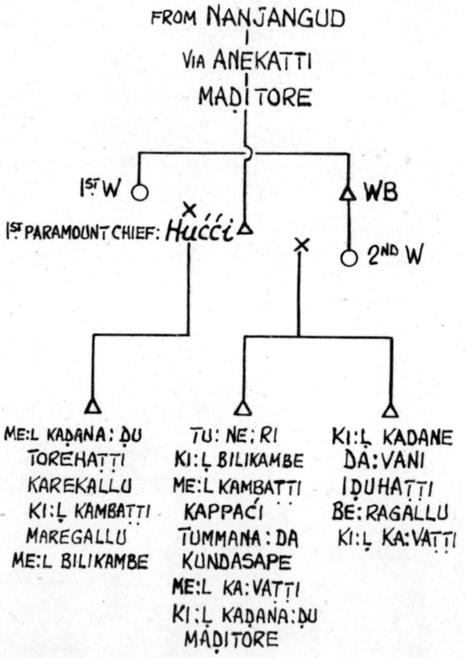

Diagram 5. The villages of Ma:ri clan of Gaudas.

the Gaudas must approach a hundred; some have legends of origin, too, as do the clans. Ma:ri clan, for instance, to which the paramount chief belongs, migrated from villages near the great temple of Nanjangud bearing an image of the goddess Ma:ri;[26] the Nilgiri villages founded by them are listed in Diagram 5. The Beḷḷi clan, supposedly descended from silversmiths *(beḷḷi,* 'silver'), may be an example of the various lineages started by itinerant tradesmen: usually these can intermarry with any other Gauda lineage or clan. The Selandi sept preserves a vestige of totemism in that the members may not kill spiders *(selandi).*

On the fringes of the plateau one can find quite atypical marriage arrangements. In the southern village of Kiṇṇakore, for example, Gaudas have a lineage intermarrying with Gaudas of the other Kundena:ḍu villages and also with Gaudas and Kanarese Okkaligas living at the foot of the hills in Attapaḍi and Pu:du:r.[27] In eight villages around Ha:sanu:ru, forty kilometres northeast of the plateau, there live about 800 Badagas forming three phratries. They generally find it more convenient now to intermarry among their neighbours (observing clan and sept exogamy) than make the long journey to the Nilgiris in search of spouses.

WAINAD GAUDAS

There is no doubt that the small community of Wainad Gaudas (totalling 951 in 1970) is descended from Badaga Gaudas. Apart from their own assertion of it and their continuing intermarriage with Gaudas of Todana:ḍu, certain aspects of their material culture underline the connection: similar nose, ear, finger and ankle ornaments are worn by both communities; they have the same typically Badaga cuisine; and their two dialects are very similar. Furthermore, it is recognized that the people of Nandaṭṭi (in the Wainad), for instance, are agnates to the people of Nunduwa and Ta:mbaṭṭi (in the Nilgiris), although the Nandaṭṭi Gaudas had settled at Gudalu:ru in the Wainad prior to founding Nandaṭṭi twelve generations ago.[28] Once every few years a party of Wainad Gaudas attends the chariot-dragging festival in Nunduwa as a mark of their relationship. Su:lu:ru (in Todana:ḍu) has a similar link with each of the eight Wainad Villages.

The migration down into the Wainad occurred at least two

centuries ago and was prompted by shortage of land around some Nilgiri villages and by the acute poverty of farm-land in the Kundena:ḍu area. The Mauntadan Chettis amongst whom the Wainad Gaudas settled came originally from the same Koṅgu country which had been the homeland of many Gaudas. Unlike the Gaudas, however, these Chettis settled directly in the Wainad in medieval times, without pausing first on the Nilgiri Plateau. So close is the association between Mauntadan Chettis and the Todana:ḍu Badagas that these two communities also used to exchange visits on the occasion of some festivals and funerals. Certain Chettis living in the Muḍumalai National Park of the Wainad are called Huliala Gaudas: they went there from the nearby Badaga village of Hullaṭṭi, on the Nilgiris, but now intermarry only with Mauntadan Chettis. The Wainad Gaudas otherwise do not marry with these Chettis although they did so in previous centuries. The two communities interdine and attend each other's ceremonies.

BADAGAS OF HA:SANU:RU

Some seven kilometres east of Ha:sanu:ru in the Biligiri Rangan Hills are seven Badaga villages; an eighth lies in Karnataka, thirteen kilometres to the north of that town. These villages are in jungle clearings at an elevation of a thousand metres and were established there at least two centuries ago by Badagas who were forced out of the northern part of the Nilgiris by a famine.[29] The Ha:sanu:ru Gaudas are explicit that they had been Gangadikara Gaudas in Mysore; and they retain precisely the same stories about their flight as are still recounted in the Nilgiris (see above, particularly note 10; Thurston, 1909, Vol, I, 75, and Vol, III, 256; Nambiar, Bharathi, 1965, 3).

TOREAS

No legend of a separate origin has been collected from the Toreas. There is a caste of Kannada-speaking Toreas now living in Coimbatore, Salem and Mysore Districts, with whom Badaga Toreas occasionally arrange marriages; but since the dialects of the two differ the practice is most uncommon. Those found in the plains are said to have once been fishermen and palanquin bearers and are now cultivators, contractors, petty tradesmen and police constables (Thurston, 1909, Vol. VII, 176). Although it is possible that certain Toreas of this caste went to the Nilgiris, at first as palanquin bearers, their occupations in the hills have been cultivators, messengers for the commune headmen and till the mid-nineteenth century weavers; and they were reportedly menials and watchmen for ancestral Badagas even in Mysore (Harkness, 1832, 112; Metz, 1864, 59–60). A common origin for some Nilgiri and lowland Toreas is possible as both belong to the Na:ga and Beḷḷi septs, among several others. (as do the A:lu Kurumbas).

Those of the Nilgiris claim their origin in the Gauda phratry and explain their status as the descendants of sons deputed to do certain chores. The Gaudas and Ha:ruvas still call them 'sons,' an ambiguous term that may either refer to their servile status or suggest they are descended from the unsanctioned unions of Gaudas (possibly with non-Gaudas). One astute nineteenth-century observer said of them: '... they are prohibited from intermarrying with the other or high-caste Badagas, as long as they are sons to them. ...'[30]

BE:DAS, KUMBA:RAS AND HILL FORTS

There are two other small phratries, the Be:das and Kumba:ras, whose origins can best be explored in the context of the hill fortresses where they lived. These forts were outposts of Ummattu:r, a small town in southern Mysore which was tributary to the kings of Vijayanagar in the fifteenth and sixteenth centuries, and then to the kings of Mysore in the seventeenth and early eighteenth centuries.

> In 1610 one of these, king Rája Wodeyar (Udaiyar) of Mysore, drove out of Seringapatam the Vijayanagar general; and two years later he was granted that place and the Ummattúr country near it by the then nominal king of Vijayanagar... Thenceforth the kings of Mysore became rulers of the Wynaad and titular possessors of the Nilgiri hills, and the latter were apparently under the immediate rule of dependents of theirs called the Udaiyars or Rájas of Ummattúr... (Hayavadana Rao, 1908, 93; cf. Rice, 1897, vol. I, 357, 364; Rea, 1910, 115; Hayavadana Rao, 1930, vol. V, 861–862).

As a result of this political situation the plateau became involved in a long military struggle mainly for control of tribute collection from the Badagas. Tribute was then levied mostly in the form of grain, which Todas did not produce and which Kotas had scarcely any of. This struggle, sometimes between Moslems and Hindus, prompted the construction or capture of certain fortresses, both to terrorize the Badagas and to guard the passes around the foot of and up into the Nilgiris. The extraordinary visibility, even as far as Seringapatam, allowed commanders of the hill garrisons to detect obvious military manoeuvres in the plains and often guided them to cross the plateau and cut the enemy troops off as they came round the foot of its escarpments.

As an example of such movements a Kota historian has described how Haidar Ali attacked the 'king of Madurai', Virapandya Devan, in Dannaika Ko:ṭe in 1759 but was forced to retreat. The 'king' then sent an army into the Nilgiris to suppress Haidar's hill forts there, and this resulted in a battle at the commune of Tu:ḍu:ru (1760) in which Virapandya lost three thousand troops and Haidar emerged victorious to capture Dannaika Ko:ṭe for himself, while the beaten troops fled to Salem District.[31] Tu:ḍu:ru has since been deserted, the remnants of its nineteen-village population having settled in the nearby village of Ko:ḍe:ru.

It was during the sixteenth or seventeenth century that two important fortresses were erected, Male Ko:ṭe on the northern rim of the plateau and Hatra Ko:ṭe on the east side (reputedly founded in 1578). A third fort, Pakkasu:ra Ko:ṭe, had been built somewhat earlier on the Hulikal Drug mountain-top, to the south-east (Harkness, 1832, 107; Francis, 1908, 329. See Map 2 above, 24–25). Tradition has it that an Ummattu:r chieftain established altogether nine fortified settlements in the area, and the ruins of the remaining half-dozen are indeed still to be seen below the slopes—for example, at Ma:vanhaḷḷa; also he encouraged 350 Badaga families to migrate into the hills, doubtless scattering them in every village. (Belli Gowder, 1923–1941, 104, and 1938–1941, 8). The Kotas still recall how Umat Arč (the Lord of Ummattu:r) and Udr Arč (the Lord Udaiya Raya) came to Ke:ti 'to collect the revenue money and built houses and lived there with wife and children' (Emeneau, 1946, 259). In Badaga tradition Bijjanarasu, son of the Ummattu:r chieftain, possibly founded Ke:ti and there collected an annual tribute of five hundred gold coins from all of Me:kuna:ḍu. Another chieftain was so incensed when the unfortunate paramount chief Tonda did not pay the tribute within a week that, according to legend, 'the Rajah took his head and put it at the front door and the body was put at the back door and the arms and feet were bound on poles near the way' (Metz, 1864, 110). The efforts of the headman of Ba:kola in collecting a record amount of tribute for these chieftains were rewarded with the gift of a silver ring (still in his family) and the title of *parpati,* in Karnataka a revenue officer.[32] That *parpati* (since 1897 a disputed position) is the divisional headman for Me:kuna:ḍu. It was probably the chieftains or commanders of the three hill forts who in the seventeenth century divided the plateau into three areas of influence *(na:ḍu)* for tribute-gathering purposes: Male Ko:ṭe commanded Todana:ḍu, Hatra Ko:ṭe Poraṅga:ḍu, and Pakkasu:ra Ko:ṭe Me:kuna:ḍu. '. . . In consequence of disputes between the Burghers [Badagas] and Kothers [Kotas] regarding their respective boundaries, a general settlement of their lands took place under the auspices of the three chiefs, when the lines of demarcation were definitively fixed; and. . .ever since, up to the present time, no disputes about them have ever been known to occur.'[33] The fourth division, Kundena:ḍu, was not recognized as one until after 1830 and moreover was so poor until this century that it would have yielded scant tribute, having little cultivation and a proverbial poverty that often forced Kundena:ḍu people to subsist on bamboo shoots or even sell their children into servitude elsewhere on the plateau.[34]

The Lingayat chieftains at both Male Ko:ṭe and Hatra Ko:ṭe invited Lingayats in particular to settle in the hills (Harkness, 1832, 107, 109–110; Congreve, 1847, 122; Belli Gowder, 1938–1941, 12). This was the origin of the Wodeas who continued to be Lingayat priests, the Adikiris who were magistrates, and the Kaṇakkas, village accountants and therapists. At about the same time (early seventeenth century) the Be:das were brought to the hills from Hullaṅgu:r, just to the north, as hunters or tax gatherers.[35] They were heartily disliked, but they settled permanently outside the walls of Male Ko:ṭe and probably near Hatra Ko:ṭe too. Kumba:ras also came in the palace retinue and settled near the fortresses. Some, however, who came from Veḷḷa:di in Mysore, intermarried only with Gaudas and settled at Me:lu:ru. The Gaudas of Aććaṇakal, near Ke:ti, claim descent from the Lingayats of Ummattu:r.

Male Ko:ṭe

Male Ko:ṭe ('mountain fort') was also known as Hussainabad under Tippu Sultan's régime. The fort, made of mud faced with stone, encircled by a ditch, was reputedly built some three or four centuries ago by two brothers, Sadasiva Raja and Bhujanga Raja (otherwise Bijjanarasu or Bujjaliṅgarasu). These men came from Ummattu:r in the service of its chieftain and acted as *janmis* or tribute collectors for the Nilgiri area.

A variant tradition, notable for its detail, claims that Lord Bujjaliṅga was himself the chieftain of Ummattu:r. This may have been a local misconception; but it is known that he had a son or brother named Bijjanarasu, and a son named Rudrarasu. He also had a Kaṇakka secretary by the name of Sivaliṅgayya whose younger brother Jambuliṅgayya acted as secretary to Bijjanarasu. Bujjaliṅga (presumably in the seventeenth century) wanted to incorporate the Nilgiris into his realm. He went there with a large retinue, and on the plains just to the north of the Si:gu:ru slopes he built a Lingayat monastery, the ruins of which are still to be seen at Sembanatta Math (originally called Jambunath). From there the chieftain moved to Nellapaṭṭana, a few kilometers away, and there built a fort which is still partly standing. Later he ascended the slopes and established a camp at Ko:ṭaṭṭi, near So:lu:ru; and later still he built Male Ko:ṭe nearby.

After conquering the Nilgiris the chieftain was paid an annual tribute of 900 gold coins (but whence?) by the headman of So:lu:ru. Once in control Lord Bujjaliṅga took seven men on a trip to examine Mukurti Peak.[36] On the way there one of these Badagas who was conversant with omens or astrology announced that the time was inauspicious, but Bujjaliṅga went on with the excursion. Meanwhile the watchman at Male Ko:ṭe[37] sent word to Bujjaliṅga's elder brother, who immediately captured the fort. Bujjaliṅga then moved to Nelliala in the Wainad, for he was afraid to return to Male Ko:ṭe. Later his secretary went back to the hills and built a house in the Kaṅakka village of Hajju:r (where inscribed palm leaves are now kept), while the chieftain apparently regained control of the fortress from his brother.

It is recalled that once while staying at Male Ko:ṭe he was '. . .invited by the then Náyar chief of Nelliálam to help him against his brother, who had turned him out. Bhujanga [Bujjaliṅga] did so with success; so much so that he took Nelliálam for his own and drove out the whole of the Náyar family.'[38] No wonder the brothers had found it advisable to erect sturdy mud-forts wherever they went!

Their family thus became the chieftains of Nelliala as well as tax gatherers for the Nilgiris. For their own convenience, as we have seen, the brothers brought with them some Kanarese Be:das and Kumba:ras to act as servants, and Wodeas to be their family priests. Gaudas in the commune of Tu:ḍegu:r (which surrounds Male Ko:ṭe) claim to have come from ten villages immediately north of the Nilgiri slopes, also in the retinue of these chieftains. They also maintained a small garrison, originally under Udaiya Raya (or perhaps Rudrayya), a Kanarese Lingayat who was responsible for the actual construction of Male Ko:ṭe and the more easterly fortress known as Udaiya Raya Ko:ṭe or Hatra Ko:ṭe. This man was an astute strategist; he was probably identical with Bujjaliṅga's son Rudrarasu, or otherwise an experienced military commander. In his old age he retired to Nelliala to build yet another fortress.

The tax collectors of Nelliala continued in office at Male Ko:ṭe without serious interruption until either Tippu Sultan or his father drove them back to Nelliala, mutilated the Vishnu images there and took over their Nilgiri fortress (Francis, 1908, 371). With the fleeing chieftain of the day went some Badagas, who became Wainad Gaudas, and a small party of Todas who settled near Nelliala and indeed remained there until about 1925 (Harkness, 1832, 166–167, note).

It is certain that this and the other hill-forts were occupied by Haidar Ali's troops, too. 'He . . . appears to have seized upon two of the three forts which commanded the passes . . ., viz. Hoolicul Droog and Mullaycotta, and having deepened their ditches, heightened their walls, and otherwise strengthened them, he put strong garrisons into them, which both controlled the Hill tribes, and observed and harrassed the kingdoms below them' (Ouchterlony, 1848, 82). Furthermore,

> He undoubtedly collected revenue on the plateau . . . his officers used to despoil whole villages of all their grain and force the ryots [peasants] to carry their own plundered property down to Dannáyakankóttai . . . which he had re-named Sharifábád and where he kept a strong force and a big magazine.'[39]

A worthier aspect of his revenue administration was that he 'had abolished the ancient system of division of produce and had introduced a fixed money assessment on the cultivated lands of each village' (Grigg, 1880, 312).

The last occupant of the fort was Syyud Budan, a captain *(killidar)* in charge of sixty or seventy infantrymen from Tippu's army. The fort was then named Hussainabad. It had two watchposts nearby, built by Tippu's men and armed with two small cannon, where the Moslems kept watch for forces coming from the direction of Nelliala. Every two months the garrison was relieved from Dannaika Ko:ṭe, in the Coimbatore Plain.[40] After quiet surrender to the Madras Regiment in 1791 (Phythian-adams, 1958, 87), the fort was deserted, and today stands in ruins. But meanwhile, what of the Nelliala chieftain who was attacked by Tippu's forces?

> The then chief, another Sadásiva Rája Urs, is said to have submitted to them and helped them in an attack upon Nambalakód [a neighbouring territory in the Wainad]. When Tipu's men withdrew, the chief of Nambalakód fell upon Nelliálam in revenge, and the then Arasu [chieftain] was so hard pressed that he hurriedly despatched his pregnant wife and her handmaidens into the surrounding jungle and then, to avoid capture, committed suicide in front of the gate of his fort, which was afterwards plundered by the men of Nambalakód. Such is the family tradition.[41]

But the chieftain's family lost even more than honour, leader and headquarters, for the right to collect tribute in Todana:ḍu passed after Tippu's defeat from them to the victorious house of Nambalako:du, eight kilometers away from Nelliala. Although by 1830 the Nilgiris were under the Collector of Coimbatore this headman still had the right to collect taxes in Todana:ḍu, which he referred to as *naṅgana:ḍ* ('our division') (Baber, 1830, 314–315). Early in the nineteenth century he used to receive some 6,000 rupees annually from Todana:ḍu.[42]

It is remarkable that for two centuries after the eclipse of the Nelliala chieftains with the dramatic suicide just described, the Badagas of Todana:ḍu still maintained a close relationship with this tragic family. Until about 1950 they would visit Nelliala to resolve some difficult disputes as well as to pay their respects during major family ceremonies. This family is still Lingayat and

Kannada-speaking and until fifty years ago continued to intermarry with the Lords of Ummattu:r.[43]

Hatra Ko:ṭe

Hatra Ko:ṭe otherwise known as Udaiya Raya Ko:ṭe or simply Atra, and nowadays called Ko:ṭe Ha:ḍa ('fort terrace'), has been described elsewhere (Congrëve, 1847, 121–122; Francis, 1908, 333–334; Belli Gowder, 1923–1941, 105–106) and needs little discussion here. It lies seven kilometers southeast of Kotagiri, on a terrace in Burnside Estate where no traces of the building and few of the moats can now be found. Badaga tradition suggests that Udaiya Raya, a Shaivite chieftain, also built the fort on the plains at Koḷḷandore, near Sirumuge in Coimbatore District (Congreve, 1847, 122; Francis, 1908, 333–334). He conquered all of the Porañga:ḍu villages and won from them an annual tribute of 700 gold coins. This Porañga:ḍu revenue passed through these two forts to Ummattu:r, while only the Todana:ḍu tribute was collected at Male Ko:ṭe. Hatra Ko:ṭe was captured by Haidar Ali in the late eighteenth century and was also occupied by a Moslem garrison under his son Tippu. At that time it bore the name Syyudabad, and the hundred soldiers there under a captain (a *killidar*) named Ali Khan were responsible to a commander at Dannaika Ko:ṭe in the plains below (Harkness, 1832, 126; Macleane, 1893, 1023). Here, as at Male Ko:ṭe, the garrison was 'to keep the mountaineers in check and also to assist the Sultan's servants in collecting the yearly revenue' (Ward, 1821, lxv).

To summarize our conclusions briefly, the migrations from Mysore in all probability began by the start of the sixteenth century and became more intensive during the anarchy that followed the collapse of the Vijayanagar Empire (1565). The question of when immigration ceased depends on two items of historical evidence: Finicio saw some Badagas at Me:lkunda in 1603, and scarcely any new villages have been established since the British arrived in 1819.[45] The answer thus lies between these two dates, and we conclude that before 1819 the Badagas had formed a closed community. The absence of any Vaishnavites among them favours the earlier dating for the termination of their migrations.[46] What led to their ultimate synoecism as a single community we can only guess.

NOTES

1. See Ward, 1821, lxx. *Baḍaga* is pronounced with stress on the first syllable.
2. They do not intermarry with other Badagas but find spouses either within their own phratry or from castes also called Kumba:ras and Be:das in southern Mysore.
3. The first European to write of Badagas was St. Francis Xavier, who in 1542–1544 described them as a 'horde of plundering ruffians', 'bloodthirsty horsemen' and 'savage brigands'; see Coleridge, 1872, vol. I, 218, 234–235. These people are said to have been royal tax gatherers in Travancore, where they bore the name Badagas or Vadhougers because of their northern origin. They greatly oppressed St. Francis' converts among the Travancore fisher-folk; Coleridge, 1872, vol. I, *passim,* and Thurston, 1909, vol. VII, 266. Elsewhere they are stated to have come from Vijayanagar; see Maffei, 1589, vol. I, pt. 4, 431; Bertrand, 1848, vol. II, 2; Coleridge, 1872, vol. I, 219, n. 12. It seems unlikely that they had any connexion with the Nilgiri Badagas, especially as some authorities consider them Telugu speakers; see Bertrand, 1848, vol. II, 2, n. 1; Grigg, 1880, 219; Natesa Sastri, 1892, 830–831.
4. India now has about four million Lingayats; except for the Districts of Kolhapur (Maharashtra), Hyderabad (Andhra Pradesh), Coimbatore and the Nilgiris they are found solely within Karnataka State.
5. Belli Gowder was a Badaga antiquarian; in his unpublished notes he mistakenly took this date for 1212; Belli Gowder, 1938–1941, 5.
6. Francis, 1908, 129; his claim that Baḍagu has *beṭṭa* for modern Kannada *beṭṭu* ('hill') is incorrect: the reverse would be true.
7. Congreve, 1847, 96–98; Grigg, 1880, 243; Sewell, 1882, 226. There is a grant of A.D. 1120 stating that Vishṅuvardhana, the first Hoysaḷa king, 'turned the Nīla mountain into a city'; Hayavadana Rao, 1908, 92. The Toda name for the area is *pin tiṭ,* 'gold mountain'; Francis, 1908, 357.
8. Belli Gowder, 1923–1941, 24–26; and 1938–1941, 5–6. It was the grandfather of Tu:ne:ri's founder who migrated from Mysore, at about the time the Vijayanagar Empire was destroyed.
9. He reports three 'villages' but there may have been more at the time, especially if the word *u:r* ('commune') has been incorrectly translated as 'village' or if other settlers later considered Badagas were not then treated as such or were not known of in that part of the plateau. An inscription on a dolmen at Me:lu:ru relating to a tiger and a grant bears the Śa:ka date 1518 (A.D. 1596), but since it is in Tamil it perhaps has nothing to do with the Badagas; Breeks, 1873, 102–103; Grigg, 1880, 240. Hayavadana Rao, 1908, 100, disagrees with this view; he believes the dolmen to have been erected more recently by two Gaundans.
10. Ward, 1821, lxx-lxxi; Harkness, 1832, 109. Certain villages still claim to have been founded by an official from Ummattu:r.
11. Benbow, 1930, 1–3; Karl, 1945, 1. A reference to the Mysorean practice of wearing a *sa:ri* is to be found in the funeral symbolism, wherein a female corpse is offered a piece of coloured cloth *(baṇṇa).* Legend maintains that when the seven brothers of Maduve clan were fleeing from Mysore they left behind a baby slung from the rafters in a *sa:ri.* In token of their grief the women never more used *sa:ris* or cradles after settling in the Nilgiris.

12. This usage accords with the definition in recent editions of Webster's *Dictionary,* e.g., 1967, 460. See below, p. 181, n. 2.
13. See below, pp. 223–225; also Diagram 9. There was supposedly a Christian community—but not necessarily of Badagas—near Avalanchi in the Kunden-a:ḍu division in medieval times: Finicio came in search of it, and the Todas have a legend about it; see Finicio, 1603, 719–720; Metz, 1864, 44; Hayavadana Rao, 1908, 106.
14. Metz, 1864, 53. The correct name for Seringapatam is Sri Raṅga Paṭṭana. On septs, see below, pp. 78–80.
15. The fact that Adikiris and Kaṇakkas have a dialect hardly varying from Standard Baḍagu is explained by their ready intermarriage with Gaudas, Ha:ruvas and Kaggusis; the Wodeas, Be:das, and Kumba:ras are mainly endogamous groupings.
16. Natesa Sastri, 1892, 754; Francis, 1908, 131; Thurston, 1909, vol. I, 73; Jogi Gowder, no date, 1; it is a Brahmin sept in Mysore.
17. Metz, 1864, 56; Macleane, 1893, 64. The same was true of Kaggusis; see below, p. 89.
18. Harkness, 1832, 106–107, note; Noble, 1976, 115–117; for Badaga polyandry, see Natesa Sastri, 1892, 754, 832, and Stuart, 1893, 243. Todas and Kurubas still practise polyandry; Thurston, 1906, 108–113.
19. Metz, 1864, 50–51; Belli Gowder, 1923–1941, 28. Adigaraṭṭi, derives from *adikari* ('powerful man') and *haṭṭi* ('village'). A variant of this legend has the early Adikiris following a chieftain named Kariabeṭṭa Ra:ya who, like Moses, was fated to lead them to the promised land without setting foot on it himself. After passing through Ha:sanu:ru to Nellitore and staying there for a time, they went on to Attupaḍi, at the foot of the southeast slopes, and some settled there. Their Lingayat descendants still inhabit that village but are now Gaudas. The chieftain led the remainder on to found another village called Nerben, in Kundena:ḍu; it no longer exists. After the chieftain had died there some of the settlers went on to Nedika:ḍ, near Adigaraṭṭi. and soon founded the latter village. Descendants of the chieftain's family and retinue thus came to be called 'powerful men' because of their association with him, in recognition of which the *janmis* gave them the duty of village magistrates.
20. The pollution of having eaten meat can be removed from men alone.
21. Metz, 1864, 50–54; Grigg, 1880, 221; Thurston, 1909, vol. I, 73. The correct name for the outpost usually called Dannaika Ko:ṭe or Danayakan Koṭṭe is Da:na Na:yaka Ko:ṭe, 'the fort of the commander Dana;' Nicholson, 1898, 425–426. It was established in 1318 by Madappa Daṇdanāyaka, who then was ruling over the Nilgiris and Wainad; Rea, 1910, 111; Belli Gowder, 1923–1941, 100. On Koḷḷandore, see below.
22. Belli Gowder, 1923–1941, 29–30; Karl, 1945, 2; the eldest, a cripple, settled at Ćinna Kunnu:r. Among the very early villages in *Todana:ḍu* were Kaḍana:-ḍu, settled from Ka:rahaḷḷi (near Tagadu:r); Tu:ḍegu:r E:koni, from Kava-spadi (or Agasvadi) or else Tayu:r; Ćinna Kunnu:r, from Koṅgaḷḷi (near Ummattu:r); Ebbana:ḍu, from Urigaddige or Ho:sahaḷḷi; Ku:kalu, from Guṇḍuḷupe:te; Honatale, from Honhaḷḷi; and So:lu:ru, from Su:lu:r. The earliest *Me:kuṅa:ḍu* villages were Me:lu:ru, settled from Urigaddige or Veḷḷa:di; Tu:ḍu:ru, settled by the fourth of seven brothers from Poraṅga:ḍu and later deserted; Ta:mbaṭṭi, also settled from Poraṇga:ḍu; Ki:ṛu:ru and

Nunduwa, settled from Urigaddige; Hulikal, from Honhaḷḷi; and Ke:ti, from Koṅgaḷḷi. The earliest *Kundena:ḍu* villages were also settled from Koṅgaḷḷi. Apart from Honatale, Ki:ṛu:ru and Nunduwa, each of the above Badaga villages became the head of a commune as other hamlets grew up around it; and each is marked as head of a commune by having a ceremonial stone structure called *akka bakka.*

23. Another name sometimes given the Kasturis is Gangalu:ru; Metz, 1864, 58–59. This is quite possibly a variant of Gangadikara, the name of a large section of Okkaligas.
24. Metz, 1864, 49–50; Grigg, 1880, 221; Tignous, 1911, 117. A variant account is that he thought he had eaten meat, though the item was really a wild vegetable in the curry.
25. Thurston, 1909, vol. I, 74. It may be significant that in the same census certain Okkaligas in Mysore gave their subcaste as Baḍagar; Rice, 1897, vol. I, 229. Belli Gowder, 1923–1941, 80, derives only the Kasturi clan from Gangadikar-as, but Gaudas of Ha:sanu:ru claim the same origin.
26. Metz, 1864, 47–48, 57–58; he gave the villages as Tayu:r and Tagadu:r. Tayu:r had a well-built mud fortress on a river bank. By 1801 it was in ruins and the countryside showed signs of having been much more cultivated in previous times; Buchanan, 1807, vol. II, 150–151.
27. Finicio possibly passed through Pa:du:r in 1603, causing the Badagas to flee to the jungle; Finicio, 1603, 729–730.
28. Baber, 1830, 314; for an instance of intermarriage between Nandaṭṭi and So:lu:ru see Emeneau, 1971, 611.
29. This account of their migration is confirmed by villagers in that part of the plateau.
30. Natesa Sastri, 1892, 755; Thurston, 1909, vol. 1, 73. A comparable usage is found in southern Mysore; see Epstein, 1962, 181.
31. Balu, 1960, 4. This story is not accurate in its details, for in 1760 the Governor of Madurai was an English creature, Yusuf Khan; perhaps Balu was referring to a skirmish with a tributary chieftain *(pa:layaka:r),* but one bearing a suspiciously medieval name!
32. Buchanan, 1807, vol. II, 136. This and other rings still in the possession of several headmen were given by Chikka Deva Raya (1672–1704), who supposedly took Kaḍana:ḍu from Ummattu:r in 1676; Belli Gowder, 1923–1941, 100; Wilks, 1930, vol. II, 225; Emeneau, 1971, 102.
33. Ouchterlony, 1848, 81, see below, p. 170. Pakkasu:ra, the chief of Hulikal Drug, is depicted in Badaga myth as a demon, whom the villagers had to feed with a daily cartful of rice complete with driver, until he was finally slain by the hero Bhima; compare Congreve, 1847, 142; Francis, 1908, 329. This story is a parochialized version of one in the *Mahabharata* I, 160; for 'the three kings or chiefs of the mountains,' see Harkness, 1832, 120. An inscription at Rampura, west of Nanjangud (Mysore), dated to A.D. 1504, describes one Govaṇṇa-Oḍeyar, a native of that place, as 'champion over the three kings, protector of the Nilagiri;' Rice, 1894, vol. III, 100, 191, n. 47. Emeneau, 1971, 1, records 'three kingdoms' in Toda thinking.
34. The exceptional nature of Kundena:ḍu is underlined by the common Badaga phrase, 'All the four divisions, including Kunda.' The relative recency of its settlement is also indicated by the fact that it lies to the west of Me:kuna:-

ḍu—which means 'western division.' Keys, 1812, xlviii; Macpherson, 1820, lviii; Ward, 1821, lxi; Keys erroneously calls Todana:ḍu 'Kothanaud.'

35. Previously they had come there from Na:gataḷḷi, in Mysore.
36. Their names are still recalled, and they came from the Badaga villages of Tu:ḍegu:r, Kaḍaṇa:ḍu, Ha:laṭṭi, Ebbana:ḍu and Ku:kalu. Mukurti is a celebrated landmark in the western Nilgiris, a peak reputedly formed when Ra:ma cut off the nose of Ra:vana's sister and dropped it at this place; Jagor, 1876, 202.
37. Murudan, son of a loose Badaga woman.
38. Francis, 1908, 371; thus also Belli Gowder, 1923–1941, 101. The conquered chieftain was Vandur Kovilagam.
39. Francis, 1908, 330; (he errs in identifying Pakkasu:ra Ko:ṭe as Tippu's Syyudabad); Ouchterlony, 1848, 82.
40. Harkness, 1832, 59. One of these watchposts was in fact a small natural mesa surrounded by sheer cliffs, the access to which could be controlled by two or three armed men. It stands above and to the west of the Si:gu:ru ghat road.
41. Francis, 1908, 371: 'other accounts state that the family fled from Mysore State as late as the time of Tipu and settled in Nelliálam under the permission of the Pychy rebel . . .
42. Poraṅga:ḍu and Me:kuṅa:ḍu at that time were paying a similar sum to two other *janmis,* one the Padignacar Kolgum (i.e., Padinnara Kovilagam), a chief of the Samuri (Zamorin) family, the other Pandalur Nayar, of South Malabar; Baber, 1830, 314–315; compare Finicio, 1603, 729.
43. Francis, 1908, 350, 370; Kariabettan, 1958a, 14. About fifty years ago the family of the Ummattu:r Lords in their ancestral home at Bagaḷḷi (five kilometers from Ummattu:r) sold all remaining lands and left the area. Bauramma, last Queen of Nelliala, was born about the year of the Indian Mutiny; she died at the age of 94, whereupon Raja Shankar Rayal sold what remained of the realm and retired to Mysore. The recent rulers are indicated in this diagram numbered in order of their succession.

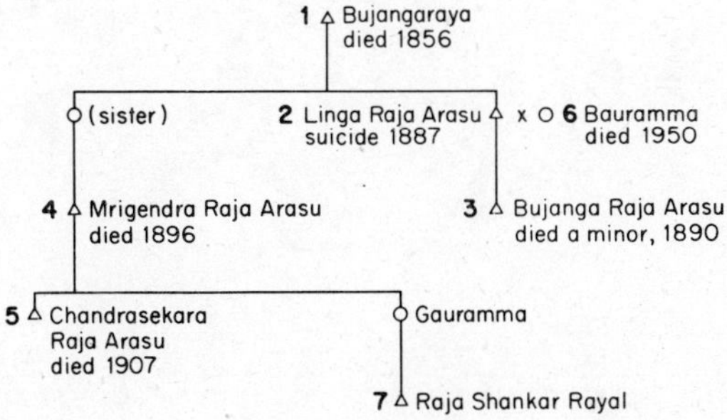

44. There are modern Badaga theorists who claim for the community an overseas origin as Jews or a northern origin as Buddhists from Bengal, Assam or Nepal; these ideas are based on very flimsy parallels in culture and vocabulary.

45. Many Badagas now believe it was the excesses of Tippu Sultan's regime that prompted the migration; but the better informed admit that this would not allow sufficient time depth to encompass the history and consolidation of the community. Da:bakambe, founded near Kotagiri around 1950, is the only case of a very new village.
46. Rhiem (1900, 499–500) claims one unidentified village as Vaishnavite. I am unable to tell which it is but feel she was misinformed; compare Jagor, 1876, 202.

2

Place–Names and Cultural Ecology

A NEW SYSTEM OF THERAPY

The Badagas thus came to the Nilgiri Plateau as refugees and settled there on land that in part they cleared from virgin tropical montane forest and that was in part granted them by a council of men from the indigenous Toda, Kota and Kurumba tribes, people who had already occupied a thin scattering of hamlets on the hills for perhaps a millennium.

The Badagas can thus be seen, at least in the first three centuries of their occupation, as frontiersmen whose population and number of settlements were slowly increasing over the decades. In 1603 there were only about 500 Badagas living in three villages (Finicio, 1603, 723). By the first British census, in 1812, they numbered 2207 people. But at this time, to judge by the same rough census (which perhaps excluded children), they had already become the numerically dominant community in the area: the Todas numbered only 179 (compared with possibly 1000 in 1603), and the Kotas 130; the Kurumbas and Irulas, two tribes living on the lower Nilgiri slopes, were not counted at all, though they were certainly there. Furthermore, during this same period of two centuries the Badaga settlement pattern became such a dispersed one that their hamlets increased in number from three to over 350. This expansion was in part the effect of fertile land being available and in part the result of an effective indigenous therapeutic system.

By the time of the first British visits, the Badagas had clearly succeeded in adapting to their new social and geographic environment. We may presume that natural selection helped the population build up a genetic resistance to whatever montane illnesses had not previously affected the people when they were living in Mysore and that some lowland disease organisms were no longer able to survive at the new elevation, either because it was too high and cold for them or because the hosts among the scattered and tiny population died off without transferring these organisms to new hosts, or more probably because the population density was so low that, after one infection by any particular disease organism, antibodies were built up that protected all Badagas from any further infection in the near future. As the settlements expanded, the increasing numbers of people permitted greater transference of disease organisms and called for greater amounts of health care; but at the same time these settlements, located in most parts of the Nilgiri Plateau within a zone that lay between 1,200m and 2,200m feet elevation, gave people opportunities to select the more healthy residential sites, to explore micro-environmental differences in the area and most importantly to discover medicinal uses for dozens of new species of plants that were in many instances confined to the Plateau. We may presume that the pharmacological uses of local plants were discovered by Badaga women who worked as goatherds and closely observed the feeding habits of their animals. While it is true that Badagas do not keep goats today, they did so during the seventeenth century and later too.

After contact with the British a new equilibrium with their changed environment was achieved by the Badagas, and their population was able to increase rapidly for several decades while there was still a very low density of population. Why? One relevant factor, I would hypothesise, was that a change in their drinking habits followed the arrival of the British (from 1819 onward) and that this was associated with greater resistance to bacteria in the drinking water. The main drinks of the community at the time were fresh milk and stream water. Yet by the 1840s arrack, a locally made liquor, as well as tea and coffee, were common Badaga preferences. Other cultural practices confined infectious bacteria to relatively limited areas. Buffalo dung tended to collect in the stone kraals built just outside the villages. Similarly, indiscriminate spitting was not tolerated and spittoons were consequently in common use. A proverb stressed that, 'If you ask for an obligation it is essential to see the right people; it is essential to spit in the proper place.' With this attitude prevalent, the spread of various viruses and of *Mycobacterium tuberculosis* has been greatly curtailed. The regular washing of the body and shaving of pubic hair have also contributed to health by restricting the incidence of bodily fungi and lice-borne diseases.

The ecological significance of these various beliefs and practices is that as the Nilgiri population increased in the nineteenth century and some village streams began to be polluted by this new pressure, the Badagas managed to avoid some contamination by switching from drinking stream water and fresh milk to tea, coffee and sometimes alcohol, all of which would be relatively free of bacterial organisms. The new balance with the environment that this change brought about was certainly one factor in the remarkable increase in the Badaga population since the advent of the British (Appendix 2).

At the same time that this change in drinking habits was occurring their eating habits were undergoing an equally radical transformation. In part this was due to the several dozen types of fruit, grain and vegetable introduced from Europe by British settlers and adopted by most Badagas. The variety of their diet was thus greatly increased.

VILLAGE NAMES

A study of the present Badaga hamlet names yields a body of insights about the early settlements formed during the two and a half centuries preceding the first British report (Keys, 1812).

Perhaps a somewhat lyrical description of the Nilgiri Plateau may at this point aid the reader's understanding of what is to follow:

> The plateau is a true tableland, its average height being very uniform. But there is not a square mile of level ground in the whole of it, its surface being broken by endless undulations which in places swell into considerable and distinct ranges. It rises most abruptly from the plains below it; and on the west, above the Ouchterlony Valley and southwards, its sides are often sheer, bare walls, hundreds of feet in height and too steep even for trees to obtain a footing on them. Elsewhere dense forest covers almost the whole of its slopes . . .
>
> It is first of all divided east and west into two fairly equal but

> dissimilar parts by a range of heights running north and south of which Dodabetta ('big mountain') is the tallest . . .
>
> East and south of the Dodabetta range . . . the plateau . . . is extensively cultivated by the immigrant tribe known as the Badagas. This does not improve its appearance; the great forests have mostly been felled and their place taken by the poorest low scrub or by fields of miserable cereals surrounding the squat red-tiled houses of numerous hamlets; the country is deeply scoured by every shower of rain until the infertile red and yellow sub-soil clays are laid bare; and, owing to the Badagas' former custom of shifting their cultivation from year to year to new patches of land, grass has been prevented from getting any firm hold on the denuded hill-sides. Only on the slopes of the plateau (which are too steep for cultivation) and in a few isolated Government reserves, does the forest flourish in its virgin beauty.
>
> West of Dodabetta, however, the Badagas are more rare; hardly a field or a village (except the little clusters of huts belonging to the pastoral Tódas) is to be seen; and the country consists of a sea of rounded green hills, rising now and again into more prominent heights and ranges, which are covered with short grass . . . These rounded hills are divided each from each by streams or bogs, and nestling in their wrinkles are beautiful little woods, . . . the edges of which have been so sharply defined by years of grazing and (perhaps) grass fires that they look almost like artificial plantations. . . .(Francis, 1908, 3–5).

A few of the village names defy any interpretation—either by me or by my best informants—probably because they have changed too much to be recognizable now as Baḍagu substantives. But leaving these aside we still have in the list of toponyms which follows a corpus of 311 meaningful toponyms for a community of about 362 hamlets, 18 of them no longer occupied. Some toponyms are repeated in several places, (e.g., Naḍuhaṭṭi, 'middle hamlet', or Hosaṭṭi, 'new hamlet'); numbers given after some explanations indicate where such a toponym occurs more than once in the Nilgiris. We will now examine the meanings of the toponyms, which are given here in a phonemic transcription of Badagu (a Dravidian language).

1. Names from a Topographic Feature or the Sky

aććanakal < aććina + kallu = well proportioned (*or* shield-like) + stone[1]
a:ka:su = very high hill
aṇehaṭṭi < aṇe + haṭṭi = water channel + hamlet
arebennu < are + bennu = large flat rock + upper part of back (i.e., curving slope)
arehaṭṭi < are + haṭṭi = large flat rock + hamlet (4)
arekombe < are + kombe = large flat rock + Kurumba hamlet
asagantore < asaga + na + tore = washerman + his + riverside
attuboyil < attu + baylu = steep place + entrance
attumaṇṇu < attu + maṇṇu = steep place + earth
attupaḍi < attu + paḍi = steep place + step
ba:muḍi < ba:mbe + muḍi = ba:mbe grass + headland
beḷḷa:ḍa < beḷḷe + ha:da = white + flat ground (2)
benaṭṭi < bennu + haṭṭi = upper part of back (i.e., curving slope) + hamlet
beṅkal < bennu + kallu = upper part of back (i.e., curving slope) + stone
beṅkala:ḍa < bennu + kallu + ha:ḍa = upper part of back (i.e., curving slope) + stone + flat ground
be:rekallu < be:re + kallu = separate + stone
beṭṭaṭṭi < beṭṭu + haṭṭi = hill + hamlet (2)
bikkekaṇḍi < bikke + kaṇḍi = olive linden + small tableland
bikko:lu < bikke + godalu = olive linden + dale between two hills
bittolakaṇḍi < bittu + hola + kaṇḍi = seed + field + small tableland
daḍahaṭṭi < daḍa + haṭṭi = way + hamlet
doḍḍhaṇi < doḍḍa + haṇi = big + swamp
eććala:ḍa < eććalu + ha:ḍa = leftover food + flat ground
eḍekallu < eḍe + kallu = middle + stone
e:koni = Milky Way, *or* the head star in it
ellenayi < elle + nayi = boundary + neck (of land)
emmale < emme + male = female buffalo + mountain
godalaṭṭi < godalu + haṭṭi = dale between two hills + hamlet
guṇḍa:ḍa < guṇḍu + ha:ḍa = boulder + flat ground (2)
ha:ḍaṭṭi < ha:ḍa + haṭṭi = flat ground + hamlet; (also called ha: laṭṭi)
ha:la:ḍa < ha:lu + ha:ḍa = milk + flat ground

ha:lke:ru < ha:lu + ke:ru = milk + pond

haṇikore < haṇi + kore = swamp + place

haṭṭa:ve < haṭṭu + ta:ve = cliff + common bracken; *or* < haeṭu + ta:ve = old, useless + common bracken

honemuḍi < hone + muḍi = St. John's wort + headland

hono:re < hone + o:re = St. John's wort + slope

hubbatale < hubble + tale = Chinese pagoda tree, hill forest indigo, New Spain senna, trifoliate tick trefoil, *Dumasia villosa, or* downy mountain senna + headland

hu:morakaṇḍi < hu: + mora + kaṇḍi = flower + tree + small tableland

iḍuhaṭṭi < iḍi + haṭṭi = dell + hamlet

iḍukore < iḍi + kore = dell + patch of cultivated ground

iṛutore < iṛu + tore = seven (i.e., many) + riverside

ittala:r < hittalu + u:ru = the back + head village

jakkakambe < jakkalu + kambe = common Nilgiri barberry + ridge (2)

jakkalo:re < jakkalu + o:re = common Nilgiri barberry + slope

jakkata (la) < jakkalu + tale = common Nilgiri barberry + headland

kalha:ḍa < kallu + ha:ḍa = stone + flat ground

kallaṭṭi < kallu + haṭṭi = stone + hamlet

kalnayi < kallu + nayi = stone + neck (of land)

kaṇḍibikke < kaṇḍi + bikke = small tableland + olive linden; (*cf.* bikkekaṇḍi)

karekallu < kare + kallu = ridge + stone

karepiḷḷu < kare + piḷḷu = ridge + narrow passage

kariyamale < kariya + male = black + mountain

kaṭṭebeṭṭu < kaṭṭe + beṭṭu = dry + mountain; *or* < several *Strobilanthes* spp. + mountain

kattuguṛi < kattu + guṛi = last point + pit

ka:vilo:re < ka:vilu + o:re = Bengal currant + slope

keṅgamudi < keṅga + mudi = flame-colour + headland

kentore < keṅga + tore = flame-colour + riverside

kerapa:ḍu < kere + pa:ḍu = natural pond + place

ke:rbennu < ke:ru + bennu = pond + upper part of back (i.e., curving slope)

ke:rbeṭṭu < ke:ru + beṭṭu = pond + mountain

kereha:ḍa < kere + ha:ḍa = natural pond + flat ground

ke:rkambe < ke:ru + kambe = pond + ridge

ke:rkaṇḍi < ke:ru + kaṇḍi = pond + flat place

ke:titore < ke:ti + tore = Ke:ti village + riverside
kiṅgare < kiṅgu + kare = red + ridge
kodamuḍi < kodaṅgu + muḍi = velvetty patchouli + headland
koṇahaṭṭi < koṇa + haṭṭi = extremity (*or* curved tip) + hamlet
koṇakore < koṇa + kore = extremity (*or* curved tip) + moor
ko:ṭenayi < ko:ṭe + nayi = fort + neck (of land)
kottibennu < kotti + bennu = wild cat + upper part of back (i.e., curving slope)
kukatore < kukalu + tore = Kukalu village + riverside
kundanayi < kunda + nayi = Kunda's + neck (of land); (Kunda is a nickname)
kuruṇevo:re < kuruṇe + o:re = creeping rose box + slope
maḍitore < maḍi + tore = worshipping place + riverside
mandaṇe < manda + haṇe = council-place + flat, grassy place
maṇikal < maṇi + kallu = bell + stone; (i.e., stone which rings when struck)
maňjakombe < maňju + kombe = cloud + Kurumba hamlet
maňjitale < maňji + tale = Nilgiri nettle + headland
maňju:ru < maňju + u:ru = cloud + head village
marlakambe < marlu + kambe = (unidentifiable) plant + ridge
maṭṭakaṇḍi < maṭṭa + kaṇḍi = extensive + small tableland
mora oḍḍe < tree + bare smooth surface of curved slope
mottakambe < motta + kambe = Kurumba hamlet + ridge
mukkumale < mukku + male = narrow corner + mountain
muḷḷimale < muḷḷi + male = bramble + mountain
naihaṭṭi < nayi + haṭṭi = neck (of land) + hamlet
ne:rikambe < ne:ri + kambe = mountain black plum + ridge
o:ranayi < o:re + nayi = slope + neck (of land)
paḍihaṭṭi < paḍi + haṭṭi = step + hamlet
pororaṭṭi < mora + o:re + haṭṭi = tree + slope + hamlet
sodalivo:re < sodali + o:re = blue-druped featherfoil + slope
so:gaṭṭi *or* so:gatore < so:ge + haṭṭi (*or* tore) = (unidentifiable) plant + hamlet (*or* riverside)
so:lu:rmaṭṭa < so:le + u:ru + maṭṭa = forest + head village + flat ground
soreguṇḍu < sore + guṇḍu = sparrow + big boulder
talemale < tale + male = top + mountain
ta:ndana:du < ta:ḷnda + na:ḍu = below the sweep of the arm + tract *or* place
torehaṭṭi *or* toreyaṭṭi < tore + haṭṭi = riverside + hamlet
tu:dale < tu:ḍe + tale = hill mango + headland; *or* < tu: + tale

= milk-giving ceremony + headland
tumbimale *or* dumbimale < tumbe + male = Nilgiri nettle + mountain; *or* < dumbi + male = bee (*or* moth?) + mountain
ulıyaṭṭi < uli + haṭṭi = waterfall + hamlet
u:rdiṭṭu < u:ru + diṭṭu = head village + hillock
u:rumale < u:ru + male = head village + mountain

2. References to Land or Quality of the Soil

attumaṇṇu < attu + maṇṇu = steep place + earth
ba:kola < ba: + hola = prosper + field
baralaṭṭi < baralu + haṭṭi = dried + hamlet
baramaṇṇu < bara + maṇṇu = dry + earth
battakore < batta + kore = any millet + patch of cultivated ground
be:bennu < be: + bennu = very fertile patch of ground + upper part of back (i.e., curving slope) (2)
be:ragaṇi < be:ru + haṇi = root + swamp
be:rakallu < be:ru + kallu = root + stone
be:rhaṭṭi < be:ru + haṭṭi = root + hamlet; (i.e., many roots there)
be:ṭḷa:ḍa < be:ṭḷu + ha:ḍa = threshing-pole + flat ground
biṅkića kallaṭṭi < biṅkića + kallu + haṭṭi = white + stone + hamlet
bittolakaṇḍi < bittu + hola + kaṇḍi = seed + field + small tableland
da:vaṇi < ta:ve + haṇi = common bracken + swamp
de:nala < je:nu + hola = honey + field
de:vanatta < de:va + natta = god's + common place
dimbaṭṭi < dimbu + haṭṭi = pillow (i.e., soft place) + hamlet
doḍḍamokke < doḍḍa + mokke = big + gravelly land
ebbana:ḍu < ebbu + na:ḍu = development + tract of land
hulla:ḍa < hullu + ha:ḍa = grass + flat ground
iḍukore < iḍi + kore = dell + patch of cultivated ground
kallakore < kallu + kore = stone + patch of cultivated ground
kamba:ḍa < kambu + ha:ḍa = pole + flat ground; (i.e., perhaps in reference to trees there looking like poles)
kammandu < kam + mandu < (?) kö + moṇ (both Toda words) + mandu = red + soil + Toda hamlet
kappaṭṭi < kappu + haṭṭi = black + hamlet
ka:rekore < ka:re + kore = cotton milk plant + patch of cultivated ground
kariyalbe < kari + kallu + bɛ̆ = charcoal + stone + fertile land

kekkaṭṭi < kekke + haṭṭi = place with uncultivable soil + hamlet
kempola < kempu + hola = reddish + field
keṅduwa < ken + to: = reddish + buffalo pen
keṅgal < keṅgu + kallu = reddish + stone
keṇgunde = reddish
koikore < koi + kore = jungle hen + patch of cultivated ground
kokala:ḍa < koe + kallu + ha:ḍa = dirt + stone + flat ground
koṇakore < koṇa + kore = extremity (*or* curved tip) + moor
koňjola < koňju + hola = tree-branches + field; (i.e., branches lying on fields to protect seed from birds)
kuruṇekore < kuruṇe + kore = creeping rose box + patch of cultivated ground
manepaṭṭu < mane + paṭṭu = house + piece of land
maňjanakore < maňjana + kore = saffron-colored + patch of cultivated ground
mavakallu < mora + kallu = tree + stone (2)
marakore < mora + kore = tree + patch of cultivated ground
mokkaṭṭi < mokke + haṭṭi = bare gravelly place + hamlet
mokkeyaṭṭi < mokke + haṭṭi = bare gravelly place + hamlet
mudugola < mudu + hola = ripe *or* well-cultivated + field
naḍuvo:re < naḍu + o:re = middle + slope
neḍugula < neḍu + hola = lengthy + field
nunduwa < nundu + hola = fertile + field; *or* < nundu + to: = fertile + buffalo pen
oḍḍe:ru < oḍḍe + e:ru = sloping land + upward (2)
pusekunnu:r < puse + kunna + u:ru = vague colour + small + head village
se:lekore < se:le + kore = Mysore fig *or* wild banyan + patch of cultivated ground
sikola < ćikka (Kannaḍa) + hola = small + field
taṭṭene:ri < taṭṭe + ne:ri = flat + mountain black plum
tumana:da < duma + na + ha:da = Duma + his + flat ground

3. *Nature of Vegetation (and Jungle Produce)*

baṇahatti < baṇa + haṭṭi = forest-garden + hamlet
bandime < pandi + me = thick grass + place
bembaṭṭi < banda + haṭṭi = burnt *or* dried + hamlet
de:nala < je:nu + hola = honey + field
de:vaso:le < de:va + so:le = god's + forest
di:naṭṭi < je:nu + haṭṭi = honey + hamlet; (i.e., much honey there) (2)

eḍeka:ḍu < eḍe + ka:ḍu = halfway *or* middle + jungle
horaso:le < hora + so:le = outer + forest
hulla:ḍa < hullu + ha:ḍa = grass + flat ground
hullaṭṭi < hullu + haṭṭi = grass + hamlet
hu:mora < hu: + mora = flower + tree
hu:morakaṇḍi < hu: + mora + kaṇḍi = flower + tree + small tableland
iruka:ḍu < iru + ka:ḍu = night (i.e., dark) + jungle
kaḍekambaṭṭi < kaḍesi + kambu + haṭṭi = last + pole + hamlet
kaḍeso:le < kaḍe + so:le = last + forest
kambaṭṭi < kambu + haṭṭi = pole + hamlet; (i.e., trees like poles there) (3)
karimora < kari + more = charcoal + tree; (i.e., black tree)
kaso:le < ka + so:le = black + forest
ka:ṭe:ri < ka:ḍu + e:ru = forest + male buffalo
koḍe:ru < ka:ḍu + e:ru = forest + male buffalo (2)
kundasappe < kunda + sappe = Kunda's (?) + clumps of tall grass
marakallu < mara + kallu = tree + stone (2)
marakore < mara + kore = tree + patch of cultivated ground
morakotti < mora + kotti = tree + wild cat
mora oḍḍe = tree + bare smooth surface of curving slope
muttina:ḍu < mutta + na:ḍu = ripe (grass) + country
pandalu:ru < pandal + u:ru = canopy (of trees) + head village
pororaṭṭi < mora + o:re + haṭṭi = tree + slope + hamlet
so:lu:rmaṭṭa < so:le + u:ru + maṭṭa = wood + head village + flat ground
so:lu:ru < so:le + u:ru = wood + head village

4. *Plant Species*

attikallu < atti + kallu = wild fig *(Ficus glomerata)* + stone
avare = beans *(Phaseolus vulgaris)*
ba:muḍi < ba:mbe + muḍi = ba:mbe grass *(Cymbopogon sp.)* + headland
battakore < batta + kore = any millet + patch of cultivated ground
bayeṅgi = Indian willow *(Salix tetrasperma)* (3)
bayigemandu < bayige + mandu = Indian willow *(Salix tetrasperma)* + Toda hamlet

bɛ̃ko:ṭe < bɛ̃ + ko:ṭe = wild plantain *(Musa superba)* + fort

bikkaṭṭi < bikke + haṭṭi = olive linden *(Elaeocarpus oblongus)* + hamlet (5)

bikkekaṇḍi < bikke + kaṇḍi = olive linden *(Elaeocarpus oblongus)* + small tableland; (*cf.* kaṇḍibikke)

bikko:lu < bikke + godalu = olive linden *(Elaeocarpus oblongus)* + dale between two hills

billikombe < billi + kombe = Nilgiri rhododendron *(Rhododendron nilagiricum)* + Kurumba hamlet

da:vaṇi < ta:ve + haṇi = common bracken *(Pteris aquilinum)* + swamp

haṭṭa:ve < haṭṭu + ta:ve = cliff + common bracken *(Pteris aquilinum); or* < haeṭu + ta:ve = old, useless + common bracken

honatale < hone + tale = St. John's wort *(Hypericum, 5 spp.)* + place

honaṭṭi < hone + haṭṭi = St. John's wort *(Hypericum, 5 spp.)* + hamlet

honemuḍi < hone + muḍi = St. John's wort *(Hypericum, 5 spp.)* + headland

hono:re < hone + o:re = St. John's wort *(Hypericum, 5 spp.)* + slope

hubbatale < hubbe + tale = Chinese pagoda tree *(Sophora glauca),* hill forest indigo *(Indigofera pulchella),* New Spain senna *(Senna laevigata)*, trifoliate tick trefoil *(Desmodium refescens), Dumasia villosa, or* downy mountain senna *(Cassia tomentosa)* + headland

imbimorahaṭṭi < imbi + mora + haṭṭi = sweet lime *(Citrus medica limetta)* + tree + hamlet

jakkakambe < jakkalu + kambe = common Nilgiri barberry *(Berberis tinctoria)* + ridge (2)

jakkalo:re < jakkalu + o:re = common Nilgiri barberry *(Berberis tinctoria)* + slope

jakkane:ri < jakkalu + ne:ri = common Nilgiri barberry *(Berberis tinctoria)* + mountain black plum *(Syzygium arnottianum); or* < jakkane:ri = type of mountain black plum

jakkata(la) < jakkalu + tale = common Nilgiri barberry *(Berberis tinctoria)* + headland

jakkato *or* sakkata < jakkalu + to: = common Nilgiri barberry *(Berberis tinctoria)* + buffalo pen

kaṇḍibikke < kaṇḍi + bikke = small tableland + olive linden

(Elaeocarpus oblongus); (*cf.* bikkekaṇḍi)
kanne:ri = type of mountain black plum *(Syzygium arnottianum)* 'which glows from its joints at night' (2)
kanne:rimukku < kanne:ri + mukku = type of mountain black plum *(Syzygium arnottianum)* + corner
ka:rekore < ka:re + kore = cotton milk plant *(Marsdenia volubilis)* + patch of cultivated ground
kaṭṭebeṭṭu < kaṭṭe + beṭṭu = dry + mountain; *or* several *Strobilanthes spp.* + mountain
kauvaṭṭi *or* kauve < kauve (+ haṭṭi) = yellow ground star *(Curculigo orchioides)* + hamlet
ka:vilo:re < ka:vilu + o:re = straight-spined Bengal currant *(Carissa paucinervia)* + slope
keććigaṭṭi < keććiga + haṭṭi = Mysore thorn *(Caesalpinia sepiaria)* + hamlet (2)
kiliňjumandu < kiliňju + mandu = pink cedar *(Acrocarpus fraxinifolius) or* red cedar *(Cedrela toona)* + Toda hamlet
kiliňjumora < kiliňju + mora = pink cedar *(Acrocarpus fraxinifolius) or* red cedar *(Cedrela toona)* + tree
kodamuḍi < kodaṅgu + muḍi = velvetty patchouli *(Pogostemon,* several *spp.)* + headland (2)
kodaṅgaṭṭi < kodaṅgu + haṭṭi = velvetty patchouli *(Pogostemon,* several *spp.)* + hamlet
kuruṇekore < kuruṇe + kore = creeping rose box *(Cotoneaster buxifolia)* + patch of cultivated ground
kuruṇevo:re < kuruṇe + o:re = creeping rose box *(Cotoneaster buxifolia)* + slope
kurutuguṛi < kurutu + guṛi = small bamboo-shoot + pit
maňjitale < maňji + tale = Nilgiri nettle *(Laportea terminalis)* + headland
marlakambe < marlu + kambe = (unidentifiable) plant + ridge
ma:siganaṭṭi < ma:siga + na + haṭṭi = forest pepper *(Toddalia asiatica obtusifolia)* + that + hamlet
ma:vaṭṭi < ma:vu + haṭṭi = mango *(Mangifera indica)* + hamlet
ma:vukallu < ma:vu + kallu = mango *(Mangifera indica)* + stone
muḷḷigu:r < muḷḷi + u:ru = bramble (*Rubus,* several *spp.,* and *Prinsepia utilis)* + head village
muḷḷimale < muḷḷi + male = bramble (*Rubus,* several *spp.,* and *Prinsepia utilis*) + mountain
muttarabikke < muttara + bikke = forefathers' + olive linden *(Elaeocarpus oblongus)*

ne:rikambe < ne:ri + kambe = mountain black plum *(Syzygium arnottianum)* + ridge (2)

ne:rimora < ne:ri + mora = mountain black plum *(Syzygium arnottianum)* + tree

perumpaḷḷi < perumbu + paḷḷi = cane + small village

sakkalaṭṭi < jakkalu + haṭṭi = common Nilgiri barberry *(Berberis tinctoria)* + hamlet; (*cf.* jakkato)

sakkata; cf. jakkato

se:lekore < se:le + kore = Mysore fig *or* wild banyan *(Ficus mysorensis)* + patch of cultivated ground

sippihaṭṭi < sippige + haṭṭi = geranium grass *(Cymbopogon martini or C. polyneuros)* + hamlet

sodalivo:re < sodali + o:re = blue-druped featherfoil *(Bridelia roxburghiana)* + slope

so:gaṭṭi *or* so:gatore < so:ge + haṭṭi (*or* tore) = (unidentifiable) plant + hamlet (*or* riverside)

suḷḷigu:ḍu < suḷḷi + gu:ḍu = fragrant garland flower *or* orange root *(Hedychium coronarium)* + nest

ta:mbaṭṭi < tappe + haṭṭi = ginger grass *(Cymbopogon flexuosus)* + hamlet

taṭṭene:ri < taṭṭe + ne:ri = flat + mountain black plum *(Syzygium arnottianum)*

ti:ḍehaṭṭi < tu:ḍe + haṭṭi = hill mango *(Meliosma wightii)* + hamlet

togalaṭṭi < togalu + haṭṭi = jungle dholl *(Atylosia trinervia)* + hamlet

tu:dale < tu:ḍe + tale = hill mango *(Meliosma wightii)* + headland; *or* < tu: + tale = milk-giving ceremony + headland

tu:ḍeguṛi < tu:ḍe + guṛi = hill mango *(Meliosma wightii)* + pit

tumbimale *or* dumbimale < tumbe + male = Nilgiri nettle *(Laportea terminalis)* + mountain; *or* < dumbi + male = bee (? *or* moth) + mountain

tumbu:ru < tumbe + u:ru = Nilgiri nettle *(Laportea terminalis)* + head village

tu:ne:ri < hu: + ne:ri = flower + common Nilgiri barberry *(Berberis tinctoria)* (3)

tu:raṭṭi < tu:ḍe + haṭṭi = hill mango *(Meliosma wightii)* + hamlet

5. *References to Local Animals*

a:nehaṭṭi < a:ne + haṭṭi = elephant + hamlet (3)

benḍaṭṭi < benḍu + haṭṭi = butterfly + hamlet (2)
hulikal < huli + kallu = tiger + stone; (i.e., stone commemorating a tiger kill)
hulisuḍu < huli + suḍu = tiger + fire
huliyaṭṭi < huli + haṭṭi = tiger + hamlet (2)
iruppukallu < iruppu + kallu = ant + stone
ka:ṭe:ri < ka:ḍu + e:ru = forest + male buffalo
koḍemu:le < koḍa + mu:le = bonnet macaque *(Macaca radiata)* + corner
koikore < koi + kore = jungle hen + patch of cultivated ground
kottibennu < kotti + bennu = wild cat + upper part of back (i.e., curving slope)
morakotti < mora + kotti = tree + wild cat
soreguṇḍu < sore + guṇḍu = sparrow + big boulder
tumbimale *or* dumbimale < dumbi + male = bee (? *or* moth) + mountain; *or* < tumbe + male = Nilgiri nettle + mountain

6. *References to Buffalo Herding*

belidada < beḷḷe + to: = white + buffalo pen
emmale < emme + male = female buffalo + mountain
ha:la:ḍa < ha:lu + ha:ḍa = milk + flat ground
ha:lakore < ha:lu + kore = milk + place
ha:laṭṭi < ha:lu + haṭṭi = milk + hamlet; (also called ha:ḍaṭṭi) (2)
jakkato *or* sakkata < jakkalu + to: = common Nilgiri barberry + buffalo pen
kenduwa < ken + to: = reddish + buffalo pen
kurukuṭti < kuri + kutti = wild sheep + herd
nunduwa < nundu + to: = fertile + buffalo pen; *or* < nundu + hola = fertile + field
pedduwa < ped + to: = big + buffalo pen
tu:dale < tu: + tale = milk-giving ceremony + headland; *or* < tu:ḍe + tale = hill mango + headland

7. *Names Showing Relation to Other Villages*

ćinna kunnu:r < ćinna + kunna + u:ru = small + little + head village

eḍapaḷḷi ‹ eḍe + paḷḷi = middle + small village
edeyu:ru ‹ eḍe + u:ru = middle + head village
ha:liyu:ru ‹ ha:ḻye + u:ru = old *or* former + head village
hosahaṭṭi ‹ hosatu + haṭṭi = new + hamlet (9)
kaḍana:ḍu ‹ kaḍe + na:ḍu = last + tract *or* place
kaḍegu:ḍu ‹ kaḍe + gu:ḍu = last + nest
ke:titore ‹ ke:ti + tore = Ke:ti village + riverside
ki:ṟaṭṭi ‹ ki:ṟ + haṭṭi = lower + hamlet
ko:ḍe:ru ‹ ko:ḍu + e:ṟu = boundary + stone
kukatore ‹ kukalu + tore = Kukalu village + riverside
mainele ‹ maiya + nele = centre + fixed permanent place;
　　(2—one is at the centre of the three old divisions—na:du—of
　　the Nilgiri Plateau)
me:laṭṭi ‹ me:l + haṭṭi = upper + hamlet (3)
me:lu:ru ‹ me:l + u:ru = upper + head village (2)
naḍuhaṭṭi ‹ naḍu + haṭṭi = middle + hamlet (7)
sikkaṭṭi ‹ ćikka (Kannaḍa) + haṭṭi = small + hamlet
sundaṭṭi ‹ sunde + haṭṭi = very small example + hamlet (3)

8. References to a Cultural Feature

aramanehaṭṭi ‹ aramane + haṭṭi = palace + hamlet
de:va:le ‹ de:va + a:le = god's + house
doḍḍamanehaṭṭi ‹ doḍḍa + mane + haṭṭi = great + house +
　　hamlet
hajju:r ‹ huzūr (Arabic) = treasury; (Arabic & Persian, 'royal
　　presence')
ki:ṟkunda ‹ kiṟ + kunda = lower + little district
kolekombe ‹ kole + kombe = magical murder + Kurumba hamlet
kolepaḷḷi ‹ kole + paḷḷi = magical murder + dangerous spot
maḍitore ‹ maḍi + tore = worshipping place + riverside
mandaṇe ‹ manda + haṇe = council-place + flat grassy place
mandaṭṭi ‹ manda + haṭṭi = council-place + hamlet (2)
manepaṭṭu ‹ mane + paṭṭu = house + piece of land
manetale ‹ mane + tale = house + headland
maṇihaṭṭi ‹ maṇi + haṭṭi = bell + hamlet (2)
me:lkunda ‹ me:l + kunda = upper + little district
nattakallu ‹ natta + kallu = erected + stone; (i.e., for memorial,
　　boundary or in a god's name)
udimandu ‹ udi + mandu = medicine bag + Toda hamlet;

(*udi* can also mean act of sorcery, contents of a medicine bag, Toda sorcery, Kurumba sorcery)
udiyakombe < udi + ya + kombe = medicine bag + of + Kurumba hamlet; (*cf.* udimandu)
uyilaṭṭi < ugal + haṭṭi = beyond the boundary + hamlet (3)

9. Fortifications

bɛ̆ko:ṭe < bɛ̃ + ko:ṭe = wild plantain + fort
koṭaṭṭi < ko:ṭe + haṭṭi = fort + hamlet
ko:ṭehaṭṭi < ko:ṭe + haṭṭi = fort + hamlet (2)
ko:ṭenayi < ko:ṭe + nayi = fort + neck (of land) (2)
Note. In addition to the above occupied villages, there are a number of other fortified sites in the Nilgiri area, now in ruins. Most are marked on Map 3 by the letter 'F':

a:nekaṭṭi	korelavadi	osahaḷḷi
ha:lako:ṭe	ko:ṭaṭṭi	pakkasu:ra ko:ṭe
hatra ko:ṭe	ma:deraṭṭi	śembanatta
ka:ramale	ma:lapuram	siru:r
kareko:ṭe	male ko:ṭe	śolapa:ḷaiyam
koḷḷandore	muttukere	yeru:r

(Exact etymologies for some of these remain uncertain.)

10. References to Badaga Men and Women or Clans

adigaraṭṭi < adigiri + haṭṭi = Adikiri clan + hamlet
asagantore < asaga + na + tore = washerman + his + riverside
kaggusi = original hamlet of Kaggusi clan
kaliganaṭṭi < kaliga + na + haṭṭi = Kaliga + his + hamlet
kundanayi < kunda + nayi = Kunda's + neck (of land); (Kunda is a nickname)
kundasappe < kunda + sappe = Kunda's (?) + clumps of tall grass
nandaṭṭi < nanda + haṭṭi = Nanda lineage + hamlet
nañjana:ḍu < nañja + na:ḍu = Nañja's + country; *or* < nañju + na:ḍu = poison + place
na:rekeri < na:re + keri = Na:re's + front yard
o:danaṭṭi < o:da + na + haṭṭi = O:da + his + hamiet

odayaraṭṭi < oḍaya + haṭṭi = Wodeya clan + hamlet (3)
puduṅgaṭṭi < puduṅga + haṭṭi = Puduṅga's + hamlet; (Puduṅga was the name of a priest from the Ha:ruva clan)
tumana:ḍa < duma + na + ha:da = Duma + his + flat ground
tumanaṭṭi < duma + na + haṭṭi = Duma + his + hamlet

11. References to Toda Men or Former Toda Sites

bayigemandu < bayige + mandu = Indian willow + Toda hamlet
kammandu < kam + mandu < (?) kö + moṇ (both Toda words) + mandu = red + soil + Toda hamlet
ke:ti < (?) ke: + ti: = Toda friend + Toda dairy-temple
kiliňjumandu < kiliňju + mandu = pink or red cedar + Toda hamlet
panneve:nu < panne + bennu = any Toda woman + upper part of back
porti < (?) po:š = name of nearby Toda hamlet; *or* < port + ti: = name of a Toda who lived there + Toda dairy temple
pudumandu < pudu + mandu = joint holding + Toda hamlet (2)
udimandu < udi + mandu = medicine bag + Toda hamlet

12. Reference to a Kota Man

o:ranaṛi < o:ra + na + haṛi = O:ṛa + his + home farm; (i.e., nickname of Kota who once owned the land)

13. References to Former Kurumba Hamlets

arekombe < are + kombe = big flat rock + Kurumba hamlet
billikombe < billi + kombe = Nilgiri rhododendron + Kurumba hamlet
de:na:ḍu < de: + na:ḍu = de: (Kurumba cry) + place; (i.e., in each of the three former divisions of the Nilgiris there was one place, called de:na:ḍu,, where Kurumbas camped during large festivals and shouted 'de:de:') (2)
hiriyasi:ge < name of former Kurumba hamlet

kolekombe < kole + kombe = magical murder + Kurumba hamlet

mañjakombe < mañju + kombe = cloud + Kurumba hamlet (which is still there)

mottakambe < motta + kambe = Kurumba hamlet + ridge

sellamotta < sella + motta = Irula's name (?) + Kurumba hamlet

udiyakombe < udi + ya + kombe = medicine bag + of + Kurumba hamlet

14. Reference to an Irula or Kasuva Site

tekali < Irula, Kasuva or perhaps Kurumba place-name (2)

SELECTION OF AN ECOLOGICAL ZONE

A brief look at this list emphasizes not only the significance of topography, soil and vegetation in naming and hence, we may presume, the choice of a new site; but also the insignificance of certain other environmental features. No toponym, for example, makes any reference to the extreme chilliness of this high elevation, even though the penetrating cold is a topic that still often recurs in the conversation of recent immigrants from the lowlands.[2] No toponyms refer to wolves, leopards or bears, although we know these animals inhabited the Nilgiris until a century ago. None refers to deities, although the Badagas worship a multiplicity of them. Very few toponyms mention Badaga settlers by name either: a marked contrast with regions developed by Anglo-Saxon colonists (e.g., Miller, 1969, 246). Most toponyms reflect an economic or aesthetic interest in the montane environment as it was several centuries ago.

What is more remarkable than these omissions is that—unlike frontier-lands elsewhere—there seem to be no instances of a hamlet acquiring the same name as the Mysore village from which its settlers had originated. This would accord with what we might expect of destitute and illiterate refugees wishing to break with their past and not give clues as to their places of origin. Yet, curiously enough, in several cases where legend does supply the name of the Mysore village whence a particular lineage of settlers had come (but where epigraphy does not come to our aid), we find a euphonious similarity with the name given to their new Nilgiri hamlet; e.g., So:lu:ru < Su:lu:r. It is as though some refugees still wanted to be reminded of their old homes but dared not be more explicit for fear of attack from the new Moslem rulers of Mysore. If there be any truth to this hypothesis, it provides an interesting instance of adaptive behaviour in a radically new environment. The following is a complete list of all Badaga hamlets for which local legend tells of a place of origin in Mysore; those marked with an asterisk are ones where the factor of euphony may have entered into the naming.[3]

kaggusi < ha:sanu:ru
e:koni < kavaspa:ḍi
*honatale < honhaḷḷi
ki:ṛu:ru < urigaddige
*hosaṭṭi < honhaḷḷi
me:lu:ru < urigaddige or veḷḷa:di
ebbana:du < urigaddige or ho:sahaḷḷi
*ku:kalu < guṇḍuḷu-pe:te (pe:te = market)
kaḍana:ḍu < karahaḷḷi
ćinna kunnu:r < koṅgaḷḷi
*so:lu:ru < su:lu:r
nunḋuwa < urigaddige
hulikal < honhaḷḷi
ke:ti < koṅgaḷḷi

Two commonly recurring elements in the Badaga toponyms are -u:ru, 'head village', and -haṭṭi, 'hamlet'. Both terms now have specific meanings in Badaga social organization that are not paralleled in Mysore, the haṭṭi being a hamlet, a cluster of contiguous homes, and the u:ru a commune or cluster of contiguous hamlets. There are some 370 hamlets divided among seven communes. Only four of the latter actually bear a toponym ending with -u:ru, however (these names being identical with the head hamlet in each commune). Yet we have seen there are a dozen toponyms ending in -u:ru. Clearly the political organization of Badaga hamlets into thirty-seven communes, and these into three (and more recently four) divisions all under one paramount chief, is an organization that is in its origin more recent than the assigning of names to the hamlets. The Kannaḍa word u:r, 'village', was initially applied by the early settlers to hamlets regardless of any status in a political or administrative hierarchy. The assigning of names to Badaga hamlets was in turn more recent than the actual founding of each hamlet. In the seventeenth and eighteenth centuries when the total Badaga population was no more than one or two thousand people, and their density of settlement only about five to ten people per square mile, it might even have taken several generations before a wooden hut or cluster of huts would have become sufficiently well known to the neighbours living some kilometers away to merit the acquisition of a site-name. 'The name of a village . . . depends for its existence upon the people in the neighbouring villages, not upon those who live in it: the latter are usually content in conversation to refer to it as "here" or "home" or "this village" as distinct from other places. It is the size of the area or population throughout which a place-name is accepted as an identificatory label that determines its persistence and permanence.' (Wainwright, 1962, 58)

As one might expect, not all of the early Badaga settlements did persist. Legend records the names of several dozen that are no longer to be found. Best remembered perhaps is the commune of Tu:ḍu:ru (× tu:ḍe + u:ru = hill mango + head village), which once consisted of nineteen hamlets.[4] 'Tradition says that the Badagas left these places and founded Athikarihatti and its hamlets instead, because the Kurumbas round about continually troubled them with their magic arts and indeed killed by sorcery several of their most prominent citizens (Francis, 1908, 316). A perhaps soberer reason for the abandonment, offered by modern informants, is that the population of all nineteen hamlets was decimated by an epidemic disease some 150 or 200 years ago.[5] Scattered elsewhere across the plateau were several other abandoned hamlets, among them Neddilu, Moritore, Billimale, Eḍeyu:-ru, and a number clustered together on land that has since been bought up by large tea plantations on the southeastern edge of the plateau, around Hulikal.[6]

It appears that during the early phase of their settlement the Badagas came into frequent contact with Todas and Kurumbas and took over a number of sites from both tribes. The unique instances of toponyms referring to Kotas and Irulas (?) suggest that these tribes, by contrast, were insignificant and perhaps not very numerous on the plateau. The Kotas today occupy only six villages there, and the Irulas fewer yet.

The question naturally arises as to how the refugees were able to displace Toda and Kurumba homes. Local tradition offers only a partial answer. As we have seen, it is recorded in Kota folklore that when the first Badaga refugees reached the Nilgiris, they met with a council from the three resident tribes: 'Because of the trouble that the Mohammedan made for us we have come, making ourselves to escape. This country is yours. We are helpless. You must help us.' (Emeneau, 1946, 257; cf. Ouchterlony, 1848, 81) The Toda sites they were given may have been uninhabited religious centers and unoccupied hamlets belonging previously to Toda clans that had died out.[7] The Kurumba sites were more probably relinquished to the Badagas only after the latter had committed some atrocities against the Kurumba sorcerers alleged to live in them. The burning of Kurumba hamlets was certainly a fairly common act of frightened Badagas during the nineteenth century, and numerous instances of it have been recorded by contemporary writers.

As an effect of the peaceful Badaga incursion, we can now identify with the help of a map (Map 3) some micro-environmental differences in the settlement patterns of Badagas, Todas and Kurumbas. The Todas now occupy the higher and more westerly plateau area commonly known as Wenlock Downs,

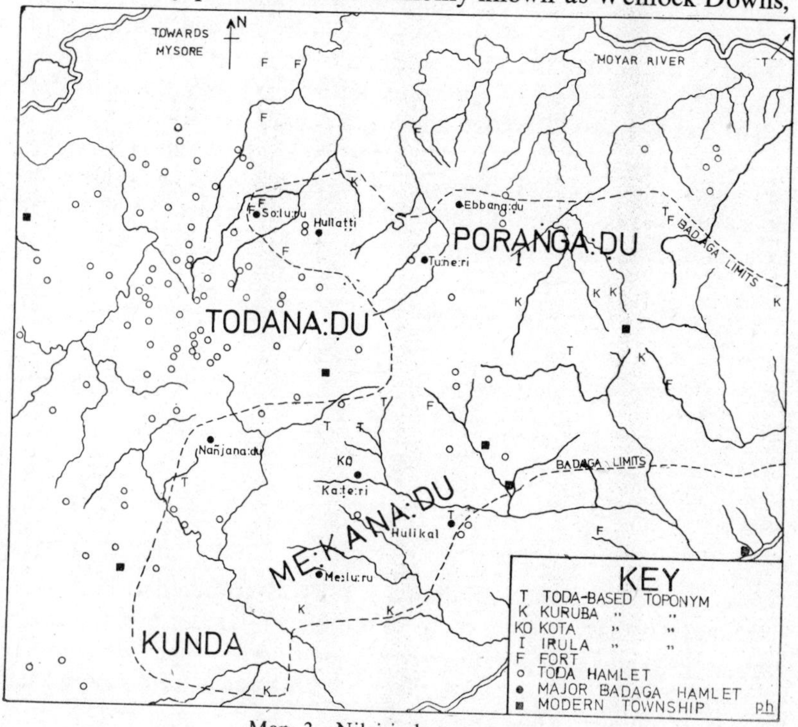

Map 3 Nilgiri place-names

an undulating grassland interspersed with temperate woodland in the dales. The elevation of their hamlets ranges from 2,400 to 2,000 meters. The Badagas now occupy the eastern half of the Nilgiri Plateau, which is heavily cultivated by them as well as by more recent settlers, and the settled parts of which range in elevation from 2,200 (Mainele hamlet) to 1,200 meters (Hiriyasi:ge). The Kurumbas and Irulas are to be found only on the jungle-covered escarpments and lower slopes of the Nilgiris, at elevations varying from 1,500 down to 450 meters. The highest Badaga hamlet with a 'Kurumba' toponym occurs however at 1,800 meters and points to the displacement of Kurumba villagers towards lower and less healthy levels. On the other hand we find that the lowest Badaga hamlet with a 'Toda' toponym (Pudumandu) occurs at an elevation of 1,700; indeed five such Badaga hamlets lie lower than any present-day Toda hamlet. This indicates a displacement of the Todas into higher elevations (by what means we cannot tell, unless it be that the Badaga immigrants introduced diseases for which the Todas had no immunity) and shows that Badaga settlement somehow resulted in the creation of a zone between 1,500 and 2,000 meters which was exclusively their own and which merged at its upper limits with the areas of Toda settlement and at its lower limits with the highest of Kurumba settlements. What was it that the Badagas found attractive about this zone in the Nilgiris?

We can find additional evidence for the kind of ecological niche in which they located themselves from the village names. A revealing break-down of those Badaga toponyms referring to vegetation is summarized here:

Number of villages with, as referrents:

forest	12
swamp	5
grass	13
bracken	2
tree	33
shrub	19
other plant species	17

Some further information about the floral chracteristics of the Badaga zone can be gleaned from a different type of break-down, one that takes into account those toponyms which refer to a particular biome or a plant species with known and somewhat restricted ecological distribution:

Number of villages with, as referents:

dense forest	28
forest verge and clearing	33
open grassland	16
swampland	5

We obviously cannot push the meaning of such figures very far, but they do suggest that (at least for floral toponyms) more often than not the Badagas settled elsewhere than in the open but exposed grasslands favoured by the Todas for grazing. Beyond telling us the obvious—that swampland was a least-favoured locale for Badaga settlement—the latter break-down does make it clear that within their zone of occupation dense forests and clearings or the verges of woodland were much favoured over grasslands or savannas for village sites. The extra work needed to make fields by slash-and-burn techniques in the forest was more than compensated for by the much richer soil available there as compared with the lateritic grasslands and swamps where the Toda buffalo herds roamed. (Hamlets with toponyms referring to rocks and stones, it is important to note, are often located in areas that are or were forested; large trees beside their temples may still bear witness to this.)

Among the toponyms referring to particular plant species there are two mentioning millet:

Battakore (any millet)—at 2,050 meters
Togalaṭṭi (jungle dholl, a wild millet)—at 1,900 meters

Gamble's admirable *Flora of Madras* lists the ranges in elevation for the following millets (among others), all of them important in the Nilgiri economy:[8]

korali —Italian millet *(Setaria italica)*—'widely cultivated'
sa:me—slender millet (*Panicum miliare*)—up to 2,150 meters
tene or navaṇe—black Italian millet *(Sacciolepis indica)*—up to 2,000 meters
baragu—Kodo millet *(Paspalum scrobiculatum)*—up to 2,150 meters
ra:gi—finger millet *(Eleusine coracana)*—up to 1,500 meters

Metz's mid-nineteenth century account of the chief millets of the Nilgiris adds a little to our understanding of micro-environmental differences in their cultivation on the plateau:

> The most common grain is what the natives call Korrali, which ... grows best in the colder districts Kundenad and Mekanad where the other finer grains do not grow.
>
> Sāmé ... which is considered the best kind of the several small grains of the Hills. It grows in the warmer districts and must have better soil.
>
> Tenney or Navoney ... which also grows only in warm places ...
>
> Varagu ... which grows only on the slopes of the Hills in feverish places and requires ... a warmer climate, than the Hill plateau affords.
>
> Ragy ... grows also only in places where the cold Monsoon wind cannot come ... (Metz, 1864, 152–153)

In general a careful observer, the Rev. Metz (who roamed the plateau daily for a quarter of a century) mentions here *baragu* and *ra:gi,* two species that were cultivated mainly by Kurumbas and Irulas on the lower slopes because of the greater warmth needed. Though grown occasionally in the lowest Badaga hamlets, neither was an important crop. The other three species were the main subsistence crops for Badagas.

We are led to the conclusion that the Badagas displaced Kurumbas and perhaps some Todas as well in the zone which they made their own, and which was best suited to dry cultivation of their millets. While the upper limits of the zone were apparently determined by the viability of these millets, the lower limits may have been determined not by horticultural requirements but by the elevation above which malarial parasites will not breed, about 1,000 meters. (The full development of the *plasmodium* parasites in mosquito requires a minimum daily temperature of 60°F (15.6°C), which is only maintained at the lower elevations relegated to the Kurumbas, Irulas and others.) In the mid-nineteenth century Hodgson (1856, 499–500) noted plateau sites 'where formerly Kurumba villages existed but where none are now found. It is well known that the Kurumbas were driven down from the healthful summit to the malarious slope of the hills. . . .'

Not only did the Badaga settlers displace residents from these several tribes: they also removed much forest cover and radically changed the Nilgiri ecology, in the view of many experts, well before the first British planters arrived in the eighteen- forties.

> There can be little question that these tracts, which are now

> given up almost wholly to the plough or hoe, were once covered with dense jungle, except the more stony ridges and heights. This is evidenced by the numerous shóla trees, single or in groups of two or three, standing generally near a rock or stream, which have owed their escape from the general destruction to the superstitious fears of the people, who regard them as the homes of the unseen genii of the place. The frequent occurrence of the suffix *kȧd,* jungle or forest, in names of localities. where now hardly a tree is to be found, is additional proof... (Grigg, 1880, 9).

This pronounced ecological change has generated a number of studies exploring the likelihood that the more westerly grasslands now occupied by the Todas were also originally heavily forested areas that succumbed to annual fires started by these herdsmen (e.g., Noble, 1967; Blasco 1971). While that question is of little significance in our present study, it does emphasize the manner in which ecological change may be so devastating as to alter the environment almost beyond recognition after a toponym has been assigned to a site there.

NOTES

1. The + used in these lists merely links the morphemes in a word, and is not to be considered as a symbol of juncture. Numbers in parentheses indicate the number of times a toponym is repeated.
2. On cold nights frost can form.
3. Euphony is an important feature of Badaga speech and is a characteristic in hundreds of their proverbs; e.g.,
   hattu jina sa:la/
   ten days debt,
   ondu jina su:la
   one day venereal disease:
   i.e., 'For ten days it will be a debt, but one day it will become a venereal sore.'
4. These were Tu:ḍu:ru, Kaṇaṭṭi, Kolekombe, Kuriyamale, Bekode, Tuha:ḍa, Hatare, Malligo:re, Tiddere, Kaggeri, Hayu:ru, Koṅamotta, Ha:ḷaṭṭaṇe, Ha:ḷa:ḍa, Honnimaṇṇu, Baṇahaṭṭi, and Gonne:ri. Since these names are almost unknown to present-day Badagas we cannot be precise about their pronunciation or meaning.
5. Remnants of this population now live in nearby Ko:ḍe:ru and can still recall something of their history.
6. These latter were named Beṭṭaṭṭi, Koṭaṭṭi, Kareko:ṭe, Baṇahaṭṭi, Ta:veka:ḍu, Beṇḍaṭṭi, and Pannamaḍai.
7. During the past century there have been several well-documented cases of Toda hamlets being abandoned.
8. It may be recalled that the Nilgiri Plateau rises to an elevation of 2634 meters in Doḍḍabeṭṭa, 'Great Mountain'.

3

Social Groupings

The extensive oral history surveyed in Chapter 1 helps clarify distinctive features of each clan and phratry, identifying their different places of origin, the various routes they took into the hills and the sequence in which they arrived.[1] These legends are more than fictional entertainment: they validate the continued occupancy of each village by members of a particular clan.

We now raise a sociological question that is intended to clarify subsequent chapters: once the migrants had settled in the Nilgiris, how was marriage regulated, and how was the continuance of social units ensured from one generation to the next? (We admit at the outset that how they happened to synoecize into the Badaga community is a question which remains unanswered.)

Indian caste society has usually been described in terms of joint family, lineage, clan and *jati* (subcaste), but in the Badaga case—which fits a caste model imperfectly—we will refer to the following categories instead. These social units are listed in order of increasing breadth:

A. Joint patrilocal family	(exogamous; occupies one village)
B. Minimal lineage	(exogamous; occupies one village)
C. Minor lineage	(exogamous; occupies one village)
D. Major lineage	(exogamous; occupies one or several villages)
E. Maximal lineage	(exogamous; occupies one or several villages)

F.	Patrilineal clan	(exogamous; widespread)
G.	Phratry	(endogamous or sometimes exogamous; widespread)
H.	Moiety	(endogamous or sometimes exogamous; Nilgiri-wide)
I.	Badaga community	(generally endogamous; Nilgiri-wide)
J.	Fourteen *kolas* or septs	(exogamous; in popular belief, South- India-wide)

THE JOINT PATRILOCAL FAMILY

The Badaga family is always patrilineal and nearly always patrilocal. Because of the power it wields a joint family is the ideal and every third generation typically passes through this desired state. Thus a young couple establish a new home in the village of the groom's father. Their children, if male, should remain in the same house with their parents, or be married into another village if female. Then the young men take brides from villages of affines, bring them to the parental home and raise their children there. At this juncture there would be three generations living under the same roof: (1) unmarried grandchildren, (2) unmarried daughters, married sons and their wives, (3) the parents. On the death of the founding father the brothers are expected to leave his house and establish separate homes. The dispersal of the household has three causes—architectural, legal, and psychological. The first is that Badaga houses have only two or three fairly small rooms and by the time that three generations, two of them with spouses, are occupying one house there is an acute shortage of space—a situation which may be aggravated by polygyny. The legal cause of dispersal is ultimogeniture: Badaga law requires that the youngest son inherit his father's house and at the same time take care of the widowed mother (Rivers, 1906, 559–560). Financial provision should be made for all older brothers to build separate houses. The psychological causes are the total lack of privacy and the elder brothers' uneasy feeling of indebtedness to the youngest brother who legitimately owns the house. A further complication is that in recent years one brother working in an office has become increasingly loath to share a relatively high income with his extended family. Thus large joint families are no longer as common as they were half a century ago: an average Badaga household today contains only 5.5 members, and the range in size is from one to perhaps twenty.

LINEAGE

Several joint families able to agree on precisely how they are descended from a common male ancestor consider themselves a *minimal* or a *minor lineage* (in Baḍagu, *guppu).* This is an exogamous and patrilineal group living in a single village and is the most important lineage for members, often the only one they know by name. It tends to split into two lineages every four or five generations. The *guppu* is a unit within which interest-free loans are obtained and which even today has a buffalo herd in common. It no longer holds land in common, though at its inception the joint family of the founder did, and each descendant is still entitled to a proportion of his land. This lineage tends to hold family ceremonies together. If further participants are wanted at such ceremonies the remainder of the *major lineage* (in Baḍagu, *kutti)* can be invited. This consists of at least two minor lineages the leaders of which can trace their ancestry back to a common founder. Very often the major lineages in one or several neighbouring villages summate to a *maximal lineage* (in Baḍagu, *kuḍumbu)* and responsible members can trace their actual descent from its founder, too. All levels of lineage can be referred to by a founder's name, though in many villages no more than one level is now recognized. Lineages of all levels may be invited to attend family ceremonies.

From the example in Diagram 6 it can be seen that a maximal lineage has a depth of about seven generations. As at O:ranayi the maximal lineage is very often coterminous with the village, which explains the exogamy of most villages. There are, however, some exceptional villages, notably those of the Wodeas and Toreas, and of the Gaudas of So:lu:ru commune and Ha:sanu:ru, which contain several distinct lineages from *different* clans within each village; so that while exogamy still marks the lineage it is not characteristic of the villages.

There is a strong sense of lineage solidarity, strongest at the minor level but still significant at the maximal. In case of a dispute

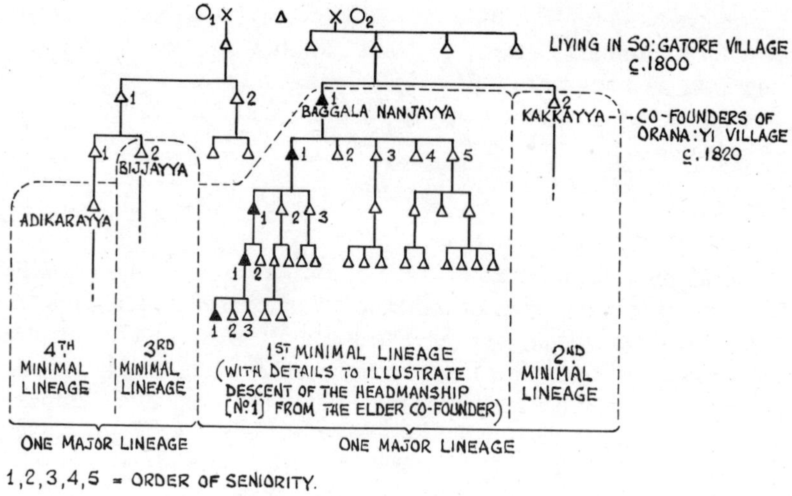

Diagram 6. O:ranayi village: A maximal lineage.

with someone outside the villager's own lineage, be it minimal, minor, major or maximal, his fellow members are usually willing to support him even though this means agreeing to false evidence. Such behaviour helps keep land and other valuables within the lineage and can also uphold the good name of a lineage and the village it inhabits. Solidarity is also expressed when a man wants to sell some land. He must offer it first to other members of his minimal or minor lineage, then to his major lineage, then to his maximal, then to any other inhabitants of his village, then to people in neighbouring villages. Only in the unusual case when nobody in this sequence will buy may he offer the land to Badagas from elsewhere. The land surrounding each village is typically owned by families of that village only.

CLAN

Several maximal lineages make up the *clan* (in American terminology, the *sib*). Like the lineage the clan is exogamous; but it is rarely confined to a single village. A lineage embraces all the patrilateral descendants of a known common ancestor (Schusky, 1965, 77) whereas a clan, made up of two or more lineages, is a unilinear kin group in which actual descent from a common male ancestor is now only a presumption (Gillin, 1948, 439; Murdock 1949, 66; Firth, 1951, 53; for fuller information on Badaga kinship, see Hockings, in press).

At this level of social organization the unit is spatially widespread: two clans are confined to a single village each (only among Kumba:ras); others are represented in clusters of nearby villages, while over half the forty-four clans are Nilgiri-wide in occurrence.

Clans are relevant in the arrangement of marriages, for there are fixed rules about which clans may marry; for example, Adikiris may marry Ha:ruvas but never Kaggusis. Clans may also form a community of interest for the pursuit of really serious disputes. In 1897, for instance, the Ha:ruvas of two different lineages in neighbouring villages were in dispute over which should have precedence during the annual fire-walking ceremony at Me:lu:ru. Having arrived at a compromise by which each group celebrated the festival on the alternate years, the whole Ha:ruva clan laid claim to a higher status than Wodeas, Adikiris or Kaṇakkas. A schism within the Ha:ruva clan has not emerged since (see below, pp. 203–204).

PHRATRY

Among the Badagas two to fourteen clans form a larger unit that we call the *phratry.* Most of these phratries and some of the clans have been called sects or subcastes by previous authors, if only because they are named social units. It is manifestly confusing, however, to apply the same term to two quite distinguishable kinds of social unit. A phratry is usually defined as a grouping of two or more clans whose members assume a conventional bond of kinship which, though undemonstrable, is at least supported with a story of their common origin. In the Badaga community most phratries are non-exogamous, but in certain cases exogamy is tolerated; no Badaga phratry is totally endogamous (Lowie, 1948, 338; compare Diagram 7). The phratries each carry a distinguishable subculture. The smallest in size are divided into two clans, identifiable as agnates and affines. Phratries with more than about a thousand members have a larger number of clans and thus a more complex internal organization. In this respect the two thousand Christians mark the extreme of complexity.

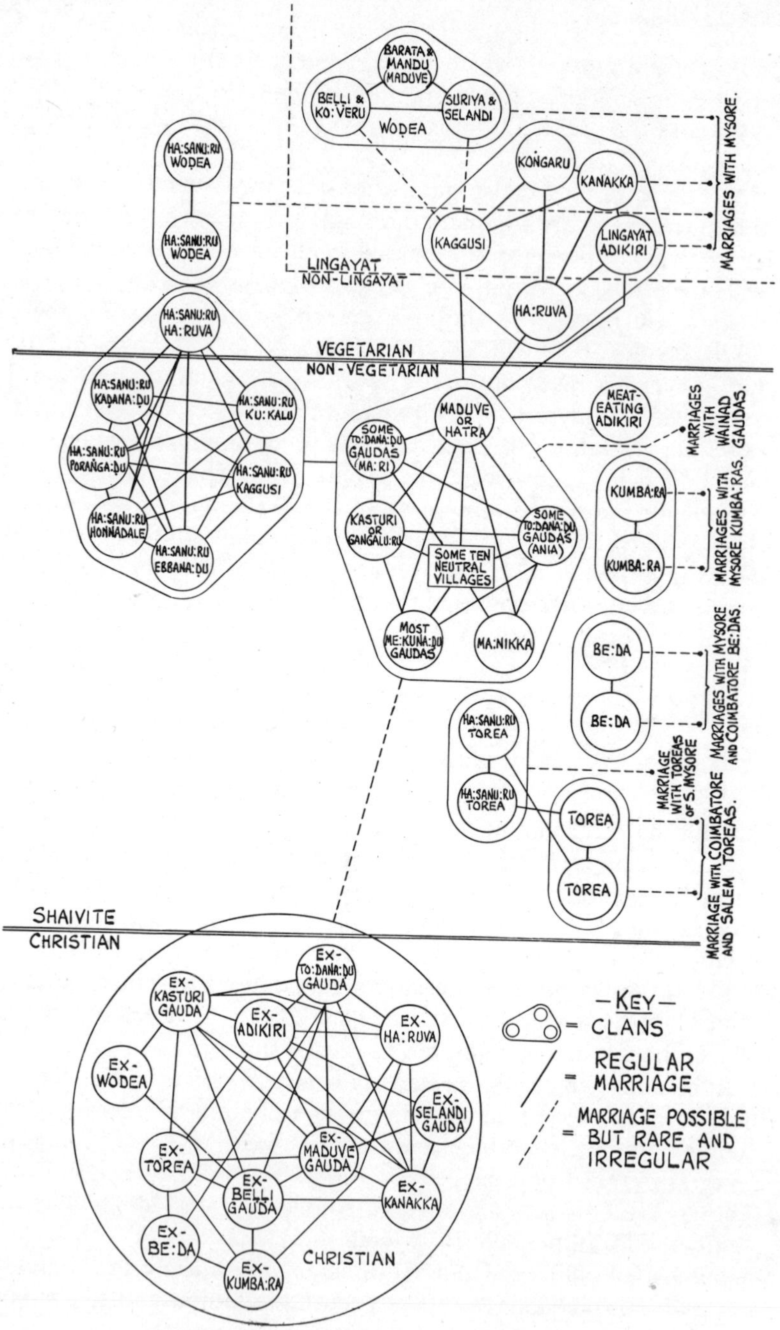

Diagram 7. The Badaga clans and phratries

MOIETIES

Some societies, among them the Todas and Australian aborigines, have only two phratries, which are then called moieties. Other societies, notably in the lowland areas of India, Pakistan, Ceylon and Nepal, have a number of endogamous phratries ranked into long-lasting social hierarchies; such units, called *jatis* or subcastes, may summate to castes or to *jati*-clusters (cf. Mandelbaum, 1970, *passim*).

Badaga society, consisting of forty-four clans and ten phratries, is now in the anomalous position of being to some extent a moiety organization, to some extent a *jati* organization. This situation has arisen, I suggest, because two different models have been available to the Badagas for emulation, a Brahminic one known to them from lowland caste society and—unique in India—a tribal one represented by Toda social organization. Their situation became yet more complex when in the nineteenth century Westernization also began, and a tenth Christian phratry grew out of six of the others. This complexity has not been properly appreciated, for though several earlier writers have described Badaga society as a hierarchy of subcastes none has considered it to have moieties. Yet the neighbouring Todas possess a well-known moiety system. In their case there are now sixteen exogamous patrilineal clans, six in Teivali (töwfiḷy) moiety and ten in Tarthar (to:ṟθas). The two moieties are endogamous, and Tarthar has a ritual superiority over Teivali which is expressed by ownership of the most sacred grades of temple and buffalo; the priests who sacrifice buffalo calves belong to Teivali.[2]

The Badagas show much more cultural diversity than the Todas, largely as an effect of having come at various times from different places and from varying caste and religious backgrounds. Nevertheless we may consider them (at least for the sake of argument) to have two well-defined, culturally heterogeneous moieties—one vegetarian, the other not. As we have already seen, the act of eating meat placed some ancestral groups definitively in one moiety, where they have since remained. In this connexion it is worth noting that while both Toda moieties are vegetarian, it is only the priests of the lower moiety (Teivali) who kill calves and also the more sacred buffaloes sacrificed at a funeral. A further parallel between the two societies is that, just as Todas of Teivali moiety have to perform certain priestly functions for Tarthar, so men in the Ha:ruva and Wodea clans perform a priestly role only for clans of the other Badaga moiety. Among Todas a kind of secondary marriage is permissible between the otherwise endogamous moieties (Rivers, 1906, 699–700); among Badagas formal marriage may sometimes occur between the usually endogamous moieties, provided that the man or woman from the meat-eating moiety abstain from meat while in the presence of the vegetarian spouse. It is important to note that the present trend in Badaga society is towards total endogamy of each moiety: Ha:ruva, Adikiri and Kaggusi marriage with Gaudas has been decreasing in this century, and Lingayats now avoid marrying into the Ha:ruva families which also have marriage connexions with Gaudas; yet hypogamy and hypergamy are both still permissible. Were the Badagas moving towards a caste model of society, one might expect hypogamy to disappear (since it is not usual in caste societies) and further culinary distinctions to be adopted. For example, distinctions might then be made, as elsewhere in India, between those who eat beef, those who take mutton but no beef, those eating eggs but no meat and those solely vegetarian. Yet no such complication is emerging: people are strengthening the boundary between households of vegetarian and of non-vegetarian diet, but no finer distinctions are drawn. The moiety of vegetarians includes all of the clans noted for their religious orthodoxy, while the larger non-vegetarian moiety includes most of the better educated, somewhat westernized and economically influential families.

SEPTS

The Badaga clans are reputedly distributed among sixteen septs which, it is asserted, cross-cut all of South Indian society. In their theory every clan of every Hindu caste is affiliated to one or more exogamous *kolas;* the Badaga clans were of the same *kolas* even before leaving Mysore, and indeed fourteen of their *kolas* are still identifiable among Mysore castes. *Kola* has thus to be defined as a sept or patrilineal descent group, 'a group of persons, all of whom believe themselves to be related, owning some relation to an object animate or inanimate, and exhibiting the taboo-behaviour towards it.... There does not appear to be any larger organisation comprising the various kulas (Srinivas, 1942, 32). Their distribution, according to Badaga elders, is as follows:

Su:riya ('sun')	former chieftains from Mysore; some Wodeas
Chandra ('moon')	servants of the former rulers, Koṅgaru (?)
Barata ('finger')	some Wodeas
Brahma (god Brahma)	Ha:ruvas
Beḷḷi ('silver')	some Wodeas, Kaggusis, Gaudas of Jakkatala and Neḍugula; some Toreas of Kaige:ru area; some Be:das
Selandi ('spider')	some Wodeas and Gaudas of Hulikal and 'Koṅgaru' Gaudas—both descended from Wodeas
Ko:ve:ru (Cauvery R.)	some Wodeas, some Adikiris, and Toreas descended from those Adikiris
Madure (holy city of Madurai)	some Wodeas
Kasturi ('musk')	some Adikiris, some Gaudas of Ke:ti, and some Toreas of Ebbana:du
Mallige ('jasmine')	some Kumba:ras and Be:das
Ania ('aliens', 'different people')	Gaudas of Ku:kalu and Nañjana:ḍu
Ma:ri (goddess Ma:ri)	Gaudas of Todana:du
Maduve ('marriage')	some Wodeas; Gaudas of Poraṅga:ḍu
Ma:nika ('gem')	Kaṇakkas (who claim their sept to be Ma:nta); some Gaudas of Jakkane:ri; some Toreas
Na:ga ('cobra')	some Toreas of Kappaṭṭi area
Samandi ('champac flower')	some Kumba:ras

Of living Badagas few, even among the elders, know much about their septs, but in earlier times these were very relevant, particularly before the society took on its present structure, and also when marriages were being arranged between families of clans not well known to each other; '... exogamy having progressed, if we may say so, more rapidly than social differentiation, it was necessary to call into question an increasingly large number of clans, to adapt the old institutions to the new rules' (trans. from Lévi-Strauss, 1968, 480). In the reorganization of social thinking that followed settlement on the hills, Badagas may well have found membership in already established septs a helpful guide, the rule of sept exogamy and the wide knowledge of their names protecting against in-breeding between families from the same descent group.

In former times the septs were quasi-totemic, as elsewhere in India.[3] One old lady of Selandi ('spider') sept recently asserted that members of that collectivity should never kill a spider; Wodeas of Beḷḷi ('silver') sept may not wear silver ornaments; Toreas, however, no longer have a special relation with the cobra though some belong to Na:ga ('cobra') sept and were formerly forbidden to kill it.

The Badagas do not distinguish between what Lévi-Strauss (following S.V. Karandikar) calls big and little *gotras* (septs). 'Big' *gotras* are said to be of recent Brahminic origin and few in number; whereas 'little' *gotras* 'appearing sometimes as territorial groups, sometimes as lineages, as clans or subdivisions of a clan, sometimes patrilineal and sometimes matrilineal, are ... the object of exogamous rules of great complexity' (trans. from Lévi-Strauss, 1968, 478–479). Clearly the Badaga septs are 'little' *gotras*. As such they were concerned, not with political divisions or different schools of ritual, but solely with the arrangement of marriage alliances. Each of their sixteen septs is distributed through one or several clans; conversely, the Gaudas belong to seven septs, and other phratries to as few as two septs.

JATI, MARRIAGE PREFERENCE AND ROLE AMBIGUITY

Although it is possible to view the society as a pair of moieties, the phratries, like social units in nearly every part of India, are ranked by members into a hierarchy about which there is considerable but not total agreement.[4]

All Hindu Badagas agree that the Christians are now the lowest phratry, and this estimation is reflected in disapproval of intermarriage and a lack of formal interdining between Christians and the higher phratries. There is also agreement that the Toreas are next lowest; higher groups should neither dine nor intermarry with them. At the other end of the scale there is near-universal accord on the supreme position of Wodeas. Though the great majority of the community are not Lingayats they cite the purity of a Wodea's vegetarian diet and the orthodoxy of his sectarian observances as support for his high rank. Many also maintain that the Wodeas were descended from ancient Virashaiva Lingayats, reached the Nilgiris before any other Lingayats and came as priests, for which reasons too they deserve primacy.

Nobody disputes with the Christians or the Toreas for their lowly position, not even the Kota tribe who find themselves ranked lower still. On the other hand there is a movement now afoot to accord the Ha:ruvas higher status than the Wodeas: this springs from the minority who support a pro-Ha:ruva and pro-music faction. The mechanics of upward mobility for Ha:ruvas, a vegetarian group since its inception, have been to abrogate marital links with lower clans. The Ha:ruvas may marry Gaudas (non-vegetarians), Koṅgaru (vegetarians), Kaṇakkas and Adikiris (both Lingayat vegetarians). At present the frequency of marriage with Gaudas is decreasing noticeably, so that the Ha:ruvas are shifting away from their lower-status affines while becoming more closely linked by marriage with the Lingayats, though not adopting Lingayat religious practices themselves.

Recently Mandelbaum (1970, 20) has described the Badagas as a *jati*-cluster. It is true that the units often identified as subcastes are now thought to constitute a hierarchy; but *none* of the ten is totally endogamous like a *jati*. Hypogamous marriages occur as often as hypergamous ones, a state of affairs not found between *jatis*, especially as marriage may take place between vegetarian and non-vegetarian Badagas. The ceremonial and economic links that one expects between *jatis* are of no consequence here except at the top of the hierarchy: Wodeas and Ha:ruvas do have attenuated ritual roles to play for the rest of the community, though over the past forty years these have been almost abandoned. Such linkages between the groupings are slight as compared with the economic and ceremonial ties between any Badaga village and its nearest Kota neighbour. These facts do not really justify calling the Badaga community a hierarchy or cluster of *jatis*: the concept of *jati* is unnecessary to this analysis. Phratry is the usual word by which anthropologists identify a grouping of clans, and there is no need to depart from that form here, especially as by doing so we might conjure up ideas of multi-caste villages, *jati* endogamy and *jati* occupational specialization which find no place in Badaga social organization although they are widespread in India.

M.N. Srinivas (personal comment, 1965) is probably right in suggesting, however, that at some point in the past, perhaps a couple of centuries ago, the Badagas adopted a caste model of society (or revived memories of the old Mysorean one) and attempted with only moderate success to fit their collection of lineages to it: indeed this perhaps was the act of synoecism. The inadequate fit that they achieved is reflected both in recent shifts in the ranking and in the ambiguous position that the claim to Brahminic status has brought to the Ha:ruvas. This group long ago adopted the 'sacred' thread,[5] a vegetarian diet and the role of priests, but they have no initiation ceremony, no *śra:ddha* for the dead and—having been illiterate—no Sanskrit or other holy writings. In the mid-nineteenth century they were still quite ignorant of Hindu scriptures, (B.E.M.S., 1867, no. 28, 73). They now find themselves caught between two models, as it were, for while they are trying to develop the image of orthodox Brahmins other Badagas find that model much less appealing then a new westernizing model upheld by Christians and by the large, dominant Gauda phratry, a model that displaced their older tribal model nearly a century ago. A more general ambiguity is expressed by shifts in the ranking of the hierarchy as certain Badagas attempt to achieve a more convincing accord between recently learnt Brahminic ideals and local needs. Since the Badagas have shown little willingness to modify the customary marriage patterns they are obliged to accept the anomaly of a hierarchy relevant only for ritual and not for marriage purposes: this sets them off from the usual model of caste society in which the units of the hierarchy are clearly delineated by marriage rules.

Another explanation for the lack of concern about status congruence when a marriage is being arranged is that the social status of a young girl is determined by the village where she lives. Girls before puberty are for many purposes treated as children of the entire village rather than of one particular family. Once a girl has attained menarche (in earlier days, before that) she should be married into another village, where she becomes identified with her husband's family and where her status is determined only by the clan and the affluence of that family, never by her own father's. The same attitude towards women is clearly reflected in the kinship system, where only the males' generation level is important in determining relationships. The generation level of a woman is that of her husband and can actually change as she marries successive husbands from different generations.[6] Though a cross-cousin is preferred, a Badaga may marry women, either concurrently or sequentially, from his aunts' and nieces' generation levels as well as from his own: such co-wives would all attain the generation level of their husband by these marriages. It is this outlook on women that permits Badaga marriages even between differently ranked clans without any thought of hypergamy being advantageous or hypogamy reprehensible.

Marriage between cross-cousins is the ideal, but because a young man's spiritual guidance is the responsibility of the mother's brother his daughter is less preferable as a bride for that youth than the father's sister's daughter. The mother's brother, called a *guru,* has a distinctly superior status to his nephew's, yet as giver of a daughter in marriage he must occupy an inferior position in the eyes of the groom and the groom's parents. This is because the bride's father feels under some obligation to the family who will take away his daughter. As one old man explained the matter, the feeling is expressed in the newly emerging practice of offering gifts of some thousands of rupees to 'bribe' a youth into a marriage. The likelihood of role ambiguity in cases where a man marries his *guru's* daughter is avoided either by searching out a classificatory cross-cousin, or by choosing the daughter of a mother's brother other than the spiritual guide or by marrying a father's sister's daughter. (Only among the Toreas is marriage with a classificatory niece permissible: she is a father's brother's daughter's daughter.)

Role ambiguity may also affect the women in a household where a man has married his *guru's* daughter. In that situation the bride's aunt (her father's sister) is also her husband's mother. The bride, relying on her father's influence over his own sister, tends to quarrel more with her than in the alternative case where a man has married his father's sister's daughter: the latter should be more timid and controllable and thus more appreciated.

A further reason for preferring marriage with a daughter of the father's sister is the need for reciprocity in bride-giving between exogamous villages. If a man marries his mother's brother's daughter, he is *taking* a girl from the same village, lineage and family whence his own father also *took* a wife. On the other hand a reciprocal relationship has been honoured, Badagas feel, when the youth *takes* his bride (the father's sister's daughter) from the same village, lineage and family to which his father's father *gave* a daughter in marriage. Since bride-giving is thought to be somewhat demeaning, this reciprocity allows the families to maintain their relative social standing.

Another factor entering into the choice of a bride is expressed in the proverb, 'Have the girl from a far-away place; have the cow from a nearby place.'[7] It is generally felt that a woman from a distant village who is a classificatory cross-cousin will make the best of wives, for she will not take too many liberties with affines who are not previously well-known to her, and at the same time she will be unable to run home to her parents too often; in short, she is likely to remain in the marital home and work adequately there. An example of an ideal marriage with a classificatory father's sister's daughter is to be seen in Diagram 9 (p. 179) (the man marked X). The principle of 'equivalence' of brothers in this kinship table makes X's wife a cross-cousin to him.

In Chapter 10 we will discuss the manner in which the modern Badaga community is becoming a class society. We should nonetheless note here that already by the nineteenth century a class of 'gentry' had arisen in each village. This is the term I have chosen for the families descended from the village founders and including all of the headman. As will be seen, these people had higher social status than others and a peculiar status in Badaga law, to be explored in Chapter 8.

The marriage system which now links the forty-four Badaga clans into ten phratries is a very complex one and calls for a clarifying diagram to accompany the following pages of description. Each circle in Diagram 7 represents one clan, and the intervening lines link clans which customarily intermarry. Clans have been grouped into phratries. The dotted lines mark irregular but acceptable patterns of marriage. The subcultural divisions between Lingayats and other Shaivites, between Christians and Shaivites, and between vegetarians and meat-eaters, have also been indicated.

WODEAS

The majority of Badagas rank Wodeas as the highest phratry in the community.[8] They occupy twelve villages scattered across the plateau, some very close to the villages of lower phratries. Their villages are not all exogamous. There are perhaps four thousand Wodeas, distributed among three unnamed clans, or six septs. These septs, with their variant names, are as follows:

Clan I: Ṣu:riya and Selandi (or Sedili) septs;

Clan II: Ko:ve:ru (Ko:vu:r or Koyaru) and Belli septs;
Clan III: Barata and Maduve (otherwise Maituve or Mandu) septs. This last clan, whose ancestors had come from the Aṅgala monastery where they were *Jaṅgama* priests, provides priests (Woderu) for most other Badagas.

Because the clans are not actually named, the confusing practice has grown up of referring to them either by the names of villages where they are found or by the names of their constituent septs. Further identification of the clans is found in the unusual feature of their recognizing clan deities. As with the Lingayat Mallavas of Coorg (Srinivas, 1942, 36–37), Wodeas who worship the same god may not intermarry.

Wodea marriages are arranged between members of any two of the three clans, even if between inhabitants of the same village; marriages also link those of the Nilgiris with those of Ha:sanu:ru. Since the beginning of this century marriages have been contracted with Lingayat girls from the Wodea caste of Mysore who, unlike Badaga girls, bring a dowry and are often well-educated: outsiders are thus increasingly entering the community. Some intermarriage with Kaggusis has occurred, and in a few cases Wodea girls have married Kaṇakkas.[9]

Wodeas, however, cite not only their supposed royal origins[10] but also the longer time they have lived in the Nilgiris as reasons for the near-absence of intermarriage between them and the other Lingayat clans. Initially, too, they were suspicious about whether these immigrants really were Lingayats; and furthermore the fact that people of these three clans may marry non-Lingayats is obviously not lost on the Wodeas. Locally they are considered a very conservative and orthodox Lingayat group, in the sense that they abide strictly by whatever prescriptions and proscriptions of the Lingayat creed are known to them. Lingayats of Mysore might regard them as rather unorthodox, though, for the Badagas were illiterate until this century and were thus unable to read Lingayat scriptures or even to follow the religious calendar properly (B.E.M.S., 1867, no. 28, 73). Apparently the Wodeas had established their position as a self-perpetuating phratry in the Nilgiris before the other Lingayats arrived.

In the past Wodeas did not accept food from Ha:ruvas or any socially inferior phratry but would eat in the inner room of any other Wodea house (Grigg, 1880, 220). Their food may only be cooked in metal vessels, not earthenware. Other Badagas take food (always vegetarian) only in the outer, less-sacred part of a Wodea house. Members of the Nilgiri tribes accept food from the Wodeas too, but are not allowed to pass beyond the veranda into the house.

KOṄGARU

These people, like Ha:ruvas, wear a single thread without *liṅga* and are vegetarian. They intermarry with Kaṇakkas, Ha:ruvas and Kaggusis. There are four villages of Kongaru.

HA:RUVAS

Like the Wodeas, the one clan of Ha:ruvas numbers about four thousand people. They occupy only six villages, but this does not imply that the villages are unusually large, for very often a Ha:ruva family lives permanently in a Gauda village. Perhaps half the Ha:ruvas are so distributed, as they have traditionally been priests in Gauda and Torea temples. Of the five clans making up the phratry to which they belong (the only unnamed one), Ha:ruvas alone have challenged the Wodeas for primacy in the social hierarchy. The ramifications of this claim will be explored when the Badaga factions are discussed (see below, pp. 203–204).

Ha:ruvas are vegetarian Shaivites but not Lingayats. For over a century they have been claiming that they were originally Brahmins before leaving Mysore and that they should therefore be treated as such.[11] This Brahminization, reminiscent of the nineteenth-century Kherwar movement in the Santal tribe (Orans, 1965, 36–37), has been primarily an attempt to gain higher rank. Little of Ha:ruva behaviour accords with that of true Mysore Brahmins, however. The three indicators in support of their Brahminhood are the observable facts that they are vegetarians, they wear a thread across the left shoulder and they have acted as temple priests to the great majority of Shaivite Badagas.[12]

Despite these arguments the subculture of the Ha:ruvas is for Brahmins a most atypical one: they have no special ceremony for investiture of the sacred thread and do not consider themselves 'twice-born'; the thread itself has only one strand instead of the customary three; until this century they were totally illiterate in Sanskrit, Tamil and Kannada; and they are altogether exogamous. They are in fact like any other Badaga clan in matters of marriage, having unions with other clans of dissimilar subculture, especially the Kaṇakkas, and even marrying meat-eating Gaudas.

If a Ha:ruva girl marries a Gauda then no meat is ever cooked in his house, and his wife remains a vegetarian. If her husband wants to eat meat he may arrange to have some cooked elsewhere and eat it away from home. The children of the union are fully Gaudas and will normally be non-vegetarians. When the Ha:ruva woman dies her household usually reverts to a non-vegetarian diet. It has been reported that, on the other haṇd, 'If a Badaga [Gauda] woman marries a Haruva she has to give up meat-eating and, to cleanse her, a red hot iron is put to her tongue' [13] 'After this she would not dare to eat meat . . . she would lose her eyesight' (Karl, 1945, 3). From this we can see that a woman married into a Ha:ruva family is expected to accept its dietary norms, whereas a Ha:ruva girl married into a socially lower clan is not expected to accept their diet (Tignous, 1911, 117). A Ha:ruva girl marrying into a Lingayat family does not change her diet but will have to wear the *liṅga* if it is offered her and to behave as a Lingayat. When a Ha:ruva man marries a Lingayat girl he continues to wear his thread while she usually continues to wear the *liṅga* if it has already been given her (see Plate 6).

Ha:ruvas are willing to accept food in the inner and more sacred room (where household gods are installed) of any other clan except the Toreas. They would not demean themselves by entering a Torea house; and they would probably be offered food only in the outer room of a Wodea house. Wodeas never accept food in a Ha:ruva home as they consider Ha:ruvas inferior; but the other three Lingayat clans will eat in the inner room of a Ha:ruva house. Even meat-eating Adikiris, who are not Lingayats, can be offered vegetarian food in the inner Ha:ruva room. The same holds true for visiting Gaudas and Kaggusis, people who may often come if related to the Ha:ruva household by marriage. Until the 1950s the Ha:ruvas also allowed Todas, Kurumbas, Iruḷas and Kasuvas to eat in the outer room, but Kotas were thought too polluting to pass beyond the entrance; since that time only Todas have been allowed into the house.

ADIKIRIS

The vegetarian Adikiris are a Lingayat clan numbering perhaps

3,500 people who inhabit sixteen villages scattered across the plateau. Though they should only marry with Ha:ruvas or Kaṇakkas, in the past eighty years a few Adikiri people have married girls from Lingayat families in Mysore villages. It is rare on the other hand for a girl to go from the Nilgiris to Mysore in marriage. There have also been a few irregular cases of vegetarian Adikiris marrying meat-eating Gaudas (but never meat-eating Adikiris).

The Adikiri villages come closer to being a corporate group than any of the other clans, except for the two tiny phratries of Kumba:ras and Be:das. This solidarity stems from the fact that Adikiris, alone of all the clans, hold an 'annual reunion'. Every November they go to the village of Nellitore, on the Coimbatore Plain, to worship at the place where a Lingayat saint was drowned. It was from this point that the original six Adikiris started up into the Nilgiris.[14] Today it is obligatory for at least a few men from each Adikiri village to attend the annual function, to which members of other Badaga clans are also welcome.

Despite this demonstration of Adikiri solidarity there have been several defections from the clan and its Lingayat values. In one village (Sakkata) Adikiris married with Toreas a few generations ago and now are treated as Toreas although sometimes called Adikiris. In one other Gauda village (So:lu:ru) Adikiris have intermarried with meat-eating Gaudas. In both these situations the soi-disant Adikiris are no longer vegetarians or Lingayats (Metz, 1864, 50–51). The three other meat-eating Adikiri villages do not dine with Toreas, but they may take a meal in the inner room of a Gauda house. In two villages of vegetarian Adikiris the *liṅga* is not worn, but the inhabitants retain the name and status of Adikiris and belong to the same clan, though they are not considered Lingayat.[15]

Adikiris and Kanakkas eat only in the houses of Wodeas, Ha:ruvas and Koṅgaru, where they can feel sure of receiving the correctly prepared vegetarian dishes. Adikiris, like Kaṇakkas, admit Ha:ruvas, Kaggusis and other Lingayats to the inner room for meals (though Wodeas refuse to eat with them). Meat-eating Adikiris, Gaudas and Toreas, as well as Todas, may only eat in the outer room, while other Nilgiri tribesmen may not enter the house at all.

KAṆAKKAS

There are perhaps three thousand Kaṇakkas. Although now

agriculturists like all other Badagas they once held the monopoly over literacy in the Nilgiris (Grigg, 1880, 221). Their name means 'accountant', and refers to their former position as village accountants under the Ummattu:r régime. Although the Kaṇakkas are Lingayats and today have a status equal to the Adikiris', there are some Badagas who whisper darkly that Kaṇakkas were in origin Tamilian, unlike all others. The Kaṇakka clan themselves would not own to this, for experience with Tamil Nadu officials has led most Badagas to look down upon the Tamilian.

Kaṇakkas intermarry with Adikiris, Ha:ruvas, Koṅgaru and Kaggusis and during this century some have married girls from Lingayat families of Mysore villages. A few cases of Kaṇakkas marrying Wodeas have been cited above. As Kaṇakkas and Adikiris marry much more frequently with each other than with any other clan, and as both are Lingayat groups, they are now accorded equal status by all other Badagas. The rules for Kaṇakka commensality are precisely the same as those of Adikiris.

KAGGUSIS

Among the smaller clans is the Kaggusi, numbering about two thousand. The people inhabit eight villages; they are vegetarians and Lingayats, but instead of wearing a personal *liṅga* they have one sacred *rudrakśa* bead on a string round the neck and do a daily *pu:ja* to that. Their marriages are mainly with Gaudas, though also with Kaṇakkas and occasionally Wodeas. As soon as Kaggusi men reached the plateau and married Gauda girls they left off wearing the *liṅga* and kept it in their houses, as they still do. It is noteworthy that Adikiris will not marry Kaggusis on the grounds that, as Kaṇakkas *do* marry them, the Kaggusis must be fictive brothers to the Adikiris (although the two in fact belong to different septs); yet no such argument stops the Adikiri from marrying a Ha:ruva though logic dictates that it should. An explanation lies in the higher status Adikiris accord to Ha:ruvas.

Kaggusis allow vegetarians and the meat-eating Gaudas into the inner room for a meal, but they feed the lower meat-eating phratries in the outer room. Members of other tribes may eat only on the veranda.

GAUDAS

About eighty per cent of the entire population is Gauda, so that this particular phratry is commonly called 'Badaga'. At a rough estimate it numbers eighty thousand. I prefer to use the correct but not widely recorded name Gauda, as it obviates the confusion that can arise in calling one phratry and the entire community by the same name. The word *Gauda* also points to their derivation from the Kanarese farmers and cattle-breeders known by that name (a branch of the Okkaliga caste; Thurston, 1906; vol. II, 269–272).

The Badaga Gaudas today occupy some three hundred villages; hence, unlike the members of a smaller phratry, no Gauda can hope to have friends or relatives in every village. Often a man cannot be too certain about whether a particular *distant* village belongs to his own or to another clan. This can raise difficulties when a marriage is being arranged with a village into which the groom's lineage or village has not previously married. Otherwise, the Gaudas can assign every village with which they have marriage connexions to one clan or another (aside from some special cases).

So far as I can ascertain the Gaudas have six clans plus ten 'neutral' villages which may have marriage relationships with any other Gauda village. It appears—and informants confirm this—that the unwieldly size of clans with over ten thousand different kinds of solution. The first employs divisional boundaries—the only situation in which the larger political divisions of the Nilgiris are relevant in the arrangement of marriages. Gaudas observe a rule that clan exogamy is essential only in marriages arranged between two villages *within* the same division. If the village is in any of the other three divisions, and if there is no known precedent of a marriage with that particular village, then it is usually *treated* as a member of another clan even though it would be possible to argue that it belonged to the same clan were the villagers to trace out a network of other known marriage connexions that indirectly link the two villages. If in one's own division two villages A and B have both had marriages with village C, then A and B usually belong to the same clan and call themselves 'brothers'. But if the villages A and B are in different political divisions then the fact that at some time they both married people from (or into) village C—which might be anywhere in the three other divisions of the plateau—is deemed irrelevant. In practice, where a history of marriage with C could be demonstrated for both A and B, the villagers would usually rationalize the knowledge by saying: 'After all, the connexion is too distant to matter; we are not marrying our own blood.' In effect they are giving up the ideal of clan exogamy in these cases while retaining the more meaningful ideal of village and lineage exogamy. The clans have now become so large that Gaudas can no longer look upon them as corporate groups. This adjustment in thinking is necessary because the old names for the clans have been forgotten and because the detailed knowledge Badagas carry of their kinship field—often embracing over three hundred people—coupled with the tremendous accumulation of relatives that comes from numerous births and frequent remarriages could otherwise make the ideal of clan exogamy totally unrealizable.

There is another manipulation to surmount this problem. Ten non-exogamous Gauda villages are in a sense of 'neutral' clan affiliation: that is, they may arrange marriages in their own village or with any Gauda clan without generally being accused of marrying within a prohibited degree. They thus form a kind of safety valve: the precedent of a marriage with one of these villages can be used to validate any other village's membership of a particular clan. This is possible because the six clans are not generally known by names now (though at least two of them still were in the last century): they are identified only by reciprocal terms meaning 'agnates' and 'affines' (or 'our clan' and 'another clan'). These special villages also act as a kind of reservoir of youths and girls eligible to *any* Gauda village needing spouses.

Though the vast majority of Gauda marriages are within this complicated system of clans and neutral villages, a number of permissible marriages have also been arranged with other phratries. Ha:ruvas marry into Gauda families, though now with decreasing frequency; the meat-eating Adikiris, a small clan, have no marriages outside the Gauda phratry to which they therefore belong in sense if not name.[16] A very recent development has been the marriage of a few Badaga Christian girls with Gauda boys, usually those with college education. Christian girls enjoy a certain reputation among urbanizing Badagas for their comparatively high level of education and their 'freer' interaction with men. When a Christian girl marries a Gauda her patrilineal ancestry must still trace back to a clan other than her groom's.

Gaudas, like Badaga Christians, are usually meat-eaters. They are willing to eat in the houses of any other phratry but the Toreas and the Christians. Adikiris, Kaṇakkas and Wodeas offer Gaudas food in the outer room only, whereas Ha:ruvas and Kaggusis allow them to eat in the inner room. Such dining occasions usually arise when Gaudas visit families related to them through marriage. In each of these cases the Gaudas receive only vegetarian food; more generally the vegetarian phratries do not eat with non-vegetarians. Toreas may be given food in the outer room of a Gauda home, but meat-eating Adikiris (who may marry Gaudas) eat in the inner one.

KUMBA:RAS

Few Badagas know of the existence of this phratry, so small are its numbers. They have only fifty households, or about 300 people, who live in two villages near Male Ko:ṭe, where they were once employed as potters (whence their name). Each village is an exogamous clan; when possible, alliances are arranged between the two. As one village contains four times as many families as the other the larger village has to look elsewhere for most of its spouses, however. They no longer intermarry with other Badagas but with the several thousand families of Kanarese Kumba:ras living in and near Mysore City who are believed by the Nilgiri Kumba:ras to share a common ancestry with them. The Kumba:ras living on the plateau nevertheless class themselves as Badagas and are so recognized by their neighbours as they bear a Badaga culture identical with that of the Gaudas. Among those Badagas who know the Kumba:ra villagers many consider them to be Gaudas, though only at Me:lu:ru have they been absorbed into the Gauda phratry.

The traditional occupation of Kanarese Kumba:ras was potting,[17] and although these Badagas no longer know the craft there are any number of broken sherds stratified at a depth of two or three meters in the ramparts of the old Male Ko:ṭe fortification to testify to this former industry. On the basis of their presumed (if servile) connexion with royalty the Kumba:ras claim to be the highest of all Badaga phratries; other Badagas knowing anything about them rank them below Gaudas and above Be:das and Toreas. Some Kumba:ras are vegetarians; most are not. Their rules for commensality are the same as those of Gaudas.

BE:DAS

Another small phratry neighbouring on the Kumba:ras, the

Be:das, also number about fifty families divided between two clans. Their two villages near Male Ko:ṭe each include members of both clans and thus are not exogamous (Metz, 1864, 47–48; Francis, 1908, 350, 370). Though they no longer marry with any other Badagas they, too, are undeniably Badagas. These people either marry into the other Be:da clan or arrange marriages with Kanarese Be:das (who are not Badagas) from Mysore City and Tiruppu:r (Coimbatore District).

The Be:das believe they came to the hills as hunters in service to the chieftain of Ummattu:r; the word *be:da* means 'hunter' (Thurston, 1909, vol. VII, 331; Burrow & Emeneau, 1961, 382, no. 4547). Though now only farmers they supplemented their diet until 1950 by hunting on the jungle slopes with bow and arrow. As they are eaters of meat and traditionally takers of life they are now ranked by other Badagas as lower than Kumba:ras but still above Toreas. It is worth noting that Kumba:ras and Be:das, like other non-Lingayat villagers, have their own 'commune Toreas' who act as messengers for the headmen. Most Badagas know so little about Be:das that they erroneously think of them as a group totally absorbed into the Gauda phratry. There are in fact two Gauda villages descended from unions of Gaudas with Be:das. The Be:das follow the same rules for commensality as Gaudas.

TOREAS

The Toreas were universally regarded as the lowest of Badaga phratries, but they had yielded that position to the Christians by 1900. In former times they were the poorest and least educated of Badagas (Harkness, 1832, 112). Though there are certain meat-eating Adikiris who have become absorbed into one Torea village the phratry is now endogamous. It numbers about 5000 people and occupies twenty-six villages. No historical connection can be traced between them and the Kanarese Toreas.[18]

Like all other Badagas they are primarily cultivators, but in addition they hold a traditional role of messengers and 'commune servants', even in the Be:da villages, whence their low status. Certain Toreas are even now appointed (except in Lingayat villages) for specific duties at festivals and some public ceremonies, particularly funerals. For this they receive a quarter-rupee and three measures of grain from each household. In some Torea villages, however, the Kurumba watchman has these duties.[19] It is recorded that in the nineteenth century they were also 'weaving a kind of sackcloth',[20] but today neither they nor anyone else can recall this activity.

Alone of all phratries the Toreas are under a slight disadvantage in the Badaga judicial system. In villages where other Badagas also live they may find that, while being permitted to bring cases to the village or commune council and to sit through its deliberations, they must not take part in the discussion that leads up to the headman's decision. A Torea village headman who is excluded from a meeting of the commune council may not complain about such demeaning treatment in the way that any other headman in the commune undoubtedly would. The depressed status of Toreas is symbolized by the fact that during the great memorial ceremonies for a deceased generation *(Manemale)* the Toreas have a separate, smaller catafalque beside the main one.

Many of the twenty-six Torea villages are adjuncts to Gauda villages, set off from them by a mere stone's throw; but a group of nine Torea villages on the eastern edge of the plateau are so isolated that their only close contact is with the Wodeas of De:na:du.

Toreas have two clans, and in many villages both are represented. Despite the well-known precedents in other phratries, they have not begun to marry non-Toreas.

The Toreas can be offered vegetarian food in the houses of all higher phratries and meat in those which habitually eat it themselves. Recently some Gaudas have interdined with Toreas on an equal footing, in their inner rooms, although traditionally none of the other groups would allow Toreas into the inner, more sacred room; they were expected to eat in the outer one. 'If they should eat food with other Badagas, the Toreyas must clear away all remnants of the feast—nobody else will help' (Benbow, 1930, 11). No other phratry, not even the Christians, will accept food in the house of a Torea (Tignous, 1911, 117). In terms of the commensality rules pertaining elsewhere in India the Toreas may therefore have the appearance of a low or untouchable caste; and it is true that, Christians apart, they are the lowest of the Badaga phratries. There is nevertheless a Badaga rule that 'foreigners' and plainsmen may not enter the inner room of any Badaga house: they may be offered food only on the veranda or in the outer room. Badaga commensal rules, valid as much among Toreas as among higher phratries, have often come as a surprise to visiting Brahmins, who find themselves excluded from the more sacred room or from receiving food there. Badagas, even Toreas, do not recognize high ritual status when found outside the Nilgiri system. The plains Brahmins of course rationalize the rebuff by considering the Badagas as Śudras, through whom no Brahmin would pollute himself by accepting their often non-vegetarian food.[21]

HA:SANU:RU BADAGAS

The eight villages of this community, lying in the low Biligiri Rangan Hills some forty kilometers northeast of the Nilgiris, belong to eleven clans which are distinct from those of the plateau. These clans form three phratries—Wodea, Gauda and Torea. A clan of Ha:ruvas is within the Gauda phratry.

The two Wodea clans rank highest; they intermarry with each other, with Wodeas of the Nilgiris, and recently with the Wodea caste inhabiting villages near Sa:mara:jnagar (southern Mysore). Like other Wodeas those of Ha:sanu:ru are vegetarian and Lingayat. They allow the Ha:ruva clan to eat in the inner room of their houses, but for the past century since they began intermarriage with Mysore villages these Wodeas have stopped allowing other Badagas (who are non-vegetarian) to eat in their houses.

At the other end of the social hierarchy are two clans of Toreas, who intermarry chiefly with the two clans of Nilgiri Toreas, but also with neighbours of the opposite clan in Kottadai, their village near Ha:sanu:ru, and in some cases these Toreas have intermarried with the Torea caste found near Sa:mara:jnagar.

Between these two poles are four Ha:ruva families and about one hundred and fifteen Gauda families; (the Wodeas number about twenty five families, and Toreas twenty). The Ha:ruvas and Gaudas are divided into seven clans (see Diagram 7), generally identified by their place of origin in the Nilgiris. Members of each clan may intermarry with any of the other six clans, and also with Gaudas of the Nilgiris. However, because of their common origin, the Gaudas of Ku:kalu clan, for example, may not marry Gaudas from Ku:kalu village in the Nilgiris.

There is a sort of hierarchy within this phratry, Ku:kalu clan and the Ha:ruvas ranking higher than the others. Ku:kalu dominates because of its size, for it consists of some twenty-five families, as compared with the four families in each of the four smallest clans. It is the leader of Ku:kalu clan who settles most of the disputes in these eight villages, although each of them has its own headman. When neither he nor the family elders were able to resolve difficult disputes in the past, the headman of Ku:kalu commune in the northeastern Nilgiris was asked to adjudicate.

The eight villages contain a population of about 800 Badagas, as well as several hundred Iruḷa tribesmen. While no intermarriage occurs between the two groups, there have been stray cases of Badaga men keeping Iruḷa mistresses.

The comparable situation of a peripheral Badaga community living in the Wainad will be discussed below (see pp. 129–131).

NOTES

1. Grigg, 1880, 219. Their factual legends, devoid of supernatural elements, are in sharp contrast to the origin myths of such tribes as the Toda and the Santal; compare Rivers, 1906, 184, and Orans, 1965, 5.
2. Rivers, 1906, 36; Emeneau, 1937, 103, where the number of clans given for töwfiḷy is incorrect; see also Lévi-Strauss, 1968, 125. On the priests who make sacrifice, see Rivers, 1906, 39–42, 71–72, 276–285, 354.
3. Srinivas, 1942, 32–38; Lévi-Strauss, 1968, 477. For the taboo on killing snakes, see Breeks, 1873, 104.
4. Diagram 7 roughly illustrates the hierarchy. A stranger to this community will hear claims of much higher ranking than the speakers would dare voice to members of other Badaga clans; here we will only present the most widely agreed-upon ranking. (The existence of a hierarchy does not *ipso facto* make this a caste society).
5. Ward, 1821, lxxi; Hough, 1829, 88. Their thread, unlike that of Brahmins, has only one strand.
6. Note, for example, the wives of Hućći in Diagram 5. The Badaga kinship terminology is of the Dakota type (Hockings, in press).
7. heṇṇa du:ranta koḷḷu/danava sa:renta koḷḷu.
8. Jagor, 1876, 202; Francis 1908, 130–131. 'At a funeral the Badagas in general take off their turbans, but the Wodearu keep theirs on. Every Native, not even excepting the petty hill-chiefs [headmen], must bow down before them and pay them adoration'; Metz, 1864, 48–49. During the great memorial ceremony Wodeas are honoured with a bed on which they are invited to sit; Belli Gowder, 1923–1941, 14.
9. There have also been a few irregular marriages of Wodea girls to men living in Mysore State and the Kollegal Hills near Ha:sanu:ru; see below, pp. 216–217.
10. Grigg, 1880, 220; Francis, 1908, 130–131; Thurston, 1909, vol. I, 72–73. The name *Wodea* actually means 'owner, lord, master, ruler'; Burrow & Emeneau, 1961, 45, n. 510.

11. Ward, 1821, lxxi, Hough, 1829, 88; Metz, 1864, 54; Grigg, 1880, 221; Francis, 1908, 131. The claim was based on their membership in the Brahma sept.
12. Kittel, 1894, 1650, gives the Kannada *Hāruva* as meaning 'Brahmin'; Burrow & Emeneau, 1961, 273, n. 3366, translate it as 'Brahmin' or 'seer'.
13. Benbow, 1930, 9. This claim is dubious, since the pollution of meat normally cannot be removed from a woman, only from a man.
14. Metz, 1864, 50–51, 63–64; see above, 21, 41. *Adikari*, meaning 'powerful man', was once used as the title of a village headman or magistrate appointed by the local chieftain, acting for the ruling power in Mysore.
15. Since about 1960 some of them have taken to wearing the *liṅga* again.
16. Most Badagas now consider these Adikiris as Gauda, as they do Be:das and Kumba:ras.
17. An art they are said to have taught the Kotas.
18. Thurston, 1909, vol. VII, 176; see above, 32–33. The Toreas of Ha:sanu:ru now intermarry with those of Mysore.
19. See below, 123. Belli Gowder, 1938–1941, 11, gives his gratuity at a funeral as 'a sum of Re. 1.25 along with ten measures of rice'.
20. Harkness, 1832, 109; Breeks, 1873, 14. It may be that these writers confused the Toreas with Kaikolans, however: twelve male and nine female Kaikolans were enumerated in Todana:ḍu early in 1821; Grigg, 1880, 26. They were a low-status caste of weavers and musicians from Coimbatore, some of whose women were dedicated in a temple to the art of prostitution; Thurston, 1907, 29–30; 'Miles', 1951, 200–202.
21. Here a note about commensality with other non-Badagas. Wodeas and other Lingayats never allow a Nilgiri tribesman to enter beyond the veranda; neither may any non-Lingayat visitor from the plains enter. Ha:ruvas and all lower phratries permit Todas and until recently Kurumbas, Irulas and Kasuvas to eat in the outer room. Kotas and any lowlander thought to be a Hindu untouchable are too polluting to be allowed past the veranda.

4

Traditional Interchange (1)

THE INTERDEPENDENCE OF THE PLATEAU COMMUNITIES

Until the First World War the Badagas were as intimately involved in the traditional system of economic and ritual interaction of the Nilgiris as were the other main participants, the Todas, Kotas and Kurumbas. Throughout the whole of the last century, from the first detailed description of the Badagas in 1812 (Keys) until Father Tignous' account in 1911, there seems to have been no essential change in the organization of this complex relationship; but since World War I the Badagas have withdrawn more and more from the obligations and privileges which had been traditionally theirs. What were these obligations and privileges? How complex were they?

Their economic and social relations have been summarized diagrammatically in the perhaps over-simplified way shown in Diagram 8.[1]

The system of interdependence that we outline here involved a complex but standardized division of labour not unlike the *jajmani* system (see Wiser, 1936; Beidelman, 1959, *passim*) commonly found in multi-caste Indian villages. In order to understand the full complexity of this system, we shall have to reconstruct it from several types of observation. The details are discussed at length by several writers, are still known to the older villagers and to some extent can yet be observed in a few dozen Nilgiri villages. Recently,

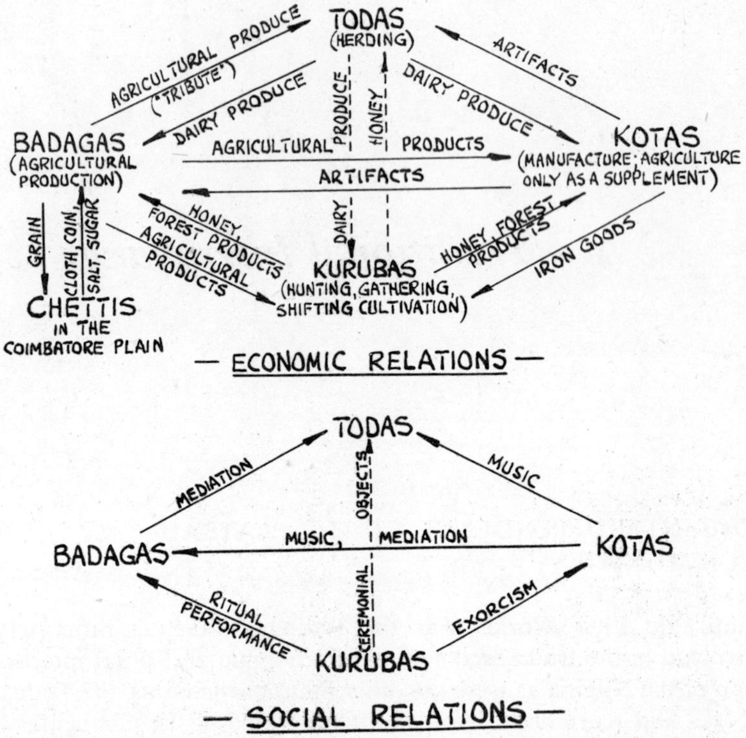

Diagram 8. Economic and social relations among the Nilgiri communities.

with the cash economy becoming almost universal among these communities and the proportion of Badagas to Todas and Kotas rising rapidly (see Appendix 2), this relationship has diminished to the point where it is today a mere skeleton of what it was prior to 1930. The breakdown is apparent in all parts of the Nilgiris although in different localities it has proceeded at differing rates depending in part on the accessibility of a bazaar.

BADAGAS AND KOTAS

The ties linking the Badagas and Kotas have always been closer and more complex than those between any other pair of Nilgiri communities, largely because the Kotas can perform a wider range of services than any other group. These inter-community ties are essentially a relationship of mutual obligation which binds a specific Badaga family to a specific Kota one and are inherited on either side through the males. A Badaga can never change to a new Kota partner unless the old one agrees to it at a joint meeting of their village councils, which rarely happens. The Kota produces certain types of artifact for a Badaga, who in return gives him grain and cloth. Because of the great disparity in numbers between the Badagas and Kotas,[2] it is necessary for each Kota family to maintain such ties with perhaps fifty to 100 Badaga households. In each case, whether or not the services required are those of a woman and whether or not the initial request comes from a woman, all mediation between the two associated families is through the male heads of each.

There are in the entire Nilgiris only seven Kota villages; but these are widely and evenly dispersed, being on the average fourteen kilometers apart (and further by road). One village at Gudalu:ru is in the Wainad, on the slope west of the Nilgiri Plateau; the larger two of the indigenous political divisions each contain two villages; and the remaining two divisions of the plateau have one village each. This distribution, whether originally so planned or not,[3] results in the Kotas being conveniently accessible to all Badaga and Toda settlements; for there is not a settlement anywhere on the plateau that would be more than a morning's walk from a Kota village. Normally each Badaga village is linked with whichever Kota village happens to be closest.

The usual pattern for activating the exchange relationship is for the Badaga to request his Kota partner's *services* whenever the need arises but to order his *products* once each year; while the Kota in turn comes for a dole of clothes and foodstuffs once a year (Harkness, 1832, 78–79; Ranga, 1934, 72). There exists a general understanding that the Kota man should inquire annually of each Badaga partner what items will be required for the coming months. The Badaga then gives him a list of items, while the Badaga's wife passes on to him another list of things required from the Kota's wife. The Kota then announces that he will be returning on a specific day (generally a Monday, the weekly holiday) just before the major Kota festival of Kambattaraya (early January), and the Badaga knows that he must have gifts ready for the Kota on this occasion. On that day the Kota usually comes with his wife and children, bringing the ordered goods if they are ready. The

Kotas then are considered guests of the partner's family, though their lower status keeps them from entering the Badaga house. The Kotas are fed on the veranda, and formerly the visiting family would simultaneously eat out of a single cloth. In recent decades that has come to be regarded as a disrespectful method of being served food; and so it is now given rather more acceptably on one large plantain leaf instead.

The traditional remuneration for Kota goods and services was not in cash, which was rare in the Nilgiri economy until the mid-nineteenth century, but in food grains, potatoes and mustard (Thurston, 1909, vol. I, 85). Today, however, Badagas prefer to pay cash for specific items they require; and some even buy goods at fixed prices from their Kota partner's stall in the market at Ootacamund, Coonoor or Kotagiri. The traditional Kota dress was a skirt-like cloth wrapped around the lower half of the body and a cloak: both were annual gifts from the Badaga partner, who had in turn acquired them from his Chetti trading partner (see below). Quantities of the two chief grains, little millet and finger millet,[4] could also be given. Whether the Badaga gave grain or cloth, or both, was a matter of personal preference. The actual volume of grain given was seemingly not fixed: it varied with the Badaga's harvest each year, according to Badagas, but according to Kotas should have been a quarter of the yield.[5] The Kota would arrange to supply a quantity of articles proportionate in value to the gifts he had received; and it is said that he was capable of remembering what each of his fifty or more Badaga partners had given him on his last visit. '...if a Kota family felt that the Badaga families for whom they provided tools and music were not giving them a rightful share of the crop at harvest, a Kota council could be called which might decree that those Badagas were to be boycotted until they paid up properly' (Mandelbaum, 1960, 275).

Instances have sometimes arisen of a Kota partner dying and leaving a wife but no son; or a wife dies and her widower has no woman in the house. Then a Badaga may want some article from the remnant of his Kota partner's family while there is actually no appropriate person left to make it. If he wants a man's product the widower can make it, and if a woman's product the widow can still make it, of course; but otherwise the surviving Kota is obliged to maintain the relationship by arranging for some kinsman to produce whatever the Badaga needs.

Kota Products and Services

The Kota friend was traditionally the only source for a Badaga's metal goods. The items which Kotas have regularly manufactured in their smithies, first from local iron ore and later from imported scrap metal, were various kinds of knives (Thurston, 1909, vol. IV, 8), adzes, crowbars, pickaxes, sickles, hoes, axes, hammers, iron cooking basins, skillets and ploughshares; and formerly they also produced stirrups, horse-bits, bows and iron-tipped arrows. Kotas were once gold- and silversmiths to the Badagas, too, and still occasionally supply them with metal ornaments. In addition to manufacturing this variety of articles, Kota partners were expected to repair them when necessary. Now they are normally given cash for any repair work done.

A second category of products over which the Kotas formerly held the monopoly is that of leather. Although not even members of the highest Badaga phratries object to handling leather goods, only the Kotas have applied themselves to the polluting task of converting buffalo hides into leather articles. The goods they have regularly prepared are horse saddles and bridles, leather ropes for ploughs and tethers (Metz, 1864, 131–132; Thurston, 1909, vol. IV, 7), leather nets used in trapping, and possibly sandals and water bags. It is worth remarking that while Badagas do not find it polluting to handle the leather on drums, they do consider it demeaning to play Kota drums; hence such instruments have never been sought from the Kotas.

Pottery is a further item over which the Kotas held the local monopoly until this century. Archaeological evidence which I collected indicates that several centuries ago the two hamlets of the Kumba:ras, a tiny Badaga phratry located on the northern edge of the plateau, were producing many kinds of wheel-made pottery. But since that time pot production has been entirely in the hands of Kota women who, it is said, had initially learnt this art from some Kumba:ras. Items which they have regularly supplied to the Badagas include household and dairy vessels, oil lamps and clay smoking-pipes. Unlike any other Kota manufactures their new pots are put through quite an elaborate purificatory ritual by Badagas before coming into daily use.[6]

The Kota partner was also a maker of leaf-umbrellas and of a wooden device not unlike a nutcracker which Badagas use for castrating their young bulls. A curious item with which Kotas must supply their Badaga partners when they find it is the bezoar, a hairy ball that accumulates in the paunch of some buffaloes. Eating a little of this is believed to make a baby strong, brave and manly; and so all Badagas—whether vegetarian or not, and even though quite cognizant of its polluting origin—feed some of it to their newborn sons.

Some Kotas are adept carpenters. In the days when Badagas were still using ploughs they obtained these from their Kota partners, who had made them from some wood supplied by the Toda partners of the Badagas. Kota men sometimes made the heavy wooden pounding-stick found in all Badaga households: in this case the wood was first obtained from the jungle slopes by the Kurumbas of one particular settlement, who passed it on to the Toda who had asked them for it. This Toda would then give the timber to the Toda partner of the Badaga needing the pounder. He in turn passed it on to the Badaga's Kota partner to whittle into a pounder. This is the most complex traditional network we know of in the Nilgiris.

Kota partners were also employed to help build houses or cattlesheds for their Badaga partners. In this case, too, if the Badaga's Toda partner were a relatively affluent man he would supply timber for the purpose. If the Kota were an affluent man he might give food to his own helpers who carried the timber from the Toda source. Similarly, the Badaga partner might get the timber that was needed for a Kota's house. There was in fact considerable flexibility in these intertribal connexions.

When a Badaga house is being built the Kota partner has to place a piece of iron in the foundations to drive away bad spirits; ghosts and demons abhor iron (as elsewhere across the Old World). A comparable ritual at the completion of a new Badaga cattleshed requires that the owner's Kota partner bring a crowbar and lay it across the threshold over which the first cow[7] to enter must step.

The Badagas very literally hold a house-warming ceremony in a newly built house, when the hearth is first built. The Kota partner of the owner must also attend this, bringing a new pot with him. This is essential, for grain has to be boiled in it during the ritual. Another Kota will also be less directly involved in this ceremony, as the mother's brother of the house owner also has to bring another pot for the same purpose from *his* Kota partner.

Until this century Kota men were usually requested to thatch Badaga houses. This service has, however, been discontinued: in

1900 or a little before, thatch was replaced by tiled rooves which were considered more convenient, safe and prestigeful; and the Kotas do not generally lay tiles.

For at least the past century Badagas and Kotas have been building their houses of locally made bricks. Kota bricklayers have built Badaga houses, and Badaga bricklayers have also built Kota houses. In either case the traditional ties are not necessarily involved, if only because so very few Badagas or Kotas can lay bricks properly. In these situations payment is generally made in cash according to recognized rates for the labour performed.

Badaga Products

Apart from the annual grant of grain and cloth to Kotas, their Badaga partners used to give them whatever cattle died. 'All the cattle that die in the villages are carried off by the Kotas, and feasted on by them . . . and at no time do the Kotas thrive so well as when there is a murrain among the herds of the Todas and Badagas' (Metz, 1864, 128).

Although Badagas and Todas used to exchange cattle on occasion, no such trade ever took place between Kotas and Badagas; indeed until the mid-nineteenth century the other communities would not allow Kotas to own any buffaloes, and after they did have some they still did not milk them (Reclus, 1891; 192; Thurston, 1909, vol. IV, 7). The Kotas would eat every Badaga or Toda buffalo that died, however, or would kill and eat an aging beast (normally a bull) given them for the purpose; but it is noteworthy that once they started keeping herds they would never eat any of their own buffalo carcasses.[8]

Another item for which the Kotas looked to the Badagas in the last century was opium. Good quality opium was produced on the Nilgiris at that time, but the Badagas seem to have held a monopoly on it. Today anyone can buy poppy capsules illicitly in the town markets (Thurston, 1909, vol. IV, 9).

Irregular Services

There are certain services which Kotas are called upon to render only when some unusual situation arises. Thus Kotas do not normally help their Badaga partners to harvest the crops; but if a

Badaga had difficulties in harvesting a large crop he might until recent years ask his Kota partner's family to help. An agreement would be made for the Kotas to receive perhaps one-fourth or one-fifth of the harvest, in addition to the usual yearly gifts.

Another service which Kota friends may be expected to render irregularly, with or without a monetary incentive, is the supply of sexual partners. Affairs between Badaga men and Kota girls are supposedly forbidden, since the Kota can pollute a Badaga in a ritual sense. Nevertheless a Badaga (even a Lingayat) may occasionally ask his Kota partner to get him a Kota girl. Badagas claim that these girls have no objection in general to such arrangements for they believe that any offspring of these affairs, though brought up as Kotas, will have some of the admired qualities of the higher-status Badaga. No opprobrium attaches to Kotas said to have Badaga fathers. Intercourse between Kota men and Badaga women, on the other hand, is altogether impermissible.

Once in a lifetime a Kota should make a ceremonial visit to the house of each Badaga partner's married daughter. At a prearranged time the Kota, perhaps accompanied by his wife, goes there and presents the daughter with some woman's implement, generally a sickle. In return for this—and on behalf of her husband, not her father—the woman gives the Kota at least one item of cloth, most commonly a loincloth.

Just as there are situations in which a Badaga has to call on his Kota partner for irregular services, so are there times when the Kota may need his Badaga friend's help. In general these occur in four kind of situation. One is when a Kota wants to borrow something—usually money—that is not available in his own village. Since 1800 the Kotas have been increasingly involved in the cash economy for they have had to pay land taxes and buy musical horns and scrap iron from lowland towns, and these transactions required ready money. Secondly, a Kota may ask his Badaga partner to help him arrange for a reputable Badaga therapist to give medical treatment (Hockings, 1979b). Thirdly, as not all Kotas have regular Toda trading-partners, a Kota may have to ask a Badaga partner to arrange for some needed timber from that Badaga's Toda friend. Lastly, Badaga elders may help arbitrate in disputes between Kotas, just as Kota headmen in former times might become the judges for a serious dispute in the nearby Badaga communes.[9]

Badaga Rituals

The role of the Kotas in Badaga ritual is, or at least was until 1930, a crucial one, since custom required that Kotas provide the music at Badaga funerals, weddings and certain festivals (Ward, 1821, lxxvii; Harkness, 1832, 78–79).

Badaga funerals take place in the village of the dead person. Whether they involve the Lingayat practice of inhumation or the general Shaivite practice of cremation, the ritual is not considered completely performed if a Kota band does not come to play dance music and lead the cortège. Thus as soon as a Badaga dies his village headman sends out word of the funeral plans, not only to other Badaga villages but also to the Kota partner of the dead person. This man will then arrange a party of eight Kota musicians to play at the funeral. The partner himself attends the ceremony but usually does not play an instrument then, for he is in mourning for his friend. The band regularly consists of two flutes, two drums, two tambourines (beaten with sticks) and two horns. The bandsmen go immediately to the bereaved house and there play music suitable for dancing.[10] It is a rule that the corpse should not be removed from the house until this performance has begun. However, if the funeral is to be on a lavish scale, word of it may have to be sent great distances—formerly by messengers on foot—and the Kotas will then have to play for two or three days before the main obsequies begin. Each time a party of visitors arrives from another village the Kota musicians go out with the headman a short way to welcome them. At night the Kotas light a fire on a veranda for warmth and sleep there if need be. If the dead man was rich his Kota partner may honour him by bringing two bands of musicians who take turns in playing through the night as well as the day. Once the corpse has been brought out in front of the house music is played for several hours while Badaga men dance around the catafalque. Each time the corpse is moved on for the next stage of the complex ritual it must be preceded by the band. When the corpse has finally been disposed of the Kotas return to their homes; they have not set foot on the burial or cremation ground and never enter a Badaga house.

There are certain definite articles that a Kota is required to bring to his Badaga partner's funeral. If the deceased was a male of a meat-eating (and so formerly a hunting) phratry, the Kota brings a roughly made bow and arrow to be burnt with the corpse.

If the deceased was a vegetarian male of the Lingayat sect a small hoe is brought instead, and this has to be used for the first strokes in digging the grave.[11] This hoe is carried anticlockwise once around the catafalque on the head of a near male relative of the deceased and is then kept underneath the corpse with other presents.[12] If the deceased were a woman the Kota partner will bring two toe-rings, one for each second toe of the corpse. In the last century the Kotas also provided a dead woman with a pounding-stick (Metz, 1864, 77); today a rough one is made by her relatives instead.

The Kota partner is often requested to supply a band of musicians for a Badaga wedding if this is to be a public one. (Many weddings are held privately, 'within the family circle', to save expenses; in which case the Kota may still come, but without musicians.) At a large-scale marriage their services may be required for several days; but while the attendance of Kotas at a funeral is imperative, it is for the groom's family to decide whether to have them at his wedding. The Kota partner may also be invited to a naming or an ear-piercing ceremony and should certainly be asked to a bull-castration.

In the early years of this century the Kota man would receive from his Badaga partner a total of two rupees or its equivalent for each day the band played at any ceremony. It is now common for less than a complete band of eight musicians to attend; but each bandsman is fed and receives five rupees a day, even more if the donor is wealthy. The Kota partner, however, gets nothing for the gifts that he must bring to a funeral.

In each commune the Badagas are supposed to hold a massive memorial ceremony whenever one generation level has altogether died out, or else when sixty years have elapsed since the previous ceremony. These events begin on a Sunday and last for eight days, during which many thousands of Badagas from all over the plateau may attend. On these rare occasions the Badaga headman informs the headman of at least the nearest Kota village (indeed, he has to seek that Kota's permission), and he arranges for all the men and boys of that village to play music at the ceremony. For this purpose the Kotas divide themselves into numerous bands of eight men each and thus the dance music can be kept going day and night for the entire period, with several of the groups playing simultaneously. At the end of the ceremony these Kotas all lead the memorial procession to the cremation ground, where a cot is incinerated along with sticks representing every member of the deceased generation. The Kotas are fed by the commune for the duration of the ceremony; after their performance each participating Kota village is given one male buffalo, and a measure of rice or other grain is given each player. All of these expenses, together with the cost of entertaining the Badaga visitors and erecting the great catafalque, are borne in common by a standard levy on each Badaga household.[13]

Kota Ceremonies

Just as the presence of Kotas at these Badaga rituals is obligatory, so are there Kota rituals that require Badaga attendance.

When there is a death in the family of a Kota, his various Badaga partners should come to the funeral with some male relatives and friends. Yet while these Badagas are expected to attend they actually play no part in the ritual: they must simply put in an appearance and make a gift to indicate their sympathy for the bereaved family. If a Badaga is rich this gift will be a male buffalo to be killed during the funeral; if poor he will give five or ten rupees, or the equivalent in grain (Thurston, 1909, vol. I, 85). The Badaga men pay no formal respects to the corpse; and they stay neither for the ceremonies nor for the exciting buffalo sacrifice. Usually they are offered tobacco or cigars by the Kotas but cannot accept food.

Badagas are also expected to attend the Kambattaraya festival every January in the villages of their Kota partners (Breeks, 1873, 44; Thurston, 1909, vol. IV, 14–17). Some days prior to this the Kotas will already have received their annual gift, which commonly includes new clothes for the festival and sometimes a temporary loan of jewellery. When the Badaga men go to a Kota village on this occasion they are accompanied by some of their female relatives. On arriving a Badaga party will halt just outside the village until the Kotas come with their musicians to escort them in. Again, the Badagas are not there to take any part in the ritual itself; but once this has been completed the visitors are expected to dance and generally enjoy themselves. After a few hours of this the Badagas return home, for they could not pollute themselves by accepting the food of Kotas (Metz, 1864, 130–131).

NOTES

1. Adapted from Zvelebil, 1955, 243–244. (For 'Kurubas' read 'Kurumbas'.) In fact a number of other tribes are interconnected socially and economically with these four, and an adequate account would embrace nearly a dozen communities.
2. Roughly one Kota to every ninety Badagas (1961); see Appendix 1 and 2.
3. 'The Todas claim that the Kotas are . . . artisans specially brought up from the plains to work for them'; Thurston, 1909, vol. IV, 7. For the location of Kota villages, see Map 2 above.
4. Respectively *Panicum miliare* and *Eleusine coracana.*
5. Emeneau, 1946, 257. Harkness (1832, 109, 135) noted: 'Each Burgher [Badaga] community now pays . . . at the rate of eighty measures [probably 65 litres] for each plough of land'. But at Kotagiri the Kotas got 182 litres from a village. Later Breeks, 1873, 42, recorded that the Kota got from each village from 37 to 74 litres of each kind of grain grown.
6. Thurston, 1909, vol. I, 85. The Wodeas alone do not cook in earthenware.
7. Nowadays any small piece of iron is used; the cow is always a gift of the Badaga's wife's father.
8. If a Toda or Badaga animal strayed into a Kota herd for one or more nights it would be returned to the owner, but the Kotas would make a point of never eating that particular animal. On nineteenth century practices, see 'Rifle', 1872, 32.
9. Emeneau, 1946, 261; Mandelbaum, 1955, 241. Each Kota village constitutes a commune, separate from the contiguous Badaga communes but answerable to the *parpati,* the Badaga head of that division *(na:ḍu)* of the plateau.
10. The music and dance are performed on the *keri,* the work-space in front of each house.
11. More practicable tools are used for the real work.
12. Today the Kota simply borrows an old hoe in the Badaga village and then covers it with mud as a gesture 'to make it into a new hoe'.
13. Belli Gowder, 1923–1941, 15. The last time these rituals were performed was in 1936, when each household in Taṅga:ḍu had to contribute a minimum of thirty rupees; see Plates 13–14.

5

Traditional Interchange (2)

BADAGAS AND TODAS

Until quite recently every Badaga family maintained an exchanging relationship with a Toda man; some still do.[1] This relationship is inherited on either side by a son from his father and usually links one Toda to an entire Badaga village. This connexion is structurally different from the ties between Badagas and Kotas, as specific Toda women are not formally involved in it in the way that Kota wives are; for in a polyandrous society like the Todas' the fact that a woman might have several husbands simultaneously could mean that if she were associated with the Badaga partner of each she would become overwhelmed by the requirements of these divided loyalties. In practice the same Toda man is normally partner to all the Badagas in a village, and some are even linked with everyone in half-a-dozen neighbouring Badaga villages.

Toda culture has seemingly changed less than either Badaga or Kota culture during the past century-and-a-half. Indeed Finicio, writing in 1603 (p. 723), describes the same economy and the same kind of interdependence with Badagas that Rivers was to find exactly 300 years later.

In the early days of European contact Harkness (1832, 39) noted:

> A very good understanding exists between these two tribes, the Tuda assuming to himself a superiority which the Burgher

> [Badaga] has no inclination to dispute; and the former, content with this privilege, willingly yields to the latter the palm of superior civilization and domestic economy; which he would think dearly bought, if at the expense of any portion of his natural liberty, or of his freedom to range, when and where he pleases, over his native mountains.

In 1963 an elderly Toda summarized the present situation: 'The Badagas now consider themselves superior to the Todas as they have risen financially. The Todas do not accept the Badaga superiority. Todas are superior because they do not eat flesh, while Badagas do.' But further questioning revealed that the attitudes recorded by Harkness still pertain.

The nature of the status difference between the two communities is shown more precisely in their customary salutations, still sometimes performed.

> Whenever a Toda meets a Badaga *monegar* (headman) or an old Badaga with whom he is acquainted, . . . the Toda stands before the Badaga, inclines his head slightly, and says "*Madtin pudia!*" ("*Madtin,* you have come.") The Badaga replies "*Buthuk! buthuk!*" ("Blessing, blessing") and rests his hand on top of the Toda's head. This greeting only takes place between Todas and the more important of the Badaga community . . . The salutation is made to members of all the various castes [phratries] of the Badagas except the Torayas. It has been held to imply that the Todas regard the Badagas as their superiors, but it is doubtful . . . The Todas themselves say they follow the custom because the Badagas help to support them. It seems to be a mark of respect paid by the Todas to the elders of a tribe with which they have very close relations, and it is perhaps significant that no similar sign of respect is shown to Toda elders by the Badagas (Rivers, 1906, 630; compare Walker, 1965, 78).

Although Badagas have in the past been strongly motivated to maintain their links with the Todas out of economic considerations, these links are apparently tinged with some distrust. While the Kurumbas are viewed by all neighbouring communities as highly dangerous sorcerers, many Badagas and Kurumbas believe Todas also have some lesser skill in sorcery; and this suspicion may in part explain why some Badagas have kept up the exchange relationship even when they might have preferred to drop it.[2]

> There is no doubt that the Badagas believe in the powers of the Toda sorcerers. I was told [in 1902] of several definite instances in which misfortunes were believed to have been brought . . . in this way, and there is little doubt that, in one case, the supposed author of the death of a child was murdered by the Badagas.
>
> If a Badaga suspects magical influence of this kind he may consult one of the Toda diviners, showing that the Badagas believe in Toda divination as well . . . (Rivers, 1906, 635; cf. Thurston, 1912, 234).

Even natural catastrophes have been attributed by Badagas to the supernatural powers of Todas.

> When any epidemic prevails among the Badagas or a murrain decimates their cattle, their first endeavour is to discover the Todas, to whose enchantments the calamity may be attributed. . . . [*c.* 1847] the whole male population of two neighbouring Toda munds [hamlets] were taken before the chief Badaga of the district and accused of having killed the cattle by means of sorcery, the Badagas threatening at the same time to withhold their usual tribute of grain unless the murrain immediately ceased. The Todas readily consented to stop their enchantments . . . Shortly after, the disease abated and the simple Badagas at once viewed this as the result of their compact with the Todas (Metz, 1864, 21–22).

Metz once rescued a Toda from fifty Badagas who were on the point of hanging him for suspected sorcery, but more recently Badagas did murder a Toda sorcerer after one of their children died (B.E.M.S., 1855, no. 15, 39; Metz, 1864, 34; Francis, 1908, 144; see below, p. 201).

Badaga Products

The above-mentioned 'tribute' of grain, or *guḍu,* is well documented by the earlier writers. Finicio (1603, 727) mentions that at the start of the seventeerth century the Todas were subject and paying tribute to the Badaga headmen. It is important to note that all later authorities talk of the Badaga headmen paying Todas; perhaps the Italian priest (who worked through an interpreter) was misinformed. In 1832 Harkness (p. 110) recorded that the Badagas were giving grain to the Todas 'rather as a free gift, than as tribute'. Ouchterlony, writing in 1848 (p. 38), considered it rent for the land (Shortt & Ouchterlony, 1868, 15; Grigg, 1880, 328). The Todas themselves think of it as a rent for certain hamlet sites their ancestors gave the Badaga settlers.

The *guḍu* was not exactly a rent for land though, for when Badagas sold land to European planters there was never any stipulation that the new owners should give anything to the Todas; nor did the Todas advance such claims against these Europeans.[3] Furthermore there is no record of Todas objecting to the government's levy of its full revenue assessment on the Badaga lands whence the *guḍu* came (Breeks, 1873, 12–13).

The amount of *guḍu* varied, possibly from one part of the plateau to another or from harvest to harvest. Harkness (1832, 108, 110–111) noted that around Kotagiri the Badagas reserved about 36 litres for the Todas, half of that for the dairyman-priest; elsewhere much less was given.[4] In 1848 Ouchterlony wrote that the contribution varied 'according to the circumstances of the inhabitants, the owner of a rich house giving usually 1 cundagum = 20 kollagums [= 74 litres]; and those less opulent from $\frac{1}{2}$ to $\frac{1}{4}$ cundagum . . .' However, he noted that although the Badagas professed to give one-sixth of their harvest, they in fact gave 'not above one-half of this proportion, if even so much, especially in the item of wheat which is so profitable to them' (Ouchterlony, 1848, 17; Shortt & Ouchterlony, 1868, 15). From this it appears that grain prices in the town markets were so high in 1847 that the Badagas chose to short-change Todas for the sake of extra cash income. In 1873 the *guḍu* was said 'formerly to represent about 1/10 or 1/8 or 1/5 of the gross produce' (Breeks, 1873, 9, note; Grigg, 1880, 333). The indefiniteness of the amount was discussed by Marshall (1873, 79):

> . . . as no very accurate accounts are kept . . . this foraging [in Badaga villages] stands with the Toda in lieu of sport . . . ; it being to the interest of the Badagas to postpone and shirk payment of grain as long as possible: whilst . . . the state of the Toda stores, and his natural persistency combined, are urging

> him on to repeat the visits.... The result being that the Toda gets exactly as much grain as will just satisfy his actual necessities.[6]

Ouchterlony traces the origin of the grain gift to the earliest Badaga settlement on the hills. He attributes the subsequent decrease in the amount to a lack of deference on the part of the Badagas:

> ... some Burghers or "Buddaghars" came up the Hills and ... asked permission to settle also and obtained it on condition of the payment of the "goodoo" or tribute of 1/6th. of their entire harvest. More Burghers soon followed the first comers; the amount of the "goodoo" became extensive; the habits of the Todars changed ... the deference of the Burghers for them diminished, and with it the amount of the "goodoo", which received a great acceleration in its decline by the coming of the Europeans ...; the Burghers observing their indifference to the alleged claims of sovereignty of their hitherto feudal landlords, gradually assumed the position of donors of the "goodoo" of free will, and as a charity; and hence reduced its amount as the circumstances of ... harvest, or their own wants and inclinations, directed. Upon this footing ... the "goodoo" appears at present to rest. The Burghers profess not to desire to be relieved from it as a tax, because to give it as a donation to the Todars has become with them a timehonored custom (Ouchterlony, 1848, 52–53; Shortt & Ouchterlony, 1868, 53–57).

Rivers, among others, suggests that the Badaga fear of Toda sorcery was one reason for the continuing payment of grain. But he adds correctly that Todas do own some disused dairies in the middle of Badaga fields, and that if the Todas became too estranged from Badagas they might re-assert their claims over these sites and so cause a few Badagas to lose farm-land. Another reason claimed for the continuing payment is that it might encourage Todas to restrain their herds from trampling the Badagas' fields (Breeks, 1873, 13; Lawley & Penny, 1914, 206; Emeneau, 1971, 45, 751). All of these arguments are denied by modern Todas, who now mention the great distance between most Toda grazing and Badaga lands, the non-existence of Toda sorcery, and the absence of any usable Toda dairies in Badaga farm-land. In the Toda view *guḍu* was never compulsory but was an annual gift the Badagas used to make in return for help rendered by Todas and for old hamlet sites the Todas had once presented to certain Badaga immigrants.

Since 1900 the grain given has not been enough to feed the Todas, so that they have also bought grain and rice at the bazaar (Breeks, 1873, 13; Rivers, 1906, 632–633). Some modern informants say the Toda associated with a Badaga village could expect roughly four litres of inferior-quality grain from each household there, but this would vary with the donor's generosity. The system of *guḍu* is still operating in some villages today, mostly those closer to the grazing lands of Todana:ḍu. Few Todas now consider it worth the trouble or the indignity of going to each house and trying to get their annual due, while few Badagas see it as a duty rather than mere charity to give visiting Todas anything.

It is traditionally in September that Todas go to collect the grain—either little or finger millet, or nowadays local potatoes or paddy rice imported from the plains. They decide among themselves how to divide up the task of collection, and then one man goes to each village and visits every house. Where practicable he will be the traditional partner of those particular Badagas (Emeneau 1938, 103). Until the early twentieth century it was unnecessary for him to call at each house because the Badaga headman himself would collect the grain from the donors beforehand.

There are other items which Todas regularly expected from their Badaga partners as well. Before the Ootacamund bazaar came into being much of their cloth came from Badagas.[8] This and the materials for embroidery were initially supplied by a Badaga's Chetti partner, or else bought directly from an itinerant Chetti (see below, pp. 143–145). In the days before the cash economy Todas could obtain from their Badaga partners salt and crude sugar, both of which were bought in the plains during the annual trading expedition there.[9] An item which Todas, like Kotas, very rarely got from Badagas was opium; today some buy poppy capsules in the market but have long ceased getting them from Badagas.

Toda Services and Products

In turn, certain necessities of Badaga life regularly came from the Todas. Of prime importance was dairy produce, mainly clarified butter but also milk and buttermilk.

A few types of basket, among them the winnows, were traditionally supplied to Badagas by Kurumbas; but the majority, including the huge grain-storage baskets, were made for the Badagas by their Toda partners, out of various types of split creeper. Certain baskets on the other hand were obtained from Kurumbas by Todas who would then weave strong edges to these before passing them on to their Badaga partners (Rivers, 1906, 630–631; Emeneau, 1938, 103).

Prior to this century, before thatched roofing fell into disfavour among Badagas, it was the Toda partner and his friends who brought the bundles of reeds needed for thatching. Until recently Todas also brought split creeper and wood needed for building the heavy wooden beds of the Badagas. Other wooden and cane items are supplied when asked for: the milk-churning stick made of cane, timber for ploughs and buildings, threshing sticks and walking-sticks with incised decorations. The flute is sometimes made by an Irula who trades it to a Toda or sometimes the Toda makes it himself to give to his Badaga partner. Until the beginning of this century Todas also made and supplied umbrellas woven of leaves. Cylindrical vessels used for milk and necessary in certain Badaga rituals, and in former days grain measures, are articles made by Todas out of wide sections of bamboo. Not only are the Badaga partners provided with such things, but sometimes a Toda will also bring a gift of fresh bamboo shoots, which are considered a great delicacy and will always draw a return gift of grain.

Cloth was formerly supplied to Todas through the Badagas, but there are two circumstances in which Todas still give Badagas an embroidered cloak. The rarer of these is when a Badaga headman needs one; for the distinctive Toda cloak was in the past virtually a symbol of office for Badaga and Kota headmen and would also be worn by other elders as a mark of respectability. It is also a custom for Badaga corpses to be covered with an embroidered cloak, obtained from his Toda partner by the husband of the daughter of the deceased. The embroidery is done by a wife or mother of the Toda (in a very shoddy manner if intended for a Badaga funeral). A coarse kind of cloth used once to be woven from the fibres of five species of local nettle, these having been supplied by Todas. Even today a bundle of these fibres (called *mañji*) is given to a female corpse during a Badaga funeral and comes from the Toda associate.

Irregular Transactions

As a general rule Badagas, Kotas and Todas shift their cattle to new grazing independently of each other, at the beginning of each year. At present Kota and Badaga cattle are so few that it is rarely necessary to move them at all; but the Todas still practise transhumance within the limits of the plateau, occasionally with Badaga cattle mixed among their own. It was previously common for Badagas to participate in the annual migration of the Toda buffaloes; and sometimes they entrusted their buffaloes to the Toda partners, to take them to better summer grazing on the southern edge of the plateau (Ward, 1821, lxxiii; Rivers, 1906, 133, 137; Ranga, 1934, 24). There the Todas would mix their own herds with the Badaga buffaloes and enjoy the use of their milk, until they were returned home at the approach of the June monsoon.

Badagas and Todas sometimes exchange buffaloes in order to get others of more useful age or yield.[10] This barter only involves female animals and is typically the exchange of one buffalo of good yield for two of lower yield. Todas may also get non-sacred buffaloes from Badaga friends when they suddenly need the animals for sacrifice at a Toda funeral or sell them to Badagas when they need cash. Any difference outstanding after such transactions was formerly paid on the Badaga side by grain, cloth, or gold and silver ornaments; and on the Toda side by various bamboo and basketry articles. More recently the differences have been made up with money alone.

Todas sometimes ask their Badaga partners for financial loans. In the nineteenth century if the request produced no immediate result they would mortgage buffaloes to wealthy Badagas as security for a loan (Marshall, 1873, 130). Today one can still find Badagas lending money merely out of fear of the Todas' sorcery.

Sometimes when a Badaga wants to indulge in some illicit sexual activity he may ask his Toda partner to lend his own wife or find him a Toda girl; but as Toda women are generally rather free in their interaction with non-Todas it is usually no problem for the Badaga to importune a girl himself. Todas on the other hand have virtually no opportunity for intercourse with Badaga women. (Such at least is what reliable Badagas have said; the Toda men deny any such relations between the two communities.)[11]

Although it has not occurred within living memory, 'It was

formerly a common practice for rich Badagas to hire forty or fifty Todas to go on wife-stealing expeditions, and carry off by force the wives of other Badagas' (Metz, 1864, 75). Today, while the practice of stealing wives may continue, assistance from the Todas is no longer required. A parallel situation in which gangs of Badagas used to help Todas steal wives is also recalled. In either case the assistants each received a few rupees.

Badagas are very fond of betting; and so when they meet informally a Badaga and a Toda sometimes have a bet over the possibility of their performing some athletic feat, such as lifting a boulder (Rivers, 1906, 597–598).

Medicine is another matter that can bring Todas and Badagas together. Although Todas have therapists in their own tribe they occasionally go to Badagas noted for particular kinds of cure (Rivers, 1906, 323, 634–635; for details of Badaga therapy, see Hockings, 1979b). A Badaga partner may help the Toda arrange treatment; but the therapist himself usually expects some fee or present from the patient.

Todas are considered moderately powerful sorcerers, despite their own recent disclaimers. It was for this reason that the parties of Badagas who went to massacre Kurumbas always included one or two Toda associates to deliver 'the first blow'.[12] This practice has not recurred since 1900; nor have Badagas murdered a Toda sorcerer since that time.

A few affluent Todas (affluent because of illicit land rentals)[13] now live in Badaga-style brick houses instead of the customary thatched huts, as the houses are more spacious and comfortable. This habit began some eighty years ago (Rivers, 1906, 29, 634). The Badaga-style houses (distinct from modern government-financed housing) are built in a Toda hamlet by Badagas hired for the purpose but not necessarily by a man's Badaga partner.

Ritual Interaction

A common setting for interaction between the two communities is ceremonial. On some Badaga festival days the Toda may be required to bring the sticks and make fire by friction or perhaps bring a new milking vessel. For the annual hunting ceremony of Be:da Sa:mi held by both Badagas and Kotas, the Toda used to bring clarified butter to smear on the weapons. Even so, no very crucial part is played by either community in the ceremonies of the other. A Badaga partner and his family or friends will often be invited to the naming, wedding or funeral of a Toda. The Badagas at these times eat Toda food provided it has been prepared in a separate pot.[14] Similarly Badagas may invite their Toda partners and friends to weddings, funerals and certain of the annual festivals, to most of which the Todas are required to bring some useful present. On these occasions the visiting Todas or Badagas should be fed, and it is also appropriate for the hosts to make small gifts; yet gift exchange is not requisite to all ceremonies.

The Toda, like the Kota, has an obligation to visit the married daughter of each Badaga partner once in a lifetime. He sends word of his intention; then comes and presents her with a buffalo heifer or perhaps something even more valuable. In return she gives him a cloak and possibly some other clothing.

Once a year each Badaga village holds a ceremony at which the cattle are given salty water. The Toda or Todas who are the associates of men in that village are invited on this occasion to take whatever salt is left over from the ceremony (Hockings, 1968c, 414).

All Todas from nearby hamlets are invited to attend the great memorial festival in which Badagas honour one generation of their dead; indeed it cannot take place without permission from some Todas of the neighbourhood. These local men bring cane to use in the catafalque and are offered Re. 1.25 in return. A Toda associated with the Badaga village may opt for the special duty of sitting at the major entrance and receiving each group of visitors. He asks every group if they include any important man—one carrying some administrative portfolio or a member of the gentry.[15] If there is such a man in the group the Toda tells them all to wait while he brings the commune headman to welcome them. Otherwise he conducts the visitors to the street where a great catafalque has been erected. The Toda is fed while he performs this service, and afterwards he gets a gift. Todas may have had a similar role during the funerals of the Badaga divisional headmen. Their main duty seems to have been policing the vast crowds that used to attend those ceremonies (Lütze, 1887, 14; see Plates 13–14).

As was mentioned earlier,

> At the present time [1902], the amount of grain supplied by the Badagas is not sufficient for the needs of the Todas, and both

> grain and rice are bought by the Todas in the bazaar. All the grain used by the *palol* [priest] must, however, be that supplied by the Badagas; but if more grain is required than the Badagas supply, it is possible that other grain may be used, though it is always in this case procured through the Badagas. The rice used at a *ti* dairy [temple] must also be procured through the Badagas (Rivers, 1906, 632–633).

This statement suggests that there used to be a separate category of Badaga associate for the priest of the *ti:* dairy-temple. This supposed institution was elaborated by Rivers (1906, 633; also 98, 630):

> The supply of grain is far from being the only duty of the Badagas to the *ti* dairies. Each *ti* has one or more special Badagas, each called *tikelfmav,* or "*ti* help Badaga," who acts as intermediary between the *palol* and the Hindus. The earthenware vessels used in the inner room, the various garments of the *palol,* and other objects are made by Hindus [the Chettis], from whom they are procured by the *tikelfmav.* I did not learn of any material recompense given to the Badagas for these services . . .[16]

Reliable Toda informants have assured me there was no such institution, even in the last century. It is true that for one month a year the *ti:* at Ȯ:nṯöw is occupied by the priest, (*pol o:ị*), and that even today Badagas give him grain during the ceremony of feeding salt to the Toda herds there at Ȯ:nṯöw.

Before 1900 the Badagas received clarified butter produced from the milk of sacred buffaloes (Metz, 1864, 41; Grigg, 1880, 195; Macleane, 1893, 905). One priest told Marshall (1873, 145) that this clarified butter from the *ti:* dairy, '. . . which we don't eat ourselves, I sell to the Badagas, who in return supply me and my family with grain, clothes, and a little money'.[17] Further, 'The *palol* wears garments of the kind called *tuni,* of a dark grey material made at Nulturs [Nellitore] in the Coimbatore District'.[18] These were sometimes brought to the priest by a Badaga who had previously acquired them from his Chetti trading partner but can in fact be supplied by anyone. The *tüṇy* cloth, a fabric quite different from ordinary Toda clothing, is also used to enshroud a corpse and was obtained from Badagas for that purpose as well

(Rivers, 1906, 236–237). A further item once acquired through Badagas was the above-mentioned vessels used in the sacred *ti:* dairy (Rivers, 1906, 90).

An occasional Toda ritual that Badagas may still attend is the rebuilding or rethatching of a temple. A day or two beforehand some Badaga elders from nearby villages should be invited by their Toda partners. At one such event in 1963 several Badagas made offerings of silver to the Toda temple and quietly made vows before it.

Sometimes when Toda men expect to be busily occupied at some such ceremony they now hire Badaga youths to prepare the food: Toda women could not do this. It is just a matter of convenience, however, and not a traditional element in the bonds between the two communities.

Although Badagas are often invited to a funeral, 'The only part played . . . is that the bell called *tukulir mani* may be kept by a Badaga or a Kota' (Rivers 1906, 633). This ancient bronze bell has to be tied round the neck of the sacred buffalo as a part of the ritual before it may be sacrificed. Some Badagas do help of their own volition with the Toda's pyre, and in the last century they used to carry the Toda headman *(manegar)* to the ceremony (Ling, 1892, 76).

A frequent guest at Toda council meetings of both a judiciary and a non-judiciary nature is the headman of Tu:ne:ri village, who is paramount chief of the Badagas. His advice is well regarded by the Todas, and he is expected to help mediate in Toda disputes whether or not Badagas are also involved in them (Rivers, 1906, 550, 633; Walker, 1965, 78, 188–189, 193). Formerly the headman of Ba:kola, who was a divisional headman *(parpati)* of the Badagas, would also attend those meetings.

BADAGAS AND KURUMBAS

The Control of Sorcery

Geographically the Kurumbas are much more isolated from the Badagas than are the Todas or Kotas; nevertheless certain Kurumbas have a crucial role in the Badaga community. A Badaga family does not have a specific Kurumba partner, but each commune appoints a particular Kurumba[19] to act as guardian and watchman to all the constituent villages. This is a lifelong appointment which passes from father to son and involves warding off magical attacks from other Kurumbas with the watchman's own sorcery. As with Toda sorcery these 'magical attacks' were once a common way of interpreting crop failures and animal diseases as well as most human ills. A Kurumba watchman is expected to spend part of the time in his Badaga commune, where he generally lives on the veranda of the headman's house.[20] If he does not appear there very often the Badagas nevertheless believe he is magically present each night or else knows by clairvoyance what is going on in the villages; yet his visits tend to be frequent, for he is fed by the commune. The standard annual remuneration should nowadays be 3.7 litres of wheat or millet from each household.

Most Badagas still believe the Kurumba is the most effective of all South Indian sorcerers: he can kill people at a distance with a spell, can secretly remove internal organs from the living, can rape women without their knowledge, can enter a locked door and can change into an insect or any sort of mammal.[21]

Until perhaps two decades ago Badaga charges were often levelled against Kurumbas; even today the suspicion directed towards them is still strong. Formal charges of witchcraft, handled by Badaga commune councils, used to unite the Badaga community against an external threat of (or target for) aggression; and the massacres which sometimes followed such charges were clearly a tension-reducing activity for the Badagas:

> In 1836, no less than fifty-eight Kurumbas were murdered, and a smaller number in 1875 and 1882. In 1891, the inmates of a single Kurumba hut were said to have been murdered, and the hut burnt to ashes, because one of the family had been treating a sick Badaga child, and failed to cure it . . . . Again, in 1900, a whole family of Kurumbas was murdered, of which the head, who had a reputation as a medicine man, was believed to have brought disease and death into a Badaga village. The sympathies of the whole countryside were so strongly with the murderers that detection was made very difficult, and the persons charged were acquitted. (Thurston, 1912, 233–234, and 1909, vol. I, 86; he partly quotes from Stuart, 1901, 5; see below, p. 200).

Metz (1864, 123) also wrote on this tension:

> When I first commenced by missionary labors on the Neilgherries, and whilst I was considered by the natives as their great friend, my object having been then but imperfectly understood, I was repeatedly asked to rid them of the Kurumbas, that is, to get them hunted down like wild beasts and exterminated, and they would remember my name with gratitude for ever.

Badagas claim that until quite recently a Kurumba council would sometimes authorize Kurumba youths to go out for a few weeks and practise the sorcery they had learned. At such times the Kurumba watchman would warn all the Badagas he was supposedly protecting that this was going on, and that they should not leave their homes after dark or take needless risks; nor should they blame him for any deaths, as each youth was permitted by the tribal council to kill one man. Since Kurumbas could also kill each other it was believed that no young sorcerer would try his skill against members of a Badaga commune protected by a more powerful Kurumba, as the latter might well retaliate out of revenge against his fellow tribesman.

Exchange of Goods and Services

Despite the tension-fraught nature of the relationship, the Kurumba watchman is no mere predator on the paranoid fears of Badagas: he does engage in economic exchange with them, too. Kurumbas are expected to supply the communes with three kinds of basket: two types of winnow and a large flat basket to hold grain while drying. They also provide their Badaga communes with certain rare species of timber found on the jungle slopes, especially the hard *ka:rča* wood needed for pounders. In the past honey, tamarind, bees-wax and knotted nets regularly came from the Kurumbas, as also did some leaf umbrellas and sleeping mats made of split cane or reeds.

One duty a Kurumba may perform for Badagas under exceptional circumstances is to remedy illnesses that Badaga therapists have failed to cure. Certain Kurumbas become noted for their abilities to cure specific ailments, either by herbal medicine or by spells, and a Badaga sufferer may arrange for treatment by them through the Kurumba watchman (Thurston, 1912, 233; Hockings, 1979b). Fees or costly presents would have to be given for this favour.

The Kurumba watchman may still play a necessary role in the ritual of his Badaga commune; but Badagas have no part whatever in Kurumba ritual. The sowing and harvest festivals in which the Kurumba must participate are the two most important in the annual cycle. In the former he must make certain ritual utterances and cut the first furrows with a plough—today with a mere ploughshare—at an early morning ceremony in January, and then he must sow the first seeds. In the harvest festival, which falls in July, he must sacrifice a buffalo calf early one morning in a Badaga's field. Two days later he leads a procession of Badagas to their temple where he assists the priest with preparations for the ritual. Then two days after this he must make a wreath of millet sheaves, attach it to a stone archh (representing a temple gateway) and then reap the first grain of the harvest. Kurumbas now claim it was they who initially taught the ancient Badagas about these two ceremonies. During the memorial ceremony for a generation that has passed away, the commune Kurumba also has an active part. On the second day (a Monday) he brings a bamboo ladder to use in building the catafalque, and he also cuts the first bamboo pole to be used in this construction. On the following Sunday and Monday he sacrifices two goats. His role throughout all of these ceremonies is that of an accessory priest, and for this he receives some fifteen rupees (Ward, 1821, lxxvi; Birch, 1838, 103, 105; Francis, 1908, 154; Belli Gowder, 1923–1941, 13–15; Noble, 1976, 118–120).

Although he does not help at any other Badaga ceremonies it used to be considered a wise precaution to invite his attendance at any auspicious ceremony, such as a wedding or naming, and then make him some small gift that might help avert the ever-threatening Kurumba malice. For a Badaga funeral he might also receive a payment (Thurston, 1909, vol. I, 86–87), although Kurumba sorcery could not affect such an inauspicious ceremony.

There are certain situations in which Kurumba musicians play at a Badaga wedding or funeral in place of the Kota band (Grigg, 1880, 211). Traditionally it could happen either when a dispute had at least temporarily alienated a Badaga family from their Kota partner or when an epidemic was rampant in the Kota's village. Now, when most Badagas have stopped inviting Kotas to any of their ceremonies, some invite Kurumba musicians instead, while others dispense with the music altogether. If the Kurumba watchman is asked to arrange for a band of musicians his own

Kurumba headman should notify the Kota headman that they will be playing at a certain Badaga village; and the Badaga inviting them should first get permission from the Kota headman to do so.[22] This set of rules is no longer followed since the feelings of Kota headmen are not respected now that Badaga/Kota relations have in general been broken off.

Until the 1930s when the institution of commune watchman began to lose currency, the Kurumba got a quarter rupee each month for every pair of oxen in the commune, or more often its equivalent in grain.[23] At harvest time he would also receive the same sum or else six litres of new grain collected from the villagers by the headman's assistant. In addition he and his family would be fed whenever in the commune.[24] The Kurumba could also rely on Badagas to satisfy all of his clothing needs, for which purpose the headman would first collect grain from the villagers with which to purchase the cloth by barter from the visiting Chetti trader. An early claim (Harkness, 1832, 109, note) that the commune Kurumba could inherit a Badaga's estate when there were no traceable heirs has never been recorded since and would not be possible today.

When a Kurumba watchman dies the headman of the Badaga commune should collect some gifts from the villagers and take them, or have them sent, to the bereaved family. This used to be imperative to secure the goodwill of the family from which the next watchman would also be drawn.

In the pre-British days the Kurumba watchmen got their only salt and crude sugar from Badagas who made annual expeditions to the plains for such needs. These had largely ceased by 1825.

BADAGAS AND IRULAS

The only Badagas having any regular contact with Irulas are those near Ha:sanu:ru and those living in the eastern sector of the Nilgiris. In this latter area Badagas probably—and erroneously—treat the Irulas as a section of the Kurumba tribe, and hence their interrelationship approximates that between Badagas and Kurumbas elsewhere on the plateau.

One of the highest mountains (1788 m.) in that particular area is Rañgasa:mi Peak (Metz, 1864, 65–66; Nicholson, 1898, 426–427; Noble, 1976, 124), important in Nilgiri culture because it is crowned by a Vaishnavite shrine (actually two megalithic circles of unknown antiquity).[25] This is controlled by Irula priests—who, unlike most South Indian tribals, are Vaishnavites. The two monoliths inside the stone circles represent the god Raṅga and his wife, to whom some of the local Badagas make a yearly offering of plantains, milk and coconuts:

> The hereditary pújári is an Irula, and on the day fixed by the Badagas for the annual feast, he arrives from his hamlet . . ., bathes in a pool below the summit, and marches to the top shouting 'Góvinda! Góvinda!' The cry is taken up . . . and the whole crowd, which includes Badagas, Irulas and Kurumbas, surrounds the enclosures while the Irula priest invokes the deities by blowing his conch and beating his drum, and pours oblations over, and decorates with flowers, the two stones which represent them. That night two stone basins on the summit are filled with ghee [clarified butter] and lighted, and the glare is visible for miles around. The ceremonies close with prayers for good rain and fruitfulness among the flocks and herds, a wild dance by the Irula, and the boiling . . . of much rice in milk. (Francis, 1908, 340; compare Ward, 1821, lxii; Breeks, 1873, 70; Macleane, 1893, 373).

While Badaga contact with the Irulas was less frequent than with other tribes, one of the major 'sanskritizing' influences in the Nilgiris was clearly constituted by the Irulas until the latter part of the last century. As Metz observed (1864, 133), 'They come up now and then . . . and divert the inhabitants with obscene theatrical performances representing passages in the life of Krishna, whom they call Govinda'. The Abbé Dubois (1906, 196) pointed out how in the early 1800s Raṅgasa:mi Peak was a place of pilgrimage for Hindus from the plains, who 'have made it a *punyasthala,* or place of virtue . . . As it is very difficult to reach the top of this mountain, a view of the summit alone . . . is considered sufficient to remove the burden of sin . . . .' Those stalwart pilgrims who did clamber up the peak could hardly have failed to influence local Badagas to some extent in pre-British times.

For such services as their Krishna dramas and occasional medical therapy Irulas used to get grain from the Badagas, a gift which was probably in the nature of a *douceur,* for Irulas were also considered sorcerers (though less powerful than the true Kurumba). Some Badagas living close to Irulas probably had a more regular exchange relationship, giving grain to the Irulas in return for honey, bees-wax, timber, nets and other jungle products (Grigg, 1880, 215–216; Macleane, 1893, 373). Like the Kurumbas, Irulas may be asked to play music for Badaga ceremonies when Kotas cannot be approached for a band. Irula women living in the Badaga villages near Ha:sanu:ru have sometimes become the mistresses of those Badagas but not elsewhere.

BADAGAS AND KASUVAS

Although it has been suggested (Thurston, 1909, vol. III, 256; Noble, 1968, 69) that the Kasuvas ('labourers') are merely Irula tribesmen who moved onto the labourer settlements in plantations over the past century, their geographical distribution does not support this. Kasuvas are only found in the Moyar Ditch north of the Nilgiri Plateau, whereas the local Irulas only live south and east of the plateau (Noble, 1968, 6, Fig. 2). At most it can be said that these are two names for people of very similar culture.

The Kasuvas perform a service for the more northerly Badagas analogous to that which the Todas perform for those living farther south: Kasuvas take Badaga cattle down into the Moyar Ditch for grazing and breeding (Francis, 1908, 209; Noble, 1968, 69–72). A Badaga owner occasionally visits his herds there, but the animals are regularly tended by a Kasuva family who jointly receive perhaps six to ten rupees weekly as well as vegetables and grain. In addition they get a ration of rice, an annual supply of clothing and occasional gifts, for example, at a Kasuva wedding. The livestock camps *(hundis)* of Kasuvas are mainly used for breeding, but large numbers of cows and buffaloes may be sent there by the Badagas when grazing on the Nilgiris is sparse. More generally,

> Dry cows are taken down, and good milk yielders are brought back up . . . Milk and buttermilk [yielded by Badaga cattle while in the Moyar Ditch] may be consumed by the Kasuva caretakers. Clarified butter carried up by Badagas or Kasuvas is either sold or consumed by Badagas (Noble, 1968, 72).

Be:ragaṇi, the only Badaga village with a sacred herd attached to its temple (Francis, 1908, 316), has for over two decades kept its hundred buffaloes permanently in the Moyar Ditch under the charge of Kasuvas because of shortage of grazing around Be:ra-gaṇi itself. The herdsmen are paid from temple funds.

As in the case of Kurumbas, Irulas and Uralis, a Kasuva band may perform at Badaga ceremonies in place of the customary Kota one. Aside from this, there is one annual ceremonial event which has brought the two communities together in considerable numbers over the past decade or so. This is a complex *pu:ja* to the goddess Sikkamma at her Kasuva-owned temple in the Moyar Ditch, held every March. Roughly five thousand Badagas and most Kasuvas attend, the highlights of the event being *pu:ja,* a free meal, and a noisy night-time procession with the goddess' image mounted on an electrically lit elephant.

BADAGAS AND URALIS

The Uralis are a tribe of gatherers and shifting cultivators who inhabit jungles on some southern slopes of the plateau. They have no regular connexion with Badagas, but as they are feared for their sorcery they can depend on alms from Badaga villagers should a crop failure force them to wander up onto the plateau, as it occasionally has. Under unusual circumstances Badagas may pay a band of Uralis to perform music at a ceremony when for some reason Kotas cannot be invited.

THE WAINAD GAUDAS AND THEIR NEIGHBOURS

The Wainad Gaudas are Badagas who settled on the lower plateau some two centuries ago. In proximity to them are various other groups: Kotas, Chettis, Panias, Irulas, Kurumbas and until 1925 some Todas. The Gaudas, a dominant community in the area, cultivate dry and irrigated rice. They claim it was the desire for rice which had prompted their ancestors to move down into the Wainad from Badaga villages on the Nilgiri Plateau.

The community consists only of Gaudas, except one commune which also has some Toreas (now calling themselves Gaudas). The 951 people live in ten communes, each made up of a few hamlets containing one lineage. Every commune has a council, and for complex cases a council of all the Wainad communes is held at

Pandalu:ru village. This system thus parallels that of the Nilgiri Badagas but does not link up with theirs: cases cannot, for example, be referred to the paramount chief of the Badagas in Tu:ne:ri, and he does not invite Wainad Gaudas to his councils. The head of the all-Wainad council is someone noted for his justice, called the Great Headman (*doḍḍa gauda*); he is selected from any of the communes. Each commune is headed by a man termed the *jammaka:ra,* under whom there are two or three lesser headmen (*kudiare*). Both of these offices are inherited fraternally; i.e., they pass from brother to brother in order of seniority, then on to the eldest brother's eldest son, and so on. Each *kudiare* is responsible for the descendants from one particular Nilgiri division: in Kolepaḷḷi, for example, there are two such headmen because its population is descended from Todaṇa:ḍu and Me:kuna:ḍu villagers. As in the hills, a legal dispute passes up this hierarchy from the *kudiare* to the Great Headman if necessary.

These Gaudas have maintained some marriage connexions with Nilgiri Gaudas, even with families of the gentry. Several communes still intermarry with the Nilgiri Badagas of So:lu:ru; but more generally all of the communes marry endogamously or exogamously within the Wainad community. Their constituent hamlets, being single lineages, are always exogamous.[26]

There is a nineteenth-century account of trading parties of Wainad Gaudas regularly visiting the Me:kuna:ḍu village of Ke:ti (and presumably elsewhere on the plateau), bringing with them buffaloes and gold dust 'for sale' (B.E.M.S., 1854, no. 14, 41).

These Gaudas had no connection with the Todas who, until the 1920s, lived on the edge of the Wainad, but some do maintain an exchange relationship with the Kotas there and also with certain Irulas and Kurumbas. The Kota partner from Gudalu:ru provides pottery as well as a pole used in Gauda funerals, to which he should also bring Kota musicians. He helps, too, with house building (Ranga, 1934, 26). In return he gets an occasional buffalo. Irulas and Kurumbas may also provide music for the funerals. Like the Panias they are valued as basket-makers but have no reputation for sorcery here as they do elsewhere. The Kurumba watchman institution is not encountered in the Wainad.

Gauda landowners have a special relationship with the Pania tribe, some of whom were their praedial slaves.[27] As if to justify this situation some Wainad natives claim the Panias originated as African slaves who escaped from two British ships in Calicut

(Kozhikode) during the reign of Tippu Sultan; but it is more likely they were local tribals or slaves (*paṇya*) who had escaped across the border from Coorg.[28] These labourers, whose services may be bought along with the land (Thurston, 1909, vol. VI, 58), and whose position there is inherited patrilineally, work without wages in return for regular meals, housing and clothes. Some of the more progressive farmers give them a little pocket-money, too, and normally pay their marriage expenses. In 1976 the Government made a serious effort to release all such people from bondage.

TRADITIONAL INTERCHANGE: A SUMMARY

Each of the four main groups—Badagas, Kotas, Todas and Kurumbas—was linked with each of the others through patrilineally descending partnerships. The men involved in these supplied each other with goods and services supplementing their own economic production and also symbolizing their social interrelationship through ritualized interaction.

Only the Badagas produced a real surplus of grain; Kotas and Kurumbas grew hardly enough crops for their own needs and Todas never grew anything. Thus the Badagas alone were in a position to pass out grain to Todas, Kotas and Kurumbas at harvest-time. They were also to some extent the suppliers of cloth, sugar and salt for these three tribes. While Badagas thus played a major part in the economy of the Nilgiri tribes their role in the rituals of these groups was minimal, probably because the form of the rituals antedated the arrival of the Badagas.

Todas specialized in dairy produce: milk and clarified butter. These they provided on occasion for Badagas, Kotas and Kurumbas. Todas were also able to supply Kotas and Badagas with various cane products: beds, flutes and certain baskets.

The Kotas possessed some buffaloes and cultivated grain, too. But they also made various artifacts for the Badagas who gave them cattle carcasses and grain and for the Todas who gave them clarified butter. The Kotas were the specialists in leather-work, carpentry, pottery, metal-working, thatching and ceremonial music. Their participation in Toda and Badaga funerals was essential.

By comparison with the Kotas, the Toda and Kurumba tribesmen maintained relatively simple relationships with the

Badagas. Most Kurumbas were kept distant from the other hill peoples because of their residence pattern and their reputation for infallible sorcery. The commune Kurumbas, or watchmen, were appointed by a Kota or Badaga commune to protect its members from Kurumba sorcery. The loyal watchman was rewarded with a dole of grain at harvest, with new cloth whenever he needed it, with meals when he was with the Badagas and in fact with anything else that he might wheedle out of his employers by supernatural threats or promises.

NOTES

1. Only four of the sixteen Toda clans keep up the relationship, and it has been totally abandoned by Christian Todas and Christian Badagas; compare Emeneau, 1939, 101. I am indebted to T. Mutiken, a Toda, for his patient criticism of these pages on Toda/Badaga relations.
2. '. . . were it not for the hold which the Todas have upon them by the pretended use of witchcraft, they would doubtless refuse payment of their accustomed tribute'; Metz, 1864, 21; compare Marshall, 1873, 145; Grigg, 1880, 328.
3. Ouchterlony, 1848, 59; Shortt & Ouchterlony, 1868, 59–60; Breeks, 1873, 12–13; Ward 1821, lxxiii, stated it was paid to Todas because they were 'the hereditary claimants of the soil'. We should note that throughout the second half of the nineteenth century the government allowed the Todas Rs. 150 annually, as 'goodoo' or compensation for former Toda lands now used by Europeans in Ootacamund Municipality; Grigg, 1880, 302, 329–331, 333–341; Price, 1908, 227–228. Similar compensation was paid for Toda and Badaga lands in Coonoor Municipality; Francis, 1908, 343.
4. Harkness (1832, 135–136) gives a general figure of 2.25 litres—probably what each household gave the Todas.
5. Ouchterlony, 1848, 59; Shortt & Ouchterlony, 1868, 59; Kotas claim it should be one winnowful (four litres) per household; Emeneau, 1946, 257.
6. Compare Shortt and Ouchterlony, 1868, 59: 'Sometimes the offerings . . . are not considered sufficient, and sometimes they refuse to give anything at all, when confusion ensues; the Todars . . . entering their houses and laying them under contribution by force.'
7. Grigg, 1880, 195; Rivers, 1906, 261; Francis, 1908, 144; compare Metz, 1864, 41; '. . . they stand in fear of the supposed power of the Pálaul to kill their cattle by sorcery.'
8. Toda men and women wear the *pu:txuḷy*—a large cloak intricately embroidered by the women—over a loincloth.
9. On occasions when the Todas did not join Badagas and Kotas in this venture.
10. Rivers, 1906, 634. Toda songs often refer to buffaloes obtained from Badagas for funeral sacrifice; e.g., Emeneau, 1971, 6, 79, 307, 448.
11. Basel Mission, 1905, 305, records the case of a Badaga Christian teacher who had relations in 1903 with a Toda girl and later with his own mare. Emeneau, 1971, 613, cites the case of a Toda woman 'raped by a Badaga'. Another

report of wife exchange between Todas and Mudugas has not been substantiated by recent investigation; see von Fürer-Haimendorf, 1954, *passim.*

12. Grigg, 1880, 212; compare Metz, 1864, 123, 'Rifle', 1872, 32; Stokes 1883a, 6. They were from one particular clan nicknamed 'Kurumba-cut-people'.
13. Francis, 1908, 272; Thurston, 1909, vol. VII, 115; Shaposhnikova, 1969, ch. 22; at present only two Badagas rent land from Todas.
14. Those of the high-status Ha:ruva and Lingayat clans eat only the milk products, not cooked food, if they visit Todas. For an instance of a Toda priest putting butter on the Badaga ceremonial spear, see Emeneau, 1971, 5, 744.
15. There is a kind of upper class among Badagas, which I call the gentry: families claiming direct descent from the founder of their village. It is from these families that the headmen usually come; see above, Diagram 6.
16. The fact that Badagas and anthropologists may go right up to the *ti:* enclosure while Todas stay a hundred meters away perhaps led Rivers to presume his Badaga guide for the day had a special relationship with the *palol*!
17. The sanctity of milk from sacred buffaloes has been lost once it is made into clarified butter, and this can be sold; Emeneau, 1938, 104, 112.
18. Rivers, 1906, 103. A less reliable source claims the *palol's* cloth was woven by the Toreas of Jakkane:ri; near Kotagiri; see Macleane, 1893, 905.
19. *U:r Kuruba;* Breeks, 1873, 53–54. The common spelling *Kurumba* comes from Tamil.
20. No Kurumba is allowed in a Lingayat house, as he is believed capable of polluting it. Other phratries allow him as far as the outer room and consider him less polluting than a Kota.
21. Harkness, 1832, 84–85; Metz, 1864, 116–117; Thurston, 1909, vol. I, 86, and 1912, 232–233; 'Miles,' 1951, 71. Fifty years ago an up-to-date old lady was 'experimenting with flying'.
22. Badagas assert it would be unethical or liable to bring misfortune were Kurumbas and Kotas allowed to play music together on the same occasion.
23. Metz, 1864, 116; Thurston, however, stated this to be the *annual* tax paid by each Badaga family; see Thurston, 1909, vol. I, 86–87. According to Kotas it should be 'four annas and a meal paid by each house'; Emeneau, 1946, 257.
24. Ward, 1821, lxxvi; Harkness, 1832, 109; Metz, 1864, 116. Around Kotagiri each family gave their Kurumba 18 litres; compare Harkness, 1832, 135, note. Elsewhere he was thought to get about one-sixtieth of the harvest; Harkness, 1832, 57. Earlier his share was put at 15–37 litres per farmer, plus 'as many of the sheaves as he can well bear away on his shoulders'; Ward, 1821, lxxvi. The Kurumbas accepted cooked food from Badagas, uncooked food from Todas, but none from Kotas; Macleane, 1893, 222.
25. Though the Badagas are Shaivites there are also Vaishnavite temples in some villages, managed by Shaivite priests.
26. Marriage, which is rarely polygynous, involves payment of a bridewealth of a hundred rupees, refundable upon divorce; for an instance of marriage between So:lu:r and the Wainad Gaudas, see Emeneau, 1971, 611.
27. Ranga, 1934, 55–59; Noble, 1968, 174–175. This relationship was ended by Government action in 1976.
28. Moses, 1964, 10; Srinivas, 1965, 20–22; *paṇya* is also a section of the Yerava tribe in Coorg.

6

Early Patterns of Trade

ORIGINAL STATE OF THE ECONOMY

Little is known about the Badaga economic system prior to the arrival of British officials in 1812, except that the exchange of goods and services outlined in the previous two chapters was undoubtedly in operation.[1] It is nevertheless worth surveying the available sources since the pre-monetary economy of the period preceding the impact of European economic ideas has till now been influential on Nilgiri cultures, despite their monetization for well over a century. Some of the most detailed information lies in the traditions of the Badagas. Because of the high degree of correspondence between tales from different parts of the plateau, their content seems to be factual rather than imaginary and can go a long way towards explaining the many vestiges of this indigenous economy that one can observe even today.

The earliest mention of Badagas in the Nilgiris is by Finicio, who reports an encounter with both Badagas and Todas. The Badagas told him they had only three villages on the plateau, but this information may be misleading.[2] Finicio describes a village called Melcuntaõ—presumably the modern Me:lkunda—which at the start of the seventeenth century already had a population of one hundred and fifty to two hundred with an adequate mixed-farming economy. The priest mentions that these Badagas had cattle, poultry, goats; that they grew lentils, 'rice' (presumably a millet), mustard seed, garlic and wheat; and they also ate honey. At this early date the Badagas were not self-sufficient, for they gave the Todas 'rice' in exchange for buffalo ghee. He added that Badagas also carried this clarified butter to a place called Manaracathe to sell (Finicio, 1603, 723). This is evidently the Manna:ru Ghat, or escarpment track, which runs from Malabar to the Sundepatti Pass, and which then leads up the south side of the plateau to Me:lkunde.[3] Whether coinage was obtainable by such transactions we are not told. The same description might well have been penned by another visitor 200 years later.

Nothing was however written about the following two centuries although that was the period when the community expanded to nearly 350 villages and consolidated itself. The next mention of Badagas is in Buchanan's survey of 1800 (1807, vol. II, 246–247), when he tells briefly of their having ploughs, practising swidden cultivation and gathering jungle produce, including honey and bees-wax.[4]

From about 1809 to 1812 several Britons explored the hills.[5] Apparently they had no impact on the local economy. The 1812 expedition was to survey the area quickly and report back to the Collector of Coimbatore, under whose charge the tract had nominally rested since the Treaty of Seringapatam in 1799. Keys' short report (1812) contains some valuable material to add to what little we glean from Finicio, Buchanan and the oldest traditions of the Badagas themselves.

In 1819 the first settler, John Sullivan, came to the plateau and set in motion a train of events which quickly and significantly transformed the indigenous economy into a monetized one. Over the succeeding years the European population slowly increased; but it was only after 1838, when coffee was introduced, that Europeans had any commercial reason for taking up residence in the area. Long after that date the great bulk of Europeans remained in the three towns of the plateau, so that their influence on the rural economy may well have been slight. Not until the 1850s is there documentary evidence of any modification of the Badaga farming economy that can be attributed directly to the British presence. What O'Malley (1941, 12) has observed for Moghul India in general is also an accurate summary of the Nilgiri situation throughout the last century:

The only contact with the villages was by means of local officials

> having their head-quarters in the towns, who were responsible for the patrolling of the main routes, the suppression of organized crime, and the realization of the land revenue. So long as it was paid, and so long as there was no disturbance of the peace endangering the general security or outbreaks of crime preventing the safe passage of travellers and merchandise, the villages were left to manage their own affairs, with headmen and councils of elders to try their petty cases and village watchmen to prevent petty crime.

A detailed account of the economy up to the year 1830 (when a large part of the plateau was transferred from Coimbatore to the Malabar administration) can be reconstructed from several reports, mainly British.[6] These provide us with a list of Badaga produce which can be amended slightly by modern informants.

The main items[7] cultivated by Badagas in the early nineteenth century were wheat, barley, panic-seed, the Italian, finger and slender millets, poppy, prince's feather, mustard seed, black gram, field peas, chick pea or Bengal gram, pepper, rose-mallow seeds; garlic, onion, fenugreek, country bean, pumpkin and gourd.

The main animal products in this period were cow and buffalo milk, clarified butter (made more by Todas than by Badagas), hides (prepared by Kotas from Badaga animals), bullocks used in ploughing and threshing, and a few large poultry. No sheep were kept, though Finicio and Birch had noticed goats in the hills (Finicio, 1603, 723; Keys, 1812, li; Birch, 1836, 103).

Materials gathered from the jungle included kitchen fuel, honey, bees-wax, hay, wild flax, gentian, sandalwood, rattan cane and black dammer or resin.

The items usually imported and exported by Badagas are also known from these same sources. The imports were coarse cloth, salt, tobacco, iron bars for the Kota blacksmith (Thurston, 1909, vol. IV, 8), coarse sugar made from a palm sap, trinkets and coinage.

Exports included wheat, barley, some superior millets, bales of millet and barley hay and wild flax (all used for fodder), poppy capsules and opium, honey, bees-wax, garlic, onion, mustard seed, pepper, fenugreek, gentian, rose-mallow seed, clarified butter, sandalwood, hides, cane—and coinage paid in land taxes to an official at Dannaika Ko:ṭe.

MARKETING BEFORE 1825

Until the British encouraged sundry traders from the plains to establish a weekly bazaar in Ootacamund around the year 1825,[8] there was no market-place on the plateau itself, and coinage did not circulate much among Badagas. Nevertheless they did participate slightly in the market economy of the plains early in the last century. Depending on the position of their villages some went down the eastern slopes to the market of Ka:ramuḍu (in Tamil, Ka:ramaḍai), others chose a route down the northern slopes to the Mysore town of Guṇḍuḷupe:te and those in Kundena:ḍu went southward (as in Finicio's day) to Sundepatti, a small market in the westernmost corner of the Coimbatore Plain.[9] Apart from visiting Ka:ramuḍu (which they called Koṅgu, meaning 'plains') they never had any occasion to travel extensively on the Coimbatore Plain. Guṇḍuḷupe:te used simply to be called Pet: this meant 'a place where people gather together', hence a market; or according to some, 'a place where cattle gather'. For a long time it was a major cattle market in southern Mysore.

Early each March the Kanarese Chettis and other people of Ka:ramuḍu held a festival to honour the god Raṅgana:tan, after which there was a large cattle fair and general market.[10] A delegation of Badaga men from villages in the eastern part of the Nilgiris attended that festival every year.[11] They would first help drag the chariot of the deity and then would barter goods for coinage and whatever else they needed. There seems to have been no fixed date for the annual visit of more westerly villagers to Guṇḍuḷupe:te, but it coincided roughly with the Ka:ramuḍu expedition. In both cases the Badagas obtained provisions for their main harvest festival, the Great Festival,[12] which falls in March or April, and salt for the ceremonial feeding of their cattle in March. In Guṇḍuḷupe:te Lingayats could also buy personal *liṅgas* at the monastery. In view of the long walk from these markets and the 1500 m. ascent, it is not surprising that the items bought were small and fairly valuable.

All three trading expeditions were organized on the same principle. Permission to go was first obtained from the village headmen, then preliminary arrangements were made as to who would go and the time of their departure. The Badaga headmen would then send a message to neighbouring Kota headmen, thus giving Kotas an opportunity to join the party, for the Kotas did not organize their own expeditions. Todas sometimes also joined, trading clarified butter and honey for tobacco, trinkets and cloth. Their clarified butter was much appreciated in the plains and was 'transported great distances, even as far as Bombay' (Hough, 1829, 72). The trading party would be at least twenty-strong, and sometimes hundreds went together—after carefully taking off all their valuables. This arrangement was important to the participants because of the dangers, real or imaginary, which they could expect as they passed through steep jungle tracks infested by tigers, elephants, wild buffalo, wolves, brigands and Kurumba sorcerers.

Until the 1830s certain Badagas, generally commune headmen, habitually walked once a year to the fort at Dannaika Ko:ṭe, below the eastern slopes.[13] The Nilgiri Plateau formed a part of the Dannaika Ko:ṭe *taluk* (revenue division) from Tippu Sultan's administration up to 1830. This was a convention important only for the collection of land revenue from the Badagas and Kotas. Each farmer was assessed a fixed rate by the officers, dependent on the total rather than the cultivated area he held; the rate did not decrease if some fields remained uncultivated one year. Traditions mention occasional visits by Tippu's officers to extract payment from the unwilling villagers (Metz, 1864, 119; Grigg, 1880, 312, 325; Emeneau, 1946, 255). In 1799, after Tippu was killed, the plateau passed into the hands of the East India Company by the Treaty of Seringapatam, and for over twenty years the British continued to collect Nilgiri revenues at Dannaika Ko:ṭe. Their estimates were now based not on acreage but on a farmer's wealth. Each year therefore the headmen carried their collected taxes down in coin. While at the fort they could also visit the nearby market towns of Sattiyamaṅgaḷa and Sirumuge (Metz, 1864, 5).

Very likely one of the reasons for the trading expeditions was to sell enough of the new harvest and other produce to get the coinage needed for the tax payment, although this could in part be paid with opium (Francis, 1908, 290; Price 1908, 224). Coinage was scarcely in circulation on the plateau at this time, especially since there was no market there until 1825. Coins had, however, found a ceremonial use. Ward (1821, lxxiii; cf. Rivers, 1906, 361–362) mentions gifts of a quarter or half rupee to Todas on the occasion of Badaga weddings. Rupee coins also reached the Todas, presumably from their transactions with Badagas and from the expeditions, for a number of the coins still displayed in Toda funerial ritual are East India Company silver rupees of the late-eighteenth century.

As further evidence of the ceremonial circulation of coinage Ward (1821, lxxi) also discusses Badaga bridewealth,[14] and the payment of twenty Cantirai fanams (coins totalling nearly six rupees) to a mother when, after divorce, she gave custody of her newborn child to her former husband. To judge by later Badaga practices it is very likely that a gift of coins[15] was already an integral part of all family ceremonies. Such a gift was actually a delayed exchange and implied that a return gift was expected later when similar circumstances arose. By 1848 only the East India Company's coinage was in circulation, but a good deal of it was also hoarded by burial or made into ornaments (Ouchterlony, 1848, 72; Shortt & Ouchterlony, 1868, 72).

This system of coinage circulation was very slow and uncertain, as it depended on the occasional celebration of weddings and other family events. Coins clearly had a ritual value for Badagas and were important in this period as a symbolic link between various social units (as to some extent they still are). We have no definite evidence that coins were used for payment of fines to the headmen as early as the eighteenth century; but throughout much of the nineteenth century a regular schedule of fines was maintained in Badaga judicial practice.[16] Coinage did not define values in a local Nilgiri market but did act as a convenient and reliable means of storing credit acquired in the lowland markets where, from 1799, the British pursued a policy of fixing local grain prices by currency values.

By the start of the last century the Badagas had become 'terribly impoverished', and most were heavily in arrears with payment of land revenue. 'The rates of assessment were undoubtedly low', were based on acreage and 'varied with the appearance of the crop at harvest-time' (Grigg, 1880, 312; Francis, 1908, 268). During the first thirty years of British rule a decline in these payments set in. From 1799 to 1813 the average annual revenue from the entire plateau was Rs. 14,762, but over the next fourteen years it fell to Rs. 6,000 (Grigg, 1880, 292; Francis, 1908, 268). In 1801 it was Rs. 13,425; in 1811 it was Rs. 15,067 (Grigg, 1880, 314); in 1821 it was Rs. 9,000 (Mackworth, 1823, 123–126); and by 1830 it was down to Rs. 6,000 (Baber, 1830, 314). There were several reasons for this decline, the most general one being the meagre control over the plateau that could be exercised from Dannaika Ko:ṭe; Sullivan attributed the low revenue to lack of a proper road (Grigg, 1880, 280–281, 314). The tax-farmers who operated for some time on the plateau, from 1807,[17] were too demanding of the dues they had paid the East India Company for the privilege of collecting, while in some other years the commune headmen were too slack about the collection. The drought of 1805–1807, the general shortage of coin, the after-effects of Tippu's plundering of Badaga villages, all perhaps contributed to the decline in the payments, if not the fortunes, of the Badagas at this period.

Despite the British policy of fixing grain prices they did show fluctuations from year to year. Sarada Raju's excellent study of economic conditions in Madras Presidency during the first half of the nineteenth century clarifies these fluctuations. He does not offer specific data for Coimbatore District (which then included the Nilgiris); nevertheless he is surely justified in his view that on a long-term basis the trend was similar in all districts (Sarada Raju, 1941, 227). As his statistical data for the Presidency adequately confirm (1941, 228–230),

> ... prices were high in the first few years of the nineteenth century. The country had just emerged from a protracted period of war and anarchy during which rival armies and plundering bands had laid whole districts desolate. Cultivators who had fled to the jungles and hills were but gradually returning to their neglected fields.... The period was also marked by a number of scarcities, more or less severe. The very first year, 1799–1800, witnessed a severe dearth and again between 1805 and 1807 occurred another famine, when prices ruled very high. After this prices were persistently low ... from 1807–8 to 1850–51 prices rose above the [economic analyst's] base only on seven occasions; and these were famine years.
>
> When the pendulum swung back, low prices ruled till 1812, when two dry seasons caused a scarcity which lasted till 1813–14. But with the coming of the rains, a lower level was reached and we hear frequent complaints of the "continued low price of grain".... All the Collectors remarked about it, affecting as it did the ryots' [peasants'] ability to pay the revenue (Sarada Raju, 1941, 231–232).[18]

While several seasons of adverse weather mentioned by Sarada Raju did give rise to famine conditions in Coimbatore District, which was one of the driest in the Presidency, it is very unlikely that famine also occurred on the Nilgiri Plateau at those times.

Because of their wetter climate the Badagas have always been able to subsist while famine ravaged the South Indian plains (Grigg, 1880, 34). Even so, Badagas were undoubtedly affected by the occasional lowland famines and by fluctuations in the grain prices, since they sold their grain surplus in the nearby lowland markets. We need hardly point out that they would have made unusually good profits from sales in the famine years, but they might also have been taxed more heavily in those years.

MARKETING AFTER 1825

Around the year 1825 the British settlers, through their officials in Ootacamund, began to encourage traders from the plains to develop a market in that town and provided government-owned land for the purpose (Price, 1908, 233). By the end of 1827,

> ...advances had been made to [immigrant] natives to open bazaars...in the place so that 'the market is now well and regularly supplied with every essential article'...a public establishment of palanquin-bearers was kept up; and...villages were beginning to spring up at the foot of the passes (Hayavadana Rao, 1908, 115; compare Grigg, 1880, 288).

The traders in those early days were Chettis from Me:ṭṭupa:ḷaya, Ka:ramuḍu and other nearby lowland villages.[19] The market in Ootacamund was held only on Monday and Tuesday of each week; every Thursday the same traders held a market in Sirumuge, and on Friday were in Ka:ramuḍu. In these places they would collect the produce from the surrounding Chetti-controlled villages, then on Friday night they would start out by bullock-cart up the long Coonoor pass to the plateau. Their merchandise included rice, salt, crude sugar, coconut and other foodstuffs[20] As the climb was entirely uphill the bullocks rested all day Saturday and Sunday on the slopes and travelled throughout the nights. Later on in the century wealthy Chettis built some free rest-houses by the roadside for these journeys. The carts regularly reached Ootacamund on Sunday evening after a forty-eight hour haul. After two days of trading the Chettis left with their loaded carts around four each Tuesday afternoon. By Friday morning they were back in Ka:ramuḍu to repeat the weekly cycle and to barter their Nilgiri acquisitions for further produce to take up to the hills.

According to modern Badaga informants their forebears did not use cash at the Ootacamund market during the first two decades of its existence. They exchanged the products of their own lands for the foodstuffs brought up by Chettis. In this way the Nilgiri Plateau was exporting a variety of goods to Ka:ramuḍu and its environs, especially clarified butter, onions, honey, coriander, opium and millet hay.

The initial period of barter in the bazaar passed as the town acquired a few regular shops. Later in the nineteenth century coinage came into use in the market, now open every day, and a government superintendent fixed the day's prices (Ouchterlony, 1848, 72; Price, 1908, 187). One could even borrow money there at 2 or 3% per month interest (depending on the security). Monday and Tuesday in Ootacamund, Thursday in Sirumuge, Friday in Ka:ramuḍu and Saturday in Me:ṭṭupa:ḷaya are however still called 'shandy days',[21] and it is still customary for Badagas to visit the Nilgiri towns on Monday, their weekly holiday, and to send truckloads of farm produce to Me:ṭṭupa:ḷaya or to Ka:ramuḍu each Friday. The transition to exclusive use of coinage in the market took a very long time, for as recently as 1924 Gaymard was able to remark that when they made their weekly trips to town some Badagas did not carry a purse but instead a basket or sackful of grain which they would exchange there for salt, pimentos, utensils and cloth (Gaymard, 1924, 2–3).

ITINERANT TRADERS ON THE PLATEAU

Both before and after these town bazaars were established the Badagas maintained another kind of link with the lowland economy. Chettis from villages lying directly east of the Nilgiris used to (and still do) come up onto the plateau once a month on foot for petty trading. Badagas call them Regional Chettis *(ṇa:ḍu cetti),* in reference perhaps to the restricted range of each man's trading itinerary. Although living in a Tamil-speaking area their native tongue is Kannada. Their settlements in and near the towns of Sirumuge, Me:ṭṭupa:ḷaya and Ka:ramuḍu are concerned with petty trade, weaving and agriculture. The Chetti and his family weave cloth in their home for the Badagas; and until the advent of the Ootacamund bazaar they were the regular source for cloth among the entire Nilgiri population.

Chetti merchandise consists of cloth, lamp-wicks and various trinkets, which are exchanged for grain or cash when available. Since the early nineteenth century these traders have also made and bartered iron measures of volume, artifacts that had previously been made out of bamboo by the Todas.[22] The Nilgiri system of measures differed significantly from that of southern Mysore, presumably because these Chettis and the officers at Dannaika Ko:ṭe imposed the standards of Coimbatore markets on the Badagas.

Each Badaga village has a traditional barter relationship with a particular Chetti man, inherited on either side by a son from his father; and despite the vast economic changes since the inception of this system some centuries ago the relationship continues today, modified only by a very considerable drop in the number of clients and volume of trade. During the ten days of his visit the Chetti works through two or three villages a day, restricting himself to the two dozen or more villages of his recognized territory, and then returns to his home in the plains. After twenty days of work there he returns to the plateau and repeats this circuit. Contiguous territories are covered by different Chettis often from the same village, so that one can send a message to his own Regional Chetti by contacting another one on tour in the hills. Although a Chetti may sometimes bring his wife with him all dealings occur between him and the Badaga men. If the Chetti's wife accompanies him it is only to strengthen the bonds of friendship with his Badaga trade associates, by making conversation with the Badaga womenfolk. During nights on the plateau the Chetti sleeps in the outer room of a Badaga friend. He is allowed to eat in that room as well but is expected to wash his own plate, an act indicative of his lower status.

The relationship between Badagas and Chettis is very different in character from that linking Badagas with Todas or Kotas. Until well into the twentieth century the latter linkages were crucial for the flow of necessary goods to members of the three communities; whereas trade with Chettis was never anything more than a convenience which in earlier times saved Badagas from extra journeys to the plains and more recently to the nearest bazaar. The Chetti is considered a foreigner as he is from the plains. Normally his Badaga friends need not visit his village: there is no ceremonial gift-exchange between the two and little participation in each other's rituals. This contrasts with the intensity of the relationships uniting the various peoples of the plateau (compare Diagram 8, p. 100).

We know of only two occasions when Chettis and Badagas do have some ritual interaction: one in the plains, the other on the hills. Perhaps two centuries ago, and certainly before British suzerainty in the area, the Chettis of Ka:ramuḍu, acknowledging that they were becoming wealthier because of trade with the Nilgiris, built a larger temple to their god Raṅgana:tan and started the annual chariot-dragging festival in his honour. It was this festival day that the Badagas always chose as the best time for their yearly trading expedition; the trading was preceded by mandatory participation in the ceremonies (Nicholson, 1898, 352; see above, p. 138).

Secondly, one of the major Badaga festivals, in honour of their goddess Hette ('grandmother'), is held in Be:ragaṇi village, where there is a special building called Weaving House belonging in common to the whole village. Several days before the annual festival their Regional Chetti comes up from near Sirumuge to sit in this house and weave a year's supply of new clothes for the priest. These are a loincloth, turban and shawl, all of cotton, for the making of which the Chetti gets a fixed amount of cash from the temple funds (Francis, 1908, 317). These men do not otherwise weave while touring the plateau.

NOTES

1. 'There are no manufactures on the hills and much less of trade'; an exaggeration from Keys, 1812, li; compare Hayavadana Rao, 1908, 108.
2. See above, p. 40, n. 9. It may be mentioned that both Ptolemy and the *Periplus Maris Erythraei* refer to a town called Nelkynda, but this was probably Nirkundram, near Kottayam in Kerala.
3. It connects with the most westerly part of the Coimbatore Plain, in the upper valley of the Bhavani, as well as with Malabar District; Hayavadana Rao, 1908, 105.
4. He did not ascend the hills but made his enquiry at the foot, on the Coimbatore side; Grigg, 1880, 277, Hayavadana Rao, 1908, 106, and Price, 1908, 2.
5. Burton, 1851, 270; Metz, 1864, 6; Balfour, 1885, 1099; Hayavadana Rao, 1908, 107, n. 1. Among these people was Colonel A. MacLeod who spent some months in military movements in the Wainad in 1804. Several Badaga boys born on the day of his visit were named MacLeod; see Metz, 1864, 6; Grigg, 1880, 312; Price, 1908, 10. Other early visitors included H. Bevan and L.G. Ford (1809), William Morrison (1812), and W. Keys and MacMahon (1812).
6. Keys, 1812, li; Sullivan, 1819, lv; Macpherson, 1820, lvii; Ward, 1821, lxiii,

lxv; De La Tour, 1822, 261; Baber, 1830, 315; Harkness, 1832, 136–137; Birch, 1838, 103; 'Stocqueler,' 1845, 579; Price, 1908, 8; Sarada Raju, 1941, 107–108. On the partition of the district, see Grigg, 1880, 290–291, 303, and Hayavadana Rao, 1908, 117. See also Hockings, 1973.

7. Botanical identifications for the species referred to in this study, here arranged alphabetically, are as follows: almonds *(Terminalia catappa),* barley *(Hordeum hexastichon),* betel or areca nut *(Areca catechu),* black dammer or resin (from *Canarium strictum*), black gram *(Phaseolus mungo),* chick pea or Bengal gram *(Cicer arietinum),* coconut *(Cocos nucifera),* coffee *(Coffea arabica),* common millet *(Panicum miliaceum),* coriander *(Coriandrum sativum),* country bean *(Dolichos lablab)* fenugreek *(Trigonella foenum-graecum),* field peas *(Pisum arvense),* finger millet *(Eleusine coracana),* flax *(Linum mysorense),* garlic *(Allium sativum),* gentian *(Gentiana pedicellata),* gourd *(Lagenaria vulgaris),* great millet *(Andropogon sorghum),* Italian millet *(Setaria italica),* Italian rye *(Lolium italicum),* lime *(Citrus aurantifolia),* mustard *(Brassica juncea),* oats *(Avena sativa),* onion *(Allium cepa),* panic-seed *(Setaria pallidifusca),* pepper *(Piper schmidtii),* poppy *(Papaver somniferum),* potato *(Solanum tuberosum),* prince's feather *(Amarantus paniculatus),* pumpkin *(Cucurbita pepo),* rattan cane *(Calamus spp.),* rose-mallow *(Hibiscus esculentus),* sandalwood *(Santalum album),* slender millet *(Panicum miliare),* tea *(Camellia sinensis),* tobacco *(Nicotiana tabacum),* turmeric *(Curcuma longa),* and wheat *(Triticum dicoccum).*
8. Hayavadana Rao, 1908, 115. This area is now the playing field between the Lawley Institute and the Botanical Gardens.
9. Baikie, 1857, 25. In the mid-nineteenth century the Sundepatti and Manna:ru Passes provided a safe short-cut for smugglers between Coimbatore and Malabar; Ouchterlony, 1848, 75; Grigg, 1880, 19, 291.
10. Nicholson, 1898, 352. Note that the deity is a Vaishnavite one; its chariot-dragging festival is still held. See above, p. 145.
11. After crossing the Bhavani River in a rattan coracle covered with skins; Mackworth, 1823, 118–119; Grigg, 1880, 295. Once a market was opened in Ootacamund Ka:ramuḍu ceased to have much importance for Badagas; Francis, 1908, 340.
12. *doḍḍa habba;* on the salt ceremony, see Hockings, 1968c, *passim.*
13. This fourteenth-century fortress, now submerged by the Bhavani Dam, controlled the important Gajalaṭṭi Pass which links southern Mysore with the Coimbatore Plain; Nicholson, 1898, 425–427.
14. Ward erroneously calls the sum a dowry.
15. Later in quarter and one rupee denominations.
16. In the amounts of Rs. $\frac{1}{4}$, $\frac{1}{2}$, 1, 3, 6, 12, 24 and 48; but see below, p. 172.
17. Also the case in some other districts of Madras Presidency; Buchanan, 1807, vol. II, 247; Grigg, 1880, 286, n. 1.
18. The years 1803–1805 were a period of drought in the Nilgiris; Grigg, 1880, 279, n. 2.
19. There were as yet no Moslem traders.
20. Cloth was not among the trade items. The Coonoor Pass was completed in 1833; Grigg, 1880, 17.
21. Shandy means 'market', from the Tamil *cantai.*
22. Foodstuffs were usually traded by volume rather than weight, for scales were never used in or near the Nilgiris.

7

Growth of the Cash Economy

IMPACT OF BRITISH IDEAS ON THE BADAGA ECONOMY (1799–1850)

During the first half of the nineteenth century the British took a number of administrative steps which moved the basal Badaga economy decisively, if unintentionally, into the status of a monetized market economy. The ceding of the Nilgiri Plateau to the East India Company by the Treaty of Seringapatam in 1799 was the first step in this process. Though it was another twenty years before any British actually settled on the plateau the demand of land-revenue payment became more insistent and regulated than it had been under Tippu Sultan's tenuous régime. Badagas must therefore have been obliged to trade more persistently with the lowlands to acquire the coinage being demanded at the Dannaika Ko:ṭe outpost every year.[1]

A second point of impact on the Badaga economy was the Company's policy of fixing grain prices. The rigid control of prices, attempted by the District Collectors throughout Madras Presidency, must have encouraged the Badagas to market grains in the Coimbatore Plain (which lay within that Presidency), where they could feel somewhat confident about getting satisfactory prices and not being cheated. Had the grain prices been more of a gamble the Badagas would have been less inclined to produce a surplus of grain and carry it the long distance down to the market.

When the pioneering John Sullivan came to the hills in 1819 he gave Badagas superior seed grains from Europe, as well as seeds of various European vegetables.[2] This increased grain production somewhat and started Badagas growing vegetables they were not accustomed to eating. And as the British population increased so did the demand for locally grown European vegetables: a handful of Badaga farmers, being able to supply them, were thus drawn further into the market economy.

One area in which the British tried to effect early changes without success was formal education. In 1820 or 1821 Sullivan founded a school at the Wodea village of De:na:ḍu, directly above Dannaika Ko:ṭe, but the enterprise (prompted no doubt by a need for local clerks) was apparently a failure (Ward, 1821, lxx; Hayavadana Rao, 1908, 113). In 1830 Sullivan founded another school at Ku:kalu, also in the northeast of the plateau, to teach Badaga boys the Tamil and Kannada languages. Another was probably founded by the Church Missionary Society in 1830 at Dimbaṭṭi (Moses, 1964, 11). Among the few youths who acquired some education there was an attitude that is still voiced today and portended changes in the occupation pattern: they considered themselves fitted by schooling for a lifetime of something better than manual labour (Harkness 1832, 69–70). Another school, the first to use English as a medium, was established by a former judge, George J. Casamajor, at Ke:ti in 1845. This became the local headquarters of the Basel Mission in the same year, and a school has been there more or less constantly ever since. (In 1901 it became the first Badaga high school [Francis, 1908, 332; Moses, 1964, 13].) In Casamajor's time parents had to be paid one anna a day before they would send their sons to the school. It was only in the latter half of the century, after the Mission was well established at Ke:ti and elsewhere and several more schools had been founded, that education became at all popular with Badagas. For this achievement German pertinacity should take some credit; but after 1856 Badagas began to realize that literacy in Tamil was the only sure road to jobs in the local bureaucracy and so started to value schooling (Grigg, 1880, 423).

In the early days of European settlement the British frequently needed day-labourers to do jobs in the developing Nilgiri towns. A large number of lowland immigrants now lived and worked in these towns, but Badagas were also occasionally hired by Englishmen and paid a daily rate in cash. Around 1827, however, it had been observed that

> The hill people are so independent...that no temptation of wages will induce them to engage... as coolies, and they are only prevailed upon to work from a conviction that, refusing to do so, Government might make some just demands against them for increase of rent [land revenue]....[4]

By the 1840s there were many Badaga families earning a certain amount during a few months of each year from townspeople, from plantations and perhaps from the new Mission (Ouchterlony, 1848, 64; Shortt & Ouchterlony, 1868, 64). Their economy was now monetized, though the majority of families were still dependent on farming for their food requirements.

EXPANSION OF THE MARKET ECONOMY (1850–1900)

During the second half of the nineteenth century far-reaching economic changes triggered by the British settlers introduced the concept of competition and the importance of valuation to the Badagas. There is little indication of any competitiveness in their indigenous exchange activities or bartering practices before about 1840.

The opening of coffee (1838) and tea (1846) plantations on the plateau called for a great deal of manual labour; and by the 1850s many Badaga men found themselves competing for the first time with immigrants in a labour market.[5] Each group constituted one-half of the work force (Grigg, 1880, 399), but the British estate owners now preferred Badaga workers to immigrants because of their diligence. The labourers were paid in cash, not grain.

Secondly, the sizeable European population on the hills was now requiring quantities of cabbage, carrot, potato and other European vegetables which some Badaga farmers were able to supply. Their tradition of intensive farming in small fields was readily adapted to the new crops (Shortt & Ouchterlony, 1868, 35); and their venture was helped by a climate not unlike that of northwestern Europe (an English poet later was to muse on 'the sweet, half-English Neilgherry air').

During the latter half of the century a wide variety of indigenous farm products also found their way into the local market.[6] These foodstuffs were local varieties of wheat and barley, Italian, finger and slender millet, prince's feather (or amaranth), mustard seed, coriander, chick pea (or Bengal gram), garlic, onion, fenugreek, as well as poultry and eggs. Though officially suppressed in 1854 and again by the Opium Act of 1878, opium continued to be produced (Ouchterlony, 1848, 27–28; Baikie, 1857, 92; Metz, 1864, 153; 'Geofry', 1881, 132; Benson, 1895, 432–433; Prince, 1908, 224).

Foodstuffs introduced by Europeans but now being grown by Badagas included:

Grains	*Root-crops*	*Vegetables*	*Fruits*	*Stimulants*
Barley (new variety)	Beetroot	Artichoke	Apple	Coffee
Fiorin grass	Carrot	Asparagus	Blackberry	Tea
Italian rye	Mangel-wurzel	Cabbage	Capers	Tobacco*
Lucern (for fodder)	Parsnip	Cauliflower	Citron	
Oats	Potato	Celery	Gooseberry	
Wheat (new variety)	Radish	French beans	Lemon	
	Turnip	Kidney beans	Loquat	
		Leek	Nectarine	
		Lettuce	Orange	
		Peas	Peach	
		Savoy cabbage	Pear	
		Sea kale	Plum	
		Spinach	Raspberry	
			Strawberry	
			Tomato	

*Reputedly a Toda import (Baikie, 1857, 95).

Trade items being imported to the Nilgiris in the late nineteenth century included four products also imported in pre-British times—sugar, salt, cotton cloth and tobacco. In addition various other Indian goods began to be imported only during the latter half of the century: almond, betel or areca, cattle, clarified butter, coconut, coriander and other spices, dried fruits, finger millet, furniture, gunpowder, Italian millet, lime, limes, oils, peas, poultry, salted fish, scrap metal, sheep, sulphur, toddy, tools, turmeric, wheat.

European articles imported to the Nilgiris in the later nineteenth century included wines, spirits, beer, clothing, candles, groceries, pottery, glass, hardware, shoes, books and stationery. It is unclear how much of these were destined for consumption by the European settlers.

Among the exports from the plateau at this time were some that had also been exported in pre-British days, namely opium, wheat and bees-wax. Other exports of the later nineteenth century were coffee, tea, potato, barley, resin, silk and hides.

AGRICULTURAL CHANGE OVER THE PAST CENTURY

Until 1863 the Badagas not only cultivated fields close to the villages but also practised shifting agriculture in the wooded areas. At that time the government abolished, at least formally, the system of swidden cultivation and thereby posed a serious threat to those Badaga farmers who had depended on it (for full details, see Grigg, 1880, 314–327). According to government experts swidden farming was wasteful of timber resources and led to soil erosion. More significantly, though, there was also an eagerness among British settlers to cover vast tracts of the Nilgiris with tea and coffee plantations. In 1863 the British abolished the revenue system current in the Kundena:ḍu area,[7] which had involved issuing a licence for each hoe and each plough without otherwise taxing or delimiting the land a man could cultivate or recording what acreage he was entitled to use. Until these restrictions came into effect many Badaga farmers made periodic use of lands five to ten times as extensive as their revenue assessments justified.[8] By about 1880 these restrictions, legislated during 1862–1864, had become realities in all parts of the Nilgiris.

The rapidly increasing Badaga population was now faced with a depleted acreage of usable farmland, a situation that worsened with erosion and land sales. For the first time in history their fields, once surveyed and registered in accordance with the Land Settlement rules, came to have a monetary value—especially as under the Waste Land Rules a man's land could be auctioned and thus irretrievably lost if he became too much in arrears with the payment of land revenue. A farmer therefore tried to hold on to as much registered land as he could.[9]

The British land legislation did not cause an immediate shortage of land among the Badagas. On the contrary, Grigg notes (1880, 480) that in the 1870s land was so 'cheap' that the Badagas who did own some or bought more tried to cultivate areas that were too large for their resources, with the result that their labour and capital were spread too thinly across the land to produce adequate returns. The slim yield of soil not properly fertilized and skimpy cultivation of too large an area impelled the poorer farmers of the late nineteenth and early twentieth centuries to sell land to British planters or to engage in new occupations so as to earn enough cash to maintain themselves and pay the revenue assessments on their land (Shortt & Ouchterlony, 1868, 64; Grigg, 1880, 325, 471, 480; Ranga, 1934, 11–14). Those made landless by the restrictions on forest swidden cultivation and also the labour surplus of the immigrant and rapidly expanding population were obliged to work in the plantations for wages, which were primarily used for buying grain in the markets. By 1870 Badaga men were getting contracts as construction gangs, a few women were picking tea or coffee-beans and young boys could be seen breaking stones by the roadside.[10]

Early in this century most Badaga families still owned and cultivated land within two kilometres of their homes. This land was usually hilly and always unirrigated. There was relatively little terracing on the hill-slopes (Grigg, 1880, 470), and most tilling was still done with ploughs and oxen.[11] The best fields lay in the valley flats, not so much because of the proximity of stream water as because of the rich deposit of topsoil. Badagas had long recognized the differences in soils and terrain, both when choosing where to plant crops and when dividing up the patrimony. Soil distinctions were important to them, but distance from the home was even more significant. Land was therefore categorized by Badagas primarily as home-farm (within a half kilometre), outfield, or jungle clearings.[2] The first type got much of the cattle manure and all human refuse; more distant land received little manure and was often left fallow (Grigg, 1880, 319–320, quoting from a Revenue Board Report probably of 1863); jungle clearings were never manured and could lie fallow for several years. Weeding, like manuring, was mostly confined to the more valuable crops growing near the home.

A majority of the cultivable land on the plateau has always belonged to the Badagas; in the mid-nineteenth century this amounted to 12,750 hectares, of which some 6,900 ha. were cultivated each year; but thirty years later 'the occupied area of the plateau has trebled itself... mainly due to the extension of cultivation by the Badaga villagers'. During the twentieth century virtually all of the land under subsistence crops (barley, millets and wheat) as well as plateau land growing market vegetables and fruits was farmed by Badagas and Kotas. On the other hand a majority of the land devoted to tea, coffee and cinchona was in British-owned plantations. Few reliable figures are available for the total area under crop by Badagas.[14] In the case of the administrative 'village' of Sholur nevertheless good data (McIver & Stokes, 1883; Benson, 1884; Arputhanathan, 1953, 43; Subrahmanyam, 1962, 3–4) allow a realistic comparison with the recent situation (see Table 1). This 'village' (actually a commune) may be considered typical of Badaga settlements and has hardly changed its official boundaries since the Land Settlement of 1884.[15]

Table 1. *Sholur (So:lu:ru) 'Village': eighty years of agricultural change*

Total 'village' area, 1884	9113 hectares
Total 'village' area, 1961	9111 ha.
Registered *patta* lands, 1884	913 ha., all held by Badagas
Registered *patta* lands, 1962	1619 ha., nearly all held by Badagas
Number of *pattas*, 1884	49 single registrations, 63 joint ones (i.e., total of 112 *pattas)*
Number of *pattas*, 1962	372 in total
Population, 1881	1772, all communities, in 384 houses
Population, 1961	8518, all communities, in 930 houses
Estimate of cropped area, 1880–1881	749 ha.
Estimate of cropped area, 1962	607 ha.

From Table 1 evidence of several important shifts emerges:

A. In eighty years the population increased fivefold.

B. In eighty years the size of households doubled, from an average of 4.61 to an average of 9.15.[16]

C. In eighty years the number of registered land holdings *(pattas)* more than tripled.

D. In eighty years the area of *patta* land doubled through release of government-held reserves (but was not all cropped).

E. Fragmentation of holdings has thus been taking place.

F. The estimate of the total cultivated area in 1962 was a little below that for 1880–1881.

G. Average cultivated area has thus dropped from 0.42 ha. per capita in 1881 to 0.07 ha. per capita around 1961; in other words, only one-sixth as much cropped land is being used as there was in 1881 for each person.

We may conclude from the recent situation at Sholur (So:lu:ru) that agricultural production is hardly managed more efficiently today than it was nearly a century ago and that food production cannot have kept pace there with the vast increase in population.

> Major changes in crop emphasis from the late 1800s to the present are best revealed by statistics [relating mainly to] Badaga cultivation. In 1875 there were 15,728 acres of Italian millet, 4,662 acres of little millet, 3,761 acres of barley, 3,430 acres of finger millet, 3,199 acres of wheat, only 754 acres of potatoes, 355 acres of mustard, 169 acres of vegetables, 144 acres of fenugreek, 67 acres of horse gram..., and 66 acres of poppies grown on the Nilgiris (Grigg *et al.* 1880: xii). In 1895 Italian millet was still the leading crop, but potato acreage had risen to 2,032 acres. Poppies outlawed by the 1878 Opium Act were no longer grown (Benson 1895: 432–433). Little millet had become the most cultivated cereal in 1905, and finger millet was growing in importance (Francis 1908: 164)... In 1914 there were about 4,000 acres with potatoes on the Nilgiris, but by 1920 potato acreage had doubled (Rao and Azariah 1953: 69). Before 1925 finger and little millets became the two important cereal crops, and remained the leading cereals from that time (Wood 1927: 210–223). Potato acreage has continually increased: by 1938 there were 12,000 acres, by 1950 almost 17,000 acres, and in 1960–61 there was a total of 20,600 acres in the main season and 2,400 acres in the lesser (Rao and Azariah 1953: 69; Krishnamurthi 1953: 193)... (Noble, 1968, 133–134).

Some official figures can be presented[17] to further illustrate the shift in importance of various crops on the entire plateau from 1905 to 1940 (see Table 2). These figures (which come from two distinct sources—Francis, 1908, 164; Madras 1949, 976), show the percentage of the total cultivated area devoted to each crop.

It may be noticed that while the figures for each *taluk* in 1905–1906 total 100%, those for 1940–1941 exceed 100%. This discrepancy reflects one important change in the thirty-five year period: mixed cropping became a fairly common practice. Thus two crops represented in Table 2 by separate figures would sometimes be growing simultaneously on the same piece of land.

There were very slight changes in the crop pattern for wheat, barley, finger millet and spices. A small area of pulses appeared only in the later figures (though pulses had in fact been grown in

Table 2. *The Nilgiri Plateau: Cropping change, 1905–1940**

	Percentage of total cropped area			
	Coonoor Taluk (Poraṅga:du and Me:kuna:ḍu)		*Ootacamund Taluk (Todana:ḍu and Kundena:ḍu)*	
	1905–1906	*1940–1941*	*1905–1906*	*1940–1941*
Mainly subsistence crops:				
Wheat	1.7%	2.8%	2.9%	3.3%
Barley	5.1%	2.7%	3.4%	4.2%
Finger millet	1.5%	1.9%	7.1%	4.5%
Slender millet	14.7%	6.3%	4.3%	6.2%
Other grains	13.1%	0.7%	27.8%	1.1%
Pulses	—	1.9%	—	0.5%
Cash crops:				
Vegetables (mainly potato) and fruits	5.2% (potato: 4.8%)	18.6% (potato: 3.2%)	3.9% —	30.3% —
Spices, condiments	0.3%	0.7%	0.9%	1.1%
Coffee	44.6%	25.6%	18.1%	15.8%
Tea	7.7%	42.7%	12.8%	32.3%
Cinchona	1.1%	0.8%	10.9%	4.0%
Miscellaneous 'industrial plants'	4.7%	5.9%	7.9%	6.6%

*All percentages are based on acreage.

the nineteenth century). As malaria became less of a problem and cures other than quinine appeared in India cinchona decreased in importance, but this was mainly on British-owned plantations. Miscellaneous 'industrial' plants, primarily eucalyptus, maintained a stable acreage. These slight fluctuations tell us very little, but others are much greater and more illuminating. The various millets lost much of their significance for Badagas even though these had previously been among their traditional staples. The land was planted with potatoes instead—especially after the start of the First World War. There were about 1600 hectares under potato cultivation on the plateau in 1914, and as we have seen by 1920 this figure had doubled (Hanumantha Rao & Azariah, 1953, 69). In the thirty-five year period spanned by Table 2 potatoes, together with some other quite minor vegetables, increased their acreage some five- or six-fold. Badagas did not eat much potato: clearly they sacrificed most of the acreage traditionally devoted to staple grains to grow marketable vegetables for cash instead.[18] Whether their diet had improved is not clear. By the Second World War a mere 3% of the entire Nilgiri population subsisted primarily on millets; the other 97% depended on purchased rice (Krishnaswami, 1947, 464). Coffee was not a successful crop in most parts of the plateau, and much of that plantation land was later given over to tea. This, together with the development of Badaga tea plantations from about 1925 onward, accounts for the great increase in tea acreage over the thirty-five year period covered in Table 2 (Ranga, 1934, 18–22).

The plantation crops called for more expertise than Badagas could usually muster and so were mostly confined to European land-holdings; even so, some Badagas were growing tea and a little coffee in the late 1920s (Ranga, 1934, 2). But potato was relatively easy to cultivate, especially as a government farm in the district helped them with seed, fertilizers and technical advice. During the past fifty years some of the more enterprising Badagas (mainly those able to obtain financial credit) have successfully cultivated tea and coffee on estates both large and small, though this was initially a ruse of theirs to increase the value of their land before selling it to Europeans.[19]

Chemical fertilizers were first used sporadically in the early 1920s; before that only cow-dung and human refuse had been available (Shortt & Ouchterlony, 1868, 44; Grigg, 1880, 468; Ranga, 1934, 14). These chemicals led to much higher yields in the European vegetable crops and helped confirm the belief that growing food for the market was a profitable occupation. Improved seeds, notably potato, and insecticides were also adopted by the Badagas (Nambiar, 1965, 23), who were 'always willing to test any new method of cultivation, or new crops brought to their notice by the Nilgiri Horticultural Society' (Thurston, 1909, vol. I, 76, quoting from *Pioneer,* 4 Oct. 1907).

The adoption of fertilizer, insecticide and good seed was soon followed by construction of more terraces on some of the sloping fields. Progress in terracing, however, was much slower than the adoption of other innovations because it demanded a greater capital outlay than many farmers could afford; and most did not possess more than a quarter-hectare of land. Even today some cultivated slopes that badly need terracing because of soil erosion remain unterraced. It is worth noting that in the past several decades the situation has much improved because of the state government's making loans available on relatively easy terms for terrace construction (Grigg, 1880, 470; Ranga, 1934, 12–13).

As a result of terracing in many places and minute subdivision elsewhere, fields are usually so small that it has become inefficient, if not impossible, to plough them (Vivekanandam Pillai, 1937, 249). For over forty years therefore the plough and oxen have rarely been seen on the plateau (Ranga, 1934, 12–13; Vivekanandam Pillai, 1937, 249; Noble, 1968, 144–145; see below, p. 167, n. 11). Much of the work load formerly carried by oxen is now taken by cheap migrant labourers from the plains; men work for daily wages of three rupees (equivalent to 40 cts. U.S.), and women for two (1970).

While the profits from potato, tea and coffee are very much higher per hectare than those from the traditional grain crops, the risks are also much greater. Not only does a farmer need ready cash to buy seed or cuttings, fertilizer and labour, but reserve cash is needed to feed his family should disease ruin the crop one season. Here the co-operative societies set up under state government guidance have helped Badagas somewhat, but less than might be expected. Short-term loans are available against land securities for all members of a society,[20] and long-term loans are obtainable from the Land Mortgage Bank (established in 1937).

Before the appearance of these facilities the money-lender (a Tamilian Chettiar, a northern Marwari or a Moslem) was an ominous figure in the lives of many Badagas; for some he still is. Early in the present century the monthly interest on his loans ranged from 3% to 12.5% of the principal, but though these rates were quite extortionate loans were in general repaid (Thurston, 1909, vol. I, 64; Madras, 1928, 55; Ranga, 1934, 4). In the previous century not even these loan facilities were accessible to Badagas: they could only borrow from wealthy Badagas, preferably those related to the borrower by marriage but living in a village at some discreet distance from him. No interest was charged on such loans then.

The first Badaga co-operative society was formed at Kereha:ḍa in 1911, the 'Kerhada Rice Rural Credit Society', named in reference to Mr. S. P. Rice, a former Collector who had initiated interest in the co-operative movement. At that time annual interest rates varied between 24% and 75% of the principal. By 1918 there were eighteen such societies, and by 1927 the plateau had fifty-four agricultural credit societies from which Badagas could get loans

(Madras, 1928, 55–57; Vivekaṇandam Pillai, 1937, 249); while at present there are nearly two hundred. By about 1920 the Badaga co-operators

> could no longer hope to repay the loan from their earnings and in almost all cases they have had to part with their property for clearing their loans. The malady was aggravated by the imperfect education in co-operation imparted and the want of adequate supervision and control in the beginning. It was then realized that co-operative credit alone was not the remedy and attempts were made to secure for these tribes their necessaries of life at moderate price and save them from the clutches of the unscrupulous shopkeepers. A Purchase and Sale Society was started in 1919, which in 1923 converted itself into the Potato Growers' Purchase and Sale Society and attempted to control the market for potatoes with a view to secure a fair price for the potato crop. In 1924 a Labour Union was organized for their benefit. But all these steps proved of no avail. Want of loyalty on their part led to the collapse of the former in 1925. The latter society is doing no work now. Attempts are now being made to increase their earning capacity by introducing among the Badagas sericulture and improved poultry farming... (Madras, 1928, 56).

In 1954 the Reserve Bank of India initiated nation-wide an 'integrated scheme of rural credit' which tied the granting of loans to the marketing of the crop rather than to the amount of land available as security. The scheme was introduced in the Nilgiri co-operatives.

> The controlled credit scheme works through a linking of the village primary societies, the Nilgiris District Central Cooperative Bank, and the Nilgiris Marketing Society. The village primary societies (and individual members of the Marketing Society) get their seeds and manure from the Marketing Society; the Marketing Society sends the relevant indents and loan applications to the Central Bank for sanction; the members market their harvests (at least enough to cover the loans) through the Marketing Society; the Marketing Society sends the sales proceeds to the Central Bank; the Central Bank deducts the loans and sends the balance to the village primary societies

or individual members.

One difficulty in the scheme is that the maximum amount which any society can lend to an individual member is Rs. 2,000. Even at the inadequate rate of Rs. 500 per acre, members can get through cooperative channels only enough finance for the cultivation of four acres. In the various societies which I visited in the Nilgiris, the officers usually were substantial people with well more than four acres. It was a curious situation to find them put in a position where to meet their current needs, they had to go to private sources... They told me that they got about half of their credit from the society and the other half from the private merchant-moneylenders. Although they sold some of their produce to the marketing society, they usually sold the major portion through the private merchants. They explained that the merchants gave them much more credit than they could get from the society, on condition that they sell their produce through the merchants. They said that the cooperatives were rather inflexible about extending loans, whereas they could count on the merchants to carry them through a bad season or two. When there is a crop failure, they have to go to the private merchant and borrow from him to pay back their loan to the cooperative society...To them this was a kind of "cooperation" and was more important than anything else.

By contrast, when their loans became overdue, the cooperative society cut off their credit. The societies went by rules and regulations which did not benefit the members. They said that from the societies they did not get real cooperation.

These statements did not conflict with what I had been told earlier in the best cooperative agricultural bank in the Nilgiris. There members and office-bearers told me that the rules laid down by Government for the cooperatives were very hard and stringent. They tied the hands of the working officials who would like to do more. Everything was rules and circulars; there was no leeway, no room for initiative. What was crucial was the Government loan, the Government grant, the Government subsidy.

Lest this seem an exaggeration, it may be observed that in Ootacamund there are no less than four Deputy-Registrars of Cooperative Societies; one is General Deputy-Registrar; another is Special Deputy-Registrar to supervise credit and agricultural marketing; a third is in charge of the Cooperative

Central Bank; and the fourth runs the Marketing Society (Thorner, 1964, 71–73).

The law today limits the monthly interest on pawned items to a rate varying from ¾% to 1½%, depending on the size of the loan. Even so, loans between Badagas now command an interest rate of 1% to 4% per month; while the professional money-lenders also secretly charge interest beyond what they are entitled to. On a loan of up to Rs. 200, for example, the Marwari lender can legally charge only 1½% per month simple interest. He gives a receipt for that rate but at the same time insists on one year's interest in advance, and compounded, at 2% per month. One can hardly castigate the Marwari for his cupidity, or the Badaga for still patronizing him, however, when one learns the scale of bribes which some local government officials expect in return for granting loans from the cooperative bank.

Yet the cooperative movement has gone a long way towards protecting Badagas from the high interest rates of private money-lenders; the Panchayat Unions and some multi-purpose societies even help farmers by supplying fertilizers, insecticides and modern equipment at cost prices. If these societies operate somewhat more effectively here than in other parts of India, the explanation lies in the fact that the Badaga societies are not in practice multi-caste institutions. They are run largely by and for the members of this one community, thus avoiding some of the factionalism and favouritism that commonly pervade such societies elsewhere.

MODERN SYSTEMS OF MARKETING

With the spread of urbanization during the mid-nineteenth century, other markets besides that at Ootacamund began to cater to the needs of local villagers. Regular weekly markets opened at Coonoor, Kotagiri, Wellington, and later in several villages at some distance from any town.[21] The use of these markets by the Badagas is related to two other developments discussed earlier: first, the payment of land revenues and the restriction on use of land caused by the Land Settlement and legislation to stop swidden farming in the forests; and secondly, the consequent movement of some Badaga labourers, including women and children, onto the tea and coffee plantations, where they earned a cash wage (Grigg, 1880, 34, 471; see above, pp. 149, 152).

Greatly increased contact with markets and with Europeans provided the impetus towards full participation in the cash economy, yet this transition took a century to complete. For the vast majority the basic requirements of food, goods and services continued to be provided either by their own efforts or by their Toda, Kota and Kurumba associates. The itinerant Chetti trader continued to make monthly visits, as he still does. From 1825 onwards Badagas could visit local markets on the plateau for what they had previously bought in Guṇḍuḷupe:te and Ka:ramuḍu, but they never sold very much in the markets and thus rarely had spare cash to spend. In the early days of cash-crop farming very few Badagas had enough knowledge or personal contacts to arrange the bulk sale of their produce in a distant market. They used to sell their crops instead to a broker in the Nilgiris, until it became known that a farmer who could find a market and negotiate a sale by himself would make bigger profits. An important motivation was the desire to acquire consumer goods that were now becoming available on a scale and in a variety never before known to the Badagas. Later in the nineteenth century there is evidence of increasing affluence which found expression in the shift from thatched to tiled rooves. '. . . in 1871 only 1,914 houses out of the 13,922 in the district were tiled; whereas now [1908] tiles are the rule . . . in Badaga villages' (Francis, 1908, 130, compare Shortt & Ouchterlony, 1868, 58; Grigg, 1880, 29, 225; 'Geofry', 1881, 132). For the farming family engaged in marketing their crops, cash was necessarily the only medium of exchange, and much of their foodstuffs had to be bought in the town bazaar. A great variety of items was also being purchased, the most obvious of which were new clothes: in the 1890s men first began to sport European-style shirts and jackets, and in the 1930s women started to wear coloured *sa:ris* (B.E.M.S., 1897, no. 58, 90; Hockings, 1979a).

We may say that their commitment to the cash economy was complete by about 1930, in which year most Badagas permanently severed their traditional exchange relationship with the Kotas. This from the Badaga point of view was an advantageous move, for it allowed them to buy pottery, ropes and metal goods in the bazaar at a lower price than the Kotas commanded, and without delays. While the Kotas had not been receiving cash, the tradition-al dole of grain they were given at each harvest was becoming increasingly valuable to the Badagas because of rising grain prices (Mandelbaum, 1955, 240).

For many Badagas with small land-holdings the transitional period between the two World Wars was marked by the frustrations of indebtedness. Pieces of their land were sometimes sold to non-Badagas in order to pay off outstanding debts—a previously inconceivable practice. Some men went as far as the Annamalai Hills for manual labouring. Badaga debtors did, however, work hard to produce profitable cash crops or at least to buy back some of their former lands (Thurston, 1909, vol. 1, 64; Ranga, 1934, 4; Vivekanandam Pillai, 1937, 249).

With the First World War, major changes in their marketing practices became apparent. Tea, coffee and cinchona, like potato, presuppose a market beyond the Nilgiris, which in turn presupposes adequate transportation. The crucial demand for vegetables to feed the numerous European troops in India, Burma, Malaya and Ceylon stimulated the change in crops documented above (see Table 2). Similar conditions arose again in the Second World War and prompted many more Badagas to try commercial farming. On each occasion cultivators took the risk of exporting potatoes and other vegetables to new and remote markets, and some made handsome profits (Francis, 1908, 167). The risks in this enterprise were real, for men could recall occasions when floods broke the road or rail connections or the goods reached their destination only after market prices had fallen heavily. The rewards of potato cultivation were, however, of critical importance in lifting the yoke of indebtedness: during World War II the British made a great deal of capital available to Badaga farmers, as part of the 'Grow More Food' campaign. This finance and the profits from selling their highly priced potatoes did more than any cooperative loan facility to relieve the indebtedness that Badagas had been suffering under for several decades.

While tea and coffee yield a higher profit per hectare than potatoes or grains, they are more susceptible to disease than the millets and require greater agricultural skill than all other Nilgiri crops if they are to attain the standards required by wholesale purchasing agents. Moreover they need to be produced in large enough quantity to warrant the processing and transportation to Bombay (since 1940, to Cochin). Middlemen, both Badagas and others, were therefore indispensable to the few Badaga tea and coffee growers of the 1920s and 1930s. Middlemen could act as a control on quality and could bring together sufficient produce to make a transaction with an exporter worthwhile. As more and more Badagas became interested in growing cash crops, middlemen appeared not only to buy up small quantities of tea, coffee and potato but also to sell seed, fertilizer and even some insurance.

After Independence profiteering by the middlemen was largely checked by the Nilgiri Cooperative Marketing Society set up with state government aid (Vivekanandam Pillai, 1937, 249). Today there are nearly two hundred cooperative societies in the Nilgiris which pool the resources of members and also supply cheap fertilizer. Many such societies own local tea-processing factories and warehouses and are dominated by Badagas. After 1957 heavy loss through potato disease caused a widespread shift to tea or coffee growing,[22] and in the 1970s large acreages have been devoted to growing a sturdy new German variety of cabbage which finds markets nation-wide. Both tea and cabbage are quite successful crops. The availability of help from the Central Cooperative Bank made these unexpected switches in crops possible, for otherwise the initial capital outlay and the small size of most estates would have rendered the new venture unfeasible. Several cottage industries have also helped diversify the rural economy over the past thirty years; in particular beekeeping, liquor distilling, milk sales, knitting and embroidery have provided new, regular sources of income for many hundreds of Badaga families.

The early twentieth century saw the rise not only of wealthy Badaga land-owners but also of large-scale labour contractors. A few men profitted by getting the contracts for gangs to dig pits for planting tea-cuttings, pick coffee-beans, build roads or construct public buildings in the district.[23] Less wealthy Badagas set themselves up as small shopkeepers, tailors or money-lenders or found work in a wide variety of urban trades.[24] Whenever possible the more resourceful reinvested their profits in land (Ranga, 1934, 10), either tea and coffee estates or farm plots formerly belonging to Kotas (Mandelbaum, 1955, 240). The other reinvestment commonly made was in college education for their sons. With the economy fully monetized the stress was now on providing stability for the coming generations.

MODERN EMPLOYMENT

Prior to World War I virtually all Badagas were cultivators, and the great majority still are today. For them the family has always been the basic unit of production. As much as five months of the year are spent non-productively (Ranga, 1934, 9–10), but during the other months every member of the family, even a child, makes some contribution to the traditional family economy. Adults work in the fields and are helped by boys and girls when necessary (Harkness, 1832, 114–115). Men do the heavier work, such as forking, ploughing or clearing stones, and women the lighter work, mainly planting, weeding and harvesting (Ward, 1821, lxx, lxxiii; Jagor, 1876, 201–202: Ranga, 1934, 8; Noble, 1968, 143–148). As well as their field-work women are responsible for cooking and for all the housekeeping, including the laundry.[25] Adolescent boys work as cowherds; girls take care of babies whose mothers are in the fields (Harkness, 1832, 113). Children also do the initial preparation of meals before the women return home each day. People too old to work in the fields stay at home minding the children and keeping an eye on what passes within the village (Jagor, 1876, 194).

This pattern has been modified somewhat by a trend among the more educated men to work away from the village. At first a few were employed in the towns as peons, clerks, builders and labourers, and throughout the district as primary school teachers.[26] During the First World War some young men began working in the munitions factory near Wellington (it still employs many Badagas). Then, in the 1920s, the first Badagas attended university and returned to professional positions in the Nilgiris. Of these professionals the most influential small group have been the parliamentarians—M.P.s and M.L.A.s—many of whom are from one extended family whose fortune was initially established by labour contraction (see Diagram 9, p. 179). More numerous today are the doctors and lawyers. Other Badagas who though less well-educated no longer follow their traditional occupation include school-teachers, government officials, bus drivers, contractors and factory workers.

A correlate of this move towards the towns has been the breakdown of customary labouring methods. There were two kinds of cooperative labour: in one a number of families (usually from one lineage) would pool their labour to farm an area and then would divide up the produce proportionately; in the other, several families would work for a particular farmer but have no share in his produce: he in turn would help them with their cultivation. For a large landowner this latter system was quite efficient and profitable, even though he had to feed those who were working in his fields and was also obliged to give them a big feast on the last day of their field-work *(kambuwa)* which enhanced social solidarity. These two techniques of co-operative labour also benefitted the landless, for they could thereby share in the harvest of someone else or at least be more regularly fed.

In the early decades of this century immigrant Kanarese and Tamilians, some of them the creditors of Badaga farmers, began to buy up former Badaga land and farm it with the help of labourers, both poor Badagas and immigrants. It was probably this trend which led those who worked on Badaga farms to expect payment in cash rather than a share of the harvest or a mutual exchange of labour. Those patterns of co-operation have passed away. The educated would now rather remain unemployed than work in a neighbour's field, and with the transition to cash-crop farming most feel it is not worth helping someone else reap his profit. Things were different when co-operative farming helped put food into the village's granary baskets.

Among rural Badagas the old order has not been replaced by a class society. We can only identify a land-owning class, a tenant class and a labouring class in the larger rural society which embraces other communities as well. The land-owners who are Badagas generally prefer Tamilian or Kanarese tenants, as it is easier to lay down stiff terms for rental and to become stern when such non-Badagas fail to pay the rent after an unsuccessful season. Badaga tenants have too many ways of pressuring their landlord into overlooking their inability to pay rent on time. The agricultural labourers are normally lowland immigrants, too. It is considered somewhat demeaning for Badagas to take on such work, especially under a Badaga proprietor. Social classes are thus not yet to be found among Badaga villagers, and the three main social categories in farming are seen by Badagas as occupational and caste differences.

The present range of occupations of both Badagas and other rural communities is suggested by Table 3, derived from a rough sample of adolescent and adult males aged 15 to 85. Clearly farm work is still the most prevalent activity, but now a substantial proportion of men in the rural population are working in occupations (categories V to IX) that typify participation in a monetary economy.[27]

Table 3. *Occupations of the interviewed males, 1963*

		Rural Badagas	*All other Nilgiri rural communities*
I	Cultivating own or rented land	59.6%	30.7%
II	Agricultural labourer	5.0%	32.3%
III	Forestry and livestock	0.0%	7.4%
IV	Cottage industries	0.7%	5.8%
V	Manufacturing	3.7%	1.6%
VI	Construction	4.0%	2.6%
VII	Trade and business	0.3%	6.9%
VIII	Transport and communications	3.7%	4.2%
IX	Teaching and 'professions'	13.0%	5.3%
X	Non-workers, students	10.0%	3.2%
		(*n*=301)	(*n*=189)

The 1970s find an increasing number of young, college-educated Badagas settling in towns with their wives and taking well-paid jobs. These people still observe community endogamy, but in other respects their behaviour suggests that the distinctive identity of the Badaga community is nearing its end. It is no longer uncommon for urban Badagas to address rural Badagas in Tamil rather than their own language: ashamed of the state government's designation of their people as a 'Backward Class',[28] they are trying to merge with the South Indian city society and deny what they consider an 'uncivilized' parentage. Few such people regularly visit their native villages now. Once marriage with non-Badagas increases and becomes acceptable the palisade around their community will have fallen.

NOTES

1. Even though there was no tax-farmer on the plateau to harrass them until 1807; Buchanan, 1807, vol. II, 247.
2. Harkness, 1832, 138, note; Shortt & Ouchterlony, 1868, 17; Grigg, 1880, 455–456; Francis, 1908, 167; Price, 1908, 23; Hockings, 1973, 867. According to Metz, 1864, 5, Sullivan came to the Nilgiris 'at the solicitation of the hill-people themselves'. Sullivan, in a letter to the Board of Revenue in 1819, explained that 'the inhabitants are extremely anxious to have their lands measured, under an idea that they are paying more than they ought to do'; Grigg, 1880, 280. Another early influence on Badaga farming may have been the experimental farm for European crops operating at Ke:ṭi from 1830 to

1836; Metz, 1864, 6–7; Grigg, 1880, 456–458; Macleane, 1893, 403; Francis, 1908, 203, 441.

3. Metz, 1864, 8–9; an anna was 1/16 rupee, worth just under one U.S. cent today.
4. Grigg, 1880, 288, quoting from a report of December 1827; yet Harkness, 1832, 111, remarked that 'The poorer Burghers form the only class of labourers now to be procured on the hills . . .'
5. B.E.M.S., 1848, no. 18, 93; 1860, no. 20, 59; Shortt & Ouchterlony, 1868, 64; Grigg, 1880, 510–511; Watt, 1889, 465; Francis, 1908, 171, 178; Tanna, 1970, 17, 37. Tea was first grown here experimentally in 1835 from Chinese seeds, and coffee in 1838; Macleane, 1893, 403.
6. Baikie, 1857, 38, 92; Markham, 1862, 367; Metz, 1864, 99, 152–154; Ouchterlony, 1848, 2, 5, 28; Shortt & Ouchterlony, 1868, 71; Grigg, 1880, 465–467. The more important items in the list are identified botanically above, p. 146, n. 7.
7. Transferred back to Coimbatore District from Malabar in 1860; Grigg, 1880, 309, 322–323; Macleane, 1893, 216; Thurston, 1909, vol. I, 78–79.
8. Grigg, 1880, 316, 321. On the shortcomings of their agriculture in this period, see Shortt & Ouchterlony, 1868, 31–36; Grigg, 1880, 480; 'Geofry', 1881, 132–135.
9. Grigg, 1880, 325. The Settlement of land holdings took place in 1864–1884; Grigg, 1880. 321–323.
10. B.E.M.S., 1858, no. 18, 93; 1860, no. 20, 59; McPherson, 1870, 15, 18, 21; Grigg, 1880, 34, 219–220. Tea-pickers were usually lowland labourers, for Badaga women were then afraid of being near jungle even when in gangs.
11. A few ploughs are still in use near the Si:gu:ru Pass; other villages preserve old ploughs to venerate at an annual ceremony; but in general ploughs went out of use fifty years ago; Ranga, 1934, 8.
12. Francis, 1908, 165–166; Ranga, 1934, 11–14. The lands are called respectively *ha:ḷihola, ka:ḍuhola* and *so:lahola;* see Plate 1.
13. Grigg, 1880, 13, citing Ouchterlony, 1848, 14; Shortt & Ouchterlony, 1868, 14. It may be illuminating to cite an example of one administrative 'village'—Ke:ti Village—which reflects how much of the plateau land was formerly owned by Badagas. The available figures come from the 1881 land settlement records and show how 3235 hectares of this particular 'village' (actually a grouping of nearly two dozen villages) were distributed in the last years before the widespread adoption there of a cash economy:

Badaga farming lands	2,083 ha.
Badaga grazing ground	204 ha.
Toda grazing lands	51 ha.
Village sites (mainly Badaga)	90 ha.
Government forest areas	123 ha.
Anglo-Indian orphanage and school	307 ha.
Plantations (mainly British-owned)	175 ha.
Government cinchona plantation	2 ha.
Available for sale	200 ha.

(Source: Benson, 1881, 188–189)

From these data it is clear that this area, by no means an atypical one, was farmed largely by Badagas. (The 200 h.a. 'for sale' is somewhat misleading; it was mostly in steep rocky places ill-suited to any cultivation.)

14. Grigg, 1880, 321, mentions there were 29,912 acres (12,105 ha.) of farming land on the plateau in 1862–1863 but considers this 'a fictitious number'. Fifteen years earlier Ouchterlony had estimated that the Badagas alone used 12,750 ha.; Grigg, 1880, 13.
15. It is 19 km. by road from Ootacamund and embraces the Badaga commune of So:lu:ru.
16. That Sholur was not atypical in this respect is suggested by the fact that in 1867 the average number of persons per Badaga household for the entire district was 4.36; Shortt & Ouchterlony, 1868, 61.
17. Land utilization figures for the entire district, 1905–1960, in Nambiar (1965), do not isolate the role of Badaga agriculture.
18. Ranga, 1934, 68. As early as 1908 Francis (p. 167) noted: 'Potatoes are much exported to Ceylon, the Straits [Malaya] and Burma . . .' It was in 1908 that the railway connecting Ootacamund with the plains was completed.
19. Ranga, 1934, 14–15, 18–22. 'In fact many planters advance money to Badagas to enable them to dig pits and plant tea . . . with the intention of being able to purchase that land'; Ranga, 1934, 15.
20. Merchants also granted credit for purchase of daily needs—at much inflated prices; Ranga, 1934, 73–74; Vivekanandam Pillai, 1937, 249. Such traders are an excellent example of Simmel's 'resident stranger', whose presence catalyses a peasant economy by affording credit; Simmel, 1923, 509–512.
21. De:vaso:le, Kolekombe, Se:las, Gudalu:ru, Manju:ru, Ki:kotagiri, Neḍugula, and Naduvatta; Baikie, 1857, 38, 88; Grigg, 1880, 471.
22. Nambiar, 1965, 23. The first time this problem beset Badaga farmers was in 1880; B.E.M.S., 1880, no. 41, 37; Grigg, 1880; 134.
23. Ranga, 1934, 7–9. Badaga contractors had been involved in such work since the mid-nineteenth century; McPherson, 1870, 21.
24. Natesa Sastri, 1892, 753; Francis, 1908, 129; Thurston, 1909, vol. I, 63; Ranga, 1934, 8; Vivekanandam Pillai, 1937, 248. These jobs included builders, blacksmiths, brickmakers, carpenters, clerks, domestic servants, painters, gardeners, washermen, teachers, printers, forest guards, tailors, barbers, water-carriers, stone-breakers, rickshaw-pullers, and even coolies and scavengers.
25. Jagor, 1876, 201–202; unlike most Hindus the Badagas do not employ washermen.
26. These were mainly Christians.
27. The categories are taken from the 1961 *Census of India.*
28. The designation is not recent; Francis, 1908, 265. On the Backward Classes generally, see Béteille, 1969, 87–145. Very recently the Nilgiri Hill Tribe Badaga Welfare Association was formed to promote government action in classifying Badagas as Scheduled Tribe, which would have material advantages for the community.

8

Administration and Law

CUSTOMARY LAW

Until the end of the last century the Indian Penal Code and the British system of local administration had little relevance to Badagas. They had their own uncodified law and their own headmen and councils to administer it.

Three periods are distinguishable in their legal history: one prior to the advent of the British when something akin to *lex talionis* was operative; a second period when Badagas still had full control of their legal procedure but operated it under the aegis of the British; and a third period, from about 1900 to the present, when litigants played off the Badaga system against the magistrate's court in an attempt to win cases through obscuration.

There are no records for the phase of *lex talionis,* but a rough account of the procedure is provided by legend. A village council sat in judgment and stipulated a time and place for punishment of the guilty. The man who had assaulted someone was to be kicked or beaten by him, the rapist had to offer his wife to the aggrieved husband, and the murderer was hanged by the family of his victim.

By the start of the nineteenth century this pattern had given way to one that is with some modification still in effect today. It originated before coinage was circulating in the Nilgiris, for the earliest fines, as among the Todas, were paid in buffaloes and not rupees. Although there are no written records the procedure can be described in detail because of its recency.

Headmen and Administrative Boundaries

As we have seen, the Nilgiri Plateau is divided into four areas, Todana:ḍu, Me:kuna:ḍu, Poraṅga:ḍu and Kundena:ḍu.[1] In each of these divisions are several communes,[2] each made up of from one to forty contiguous villages. These villages may belong to any one of the seven plateau phratries, and one of the villages, not necessarily the largest or even of the highest phratry, has permanent precedence and gives its name to the entire commune. Its headman is also head[3] of the entire commune; under him are the headmen[4] of all the other villages. The divisional headman[5] is a hereditary position in one family of a chosen village. From time immemorial the village headman of Tu:ne:ri, in Todana:ḍu, has been paramount chief[6] of the entire Badaga community.[7] Because of the extent of their duties the divisional headmen and the paramount chief do not also serve as headmen at all other levels. All of these offices are normally inherited patrilineally, save when the eldest son is deemed unfit and another relative is chosen by the council to replace him.

At each of these levels—village, commune, division and entire community—the relevant headman can call together a council (*manta*) of respected men to judge disputes. Every case has to pass up this hierarchy of councils, so that only when lower councils have failed to solve them satisfactorily do the most complicated land and marriage disputes and murder cases reach the paramount council. A dissatisfied disputant may appeal a council's decision to the next higher level of council, but high-level headmen check that a case brought to them has first passed through the lower-level councils. Badaga law has the unusual provision that if a higher-level headman considers the judgment given at a lower level to be in error he can fine the headman responsible. This was in the past an effective check against favouritism.

Procedure

In a dispute between two parties from the same village their headman called a council of the heads of each household, one of whom would be his deputy (*gaundike*). Where litigants came from neighbouring villages the case would first be heard by the commune council, which was made up of all its village headmen.

If one of the litigants was a Kota his headman would also take part in the council.

The proceedings would begin with statements from the contending parties. Male witnesses might then be brought to support these statements. Females and serfs[8] never appeared before the councils, but if their evidence were considered important it would be heard in private by the headman in charge. Toreas could make statements and attend the meeting but used not to take an active part in the council's deliberations.

A man's family and lineage would normally support him in a dispute and provided the most usual 'witnesses'. Beside their testimony other kinds of admissible evidence included written receipts, re-enactments of the event, oaths testifying to a man's innocence and pronouncements uttered by a god through the mouth of an entranced man. If necessary a postponement was allowed for additional evidence to be brought. Presentation of the evidence was followed by a council discussion, after which the headman in charge voiced his opinion and determined punishment. It was not unusual to punish both parties in a dispute.[10]

Crime and Punishment

The following partial list of punishments suggests the sanctions traditionally placed on various crimes:

Planned murder of an adult—hanging
Unpremeditated murder—Rs. 48 fine, or servitude to the victim's family
Causing someone to commit suicide—Rs. 48 fine
Failure to obey an important order of the headman—ostracism
Failure to pay a fine—ostracism
Rape of a father's wife—ostracism or Rs. 48 fine
Rape of a son's wife—Rs. 24 fine or less
Rape of a brother's wife—minimal fine
} Reduced if the woman had consented; i.e., adultery
Man beating victim with leather—Rs. 24 fine, or head shaved
Woman beating victim with boom—Rs. 24 fine, or made to parade through village with basket of ash on her head
Minor misdemeanour—bow down inside the circle of the council (the minimal punishment)
Attempted suicide—not considered an offence.

The preceding was never a fixed scale of punishments but rather a guide to how an offender would be treated in those times, 'all else being equal'. In each case the punishment could be mitigated according to the circumstances of the crime and the identity of the criminal. A poor man would be fined less than one of the gentry; and any man might plead poverty or haggle with the council to have his fine reduced. This is equally true today.

LOCAL ADMINISTRATION

Since the start of the last century Badagas were ruled indirectly by the British but contact with them had very little effect in the early years. The Badagas avoided the British legal system and its officers, and their own customary system continued to operate effectively until the end of the century when they subtly adapted their legal thinking to avail themselves of the Imperial system as well.

Village government under the British régime perpetuated the existing hereditary headmen, some of whom received the title of *manegar*. The hierarchy of headmen did not enter into the British scheme for local government however; *manegars* were typically *u:r gaudas,* headmen at the commune level. In the earliest days the British deemed it enough for a *manegar* to be a member of the gentry respected by the Badagas; but by the end of the nineteenth century the role of headman had been split: a *manegar* was appointed in the main communes by the District Collector,[11] while the Badagas still selected their own headmen at both the village and the commune levels.[12] The appointed *manegar* was preferably a literate man, and no longer merely someone with prestige (Grigg, 1880, 366). In addition the British appointed an accountant, the *karnam,* to keep village records. Both of these roles,[13] held by Badagas responsible to an outside authority, were new to Nilgiri society and were not honoured in the spirit expected by the British administration. Grigg, the Collector in 1880, noted with perhaps some exaggeration that

> The vaguest notion of their duties as village magistrate or police officer prevails among the headmen. So far from their understanding that it is their duty to repress such crime, they seem to regard it almost as a sacred duty not only to countenance and

shield the wrong-doers, but even to aid in the perpetration (Grigg, 1880, 411; Francis, 1908, 295).

The power and influence of the *manegar* was vastly greater in the last century than it now is: '... when he visited any village within his jurisdiction, the monegar had the privilege of having the best women or maids of the place to share his cot according to his choice'.[14] Girls were only one kind of bribe that might secretly be used to secure his sympathies: clothes and feasting were much commoner. The autocracy of these local officials is well illustrated by 'stories ... of a Monegar of one village who ordered an individual who had disobeyed his orders to be covered with a slab of stone' (Natesa Sastri, 1892, 831–832).

Just as alien as the British notion of a headman's role was the idea of electing a council; and yet a supposedly elected *panchayat*[15] became the official organ of local government shortly after the First World War. (Its duties today are to provide certain facilities, notably the up-keep of roads and paths, water supply, community radio, maintenance of land records and birth and death registers, and the supply of information about governmental activity.) Despite the appearance of village *panchayats* and of a state police force in some villages, the organization of celebrations and the settlement of disputes have remained very much in the hands of the traditional headman, his festival committee and his council. Criminal cases should be reported to the police and are usually handled in a lawcourt, but civil and petty criminal cases can either be settled by the village council or by an official *panchayat* court.[16]

This multiplicity of procedures exposes the Badagas to three different legal systems: their own indigenous one, still influential in establishing precedents; the present-day Badaga village council which settles disputes according to a majority opinion (an opinion voiced, however, by the headman and modified by the knowledge that the case may then be taken, together with the decision, before a court of law); and finally the increasingly popular hierarchy of government law courts.

THE PRESENT AMBILEGAL SITUATION

With such a confusion of courts, officials, regulations and legal options, how does a Badaga choose which medium to use? The prime consideration is apparently not the seriousness of the complaint but the good repute of a man's village. Even recent cases of murder and suicide were handled entirely by the traditional Badaga council in the village where the acts were committed. That procedure contravenes Indian law, for any such criminal offences should automatically be reported to the police and then examined in a magistrate's court.[17] However, whether siding with the victim, the malefactor or neither, Badagas prefer to settle such matters through the headman and his council, thus protecting the village name from the dishonour of a police investigation and loose gossip. For the same reason they also try to stop a case from reaching the higher levels of their own traditional councils.

Despite this restrictiveness, it is now very common for a case which has already been judged by the village council to be taken to a lawcourt by whichever side has lost; hence we may characterize the present procedure as 'ambilegal'. There are two factors which may prevent the loser from appealing his case to a magistrate: one is the high cost of solicitors and of bribing various petty officials; the other is the common knowledge that the decision of the village council, though often not very impartial, can be used as evidence in court, whereupon in something like '98% of cases' (in the estimate of one experienced informant) the magistrate simply reiterates this decision.

Although he usually upholds the village council's decision, it is not in itself legally binding. Therefore while an appeal to the traditional councils is normally cheaper this is done less often now than before the Second World War. As disenchanted and westernized litigants turn to the magistrates more and more frequently the traditional hierarchy of councils is proportionately sapped of the power to enforce its decisions.

A case taken from my notes may help illustrate how an individual can nowadays try to manipulate the two judicial systems to disadvantage an opponent.[18]

> Two brothers, Kallan and Jo:gi, lived together with their wives and children as a joint family in a Me:kuna:ḍu village and, as was the custom, also held joint ownership of their land, each farming as much of it as he wanted. In 1948, Jo:gi, the elder brother, died leaving his two young children and wife in the care of Kallan. One of these children was a daughter who would leave the family at marriage and would not be entitled, under

Badaga law, to any inheritance from her dead father. But Nandi, the dead man's son, would in time demand a half of the joint family's estate. Kallan knew this very well, for he could easily see how most joint families were breaking up into nuclear families; and he also recognized that with his wife, two sons and two daughters he would be making a much greater drain on the family resources than would Nandi and his mother. Kallan therefore decided soon after Jo:gi's death to secure title—under the Indian legal system—to much more than the half of the family land which he could justly claim when Nandi demanded its division, as he undoubtedly would in due course. Already arguments had arisen between Kallan and the widow over who should cultivate each part of the land.

Kallan realized that he could expect no support from his village council, for they would certainly take the just side of his victim, and Kallan himself was not wealthy or powerful enough to bribe them into doing otherwise. He therefore decided to get a legal agreement registered for transfer of land to himself without either the boy or his mother knowing about it. He mustered two men and one woman to act as witnesses, giving them handsome bribes for their services and secrecy. Two of them belonged to a different phratry than Kallan's, and all were unrelated to his family. At the land registrar's office in Coonoor, far from their village, the woman witness claimed that she was Jo:gi's widow, and that Kallan had loaned her some money against the security of about three-quarters of the land she had title to since her husband's death (i.e., on her son's behalf). The government official registered an agreement that if the sum of money supposedly lent her was not repaid within ten years the land would automatically become Kallan's property. The official did not investigate whether the woman really had any title or whether she was indeed Jo:gi's widow. As she could not write, she set her thumb-print to the document.

Kallan continued to let Jo:gi's real widow use the land she needed, hoping that she would die within the next ten years; and after eight years she did in fact pass away, presumably by natural causes. By this time her son Nandi had attained legal majority and soon found himself faced with the perennial problem of Badaga farmers, shortage of money. He went to the local co-operative society and obtained a loan of two thousand rupees against a pledge of two acres of what was assumed to be his land. The co-operative society casually enquired if the land was encumbered, but as nobody suspected that it was the loan was granted.

That year Nandi's potato crop was ruined by disease, and he was unable to repay the loan within the stipulated time. The co-operative society thereupon made preparations to seize the two acres which Nandi had pledged; at which point Kallan decided to step in, as the land was covered by his spurious agreement. He even announced that he would sue the society in court for trying to seize land that legally belonged to him. This was the first time that Nandi and the village learned about the transfer agreement registered some twelve years earlier.

In revealing the existence of that document and telling Nandi that his mother had made the agreement while he was a small boy, Kallan failed to take note of one important fact: one of the men whom he had paid to act as false witness at the registration was now president of the co-operative society! This man, Madia, now did what seemed best for his society and—without mentioning his own role in the matter—tipped off Nandi about the falsity of Kallan's agreement. Madia advised the young man to take the case to the magistrate's court and charge Kallan with false representation. This would not be difficult, for the woman who had posed as Nandi's mother was still living, and her thumb-print could thus be checked with that on the document. Such a sophisticated method of proving the falsity of a document would be beyond the capabilities of the village council and would probably win scant support for Nandi's case there. (Undoubtedly Madia had his own reasons for not wanting the matter discussed in his village.) But unfortunately Nandi had no money to initiate a hearing in the magistrate's court. He did not take the matter to his own village council either, for he knew the council has little power left to enforce its decisions, and the likelihood was high that Kallan would be able to bribe its members.

Whether bribes were in fact given or not, the council did discuss the case some fifteen years ago and advised Nandi to repay the money his mother had supposedly borrowed from Kallan. This was their compromise solution, offering Kallan a financial inducement—the money which he had never really lent—and offering Nandi tenure of the two acres he had pledged and cancellation of Kallan's spurious agreement.

Kallan was apparently willing to accept this, for he was now urging Nandi to repay the supposed loan but under no circumstances to go to a lawcourt. Now it is up to Nandi to solve the problem, still at stalemate in 1975. The solution which he chooses must be couched in the current ambilegal idiom. If he attempts a solution purely in the traditional idiom or purely in the lawcourt idiom, without taking into account the alternate system and Kallan's possible manipulation of it, then Nandi's chances of ultimate success are slim.

The point which the case of Kallan and Nandi underlines is that the introduction of British procedural law in the nineteenth century did not simply offer Badagas an alternative or more effective approach for solving conflicts in their community. The procedure in a lawcourt must have seemed capricious to a villager: it operated on the assumption that all individuals were equal before the law and that the proceedings must work directly towards a just decision; whether a man was a Torea or a member of the gentry was irrelevant to how he would be treated; his past history and his family's reputation were similarly not taken into consideration. To Kallan and Nandi, therefore, as to many of their Badaga contemporaries, the lawcourt is less a mechanism for dispensing impartial justice than a possible means of revenge and a process for overcoming one's opponent (regardless of who may actually be in the right). The use of a lawcourt can involve an opponent in crippling legal costs, and the prospect of these costs may frighten him into compliance with what is wanted of him. Threatening to go to a lawcourt after receiving unfavourable treatment from the village council can also be used to undermine the authority of the elders and cast aspersions upon the village's respectability. For over a century Badagas have had a saying that runs: 'If you prefer a complaint to a magistrate, it is as if you had put poison into your adversary's food' (Metz, 1864, 92; Grigg, 1880, 224). The belief is still voiced today; but in the interim Badagas have learned how to apply the poison effectively.

POLITICAL CHOICE

For the past five decades Badagas have been elected to seats in the state legislature, and for the past three there have been Badaga Members of Parliament. In recent years (as an effect of earlier reversals) the Congress Election Board and some other parties have been careful to choose candidates who were Badagas, since this is the preponderant community in the Nilgiris. Until 1967 the electorate was clearly more interested in the candidate than his party's platform; but in 1967 this preference was reversed, owing to opposition party propaganda and the failure of earlier Congress representatives to satisfy educated young Badagas.

The first Badaga to enter provincial politics was H.B. Ari Gowder, a university-educated Gauda. His village was close to the European towns of Wellington and Coonoor, and his father (a former cowherd) was involved in lucrative construction work on the railway. Ari served for three terms as a member of the Madras Legislative Council before the Second World War and then had three terms in the Madras Legislative Assembly. He was defeated by a Congress candidate in 1946, but in 1952–1957 had another term as an Independent M.L.A. In his early political career he was an Independent but with leanings towards the Justice Party (which tended to support British rule and oppose the dominance of the provincial administration by Brahmins); and ever after he remained an Independent, despite a general sympathy among Badagas for the Congress movement. This man clearly achieved much political influence and perhaps charisma by entering public life in 1924 and capitalizing on the wealth and popularity of his father. Up to his death in 1971 he was undoubtedly more powerful among Badagas than their paramount chief.[19]

As Diagram 9 indicates, Ari Gowder's relatives followed him into the political arena. In the 1957 elections for the State Assembly his sister's husband was elected, and in 1962 the Communist candidate was his nephew; in the same year his brother's wife, the first Badaga woman to graduate, ran for Parliament on the Congress Party ticket and was elected. In 1967 she was defeated by a former Congressman, a well-educated Gauda from the Ke:ti area who represented the rightist Swatantra Party—the first time since Independence that a winning Badaga candidate was from a party other than Congress. In the State Assembly election of that year Congress also lost to an Independent and a D.M.K. (Dravidian Progressive) candidate (both Badagas). As a result the national Congress government, which the electorate held responsible for the poor rice ration, has been trying to regain favour with Badaga voters by locating in the Nilgiris during the later 1960s a German agricultural project, a

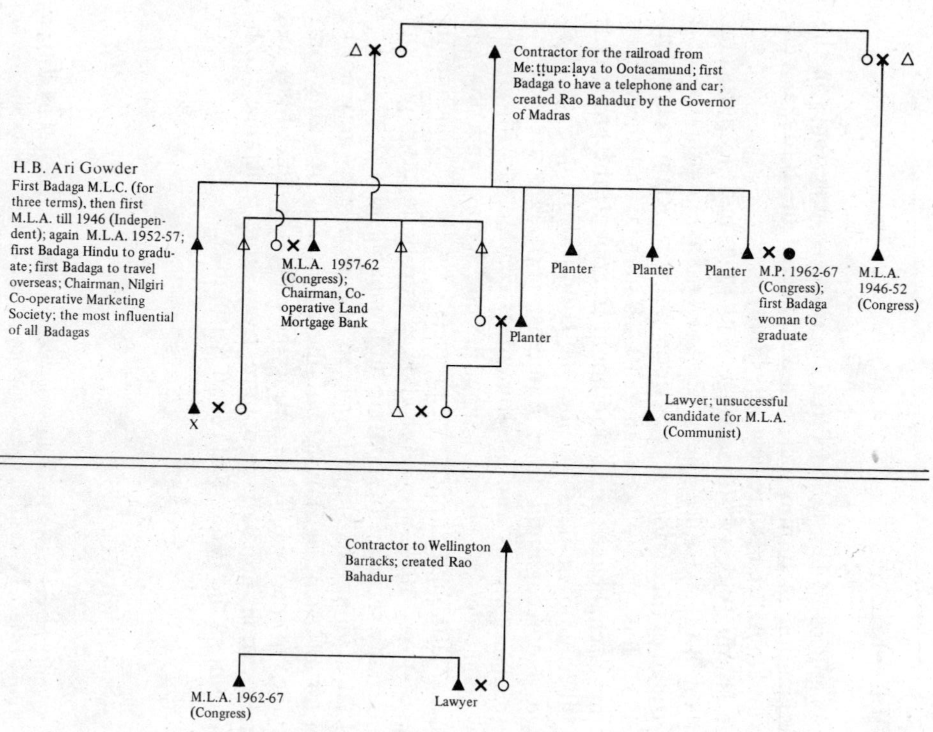
H.B. Ari Gowder
First Badaga M.L.C. (for three terms), then first M.L.A. till 1946 (Independent); again M.L.A. 1952-57; first Badaga Hindu to graduate; first Badaga to travel overseas; Chairman, Nilgiri Co-operative Marketing Society; the most influential of all Badagas
Contractor for the railroad from Me:ṭṭupa:ḷaya to Ootacamund; first Badaga to have a telephone and car; created Rao Bahadur by the Governor of Madras
X
M.L.A. 1957-62 (Congress); Chairman, Co-operative Land Mortgage Bank
Planter
Planter
Planter
Planter
M.P. 1962-67 (Congress); first Badaga woman to graduate
M.L.A. 1946-52 (Congress)
Lawyer; unsuccessful candidate for M.L.A. (Communist)
Contractor to Wellington Barracks; created Rao Bahadur
M.L.A. 1962-67 (Congress)
Lawyer

Diagram 9. The corridors of power

French-supported film factory and a protein products factory, supposedly to improve farm productivity and employ the pool of Badaga graduates.

MODERN LAWS

Certain pieces of legislation often regarded as milestones in the modernization of Indian society have affected the Badagas very little, and these we need review only briefly.

The Hindu Widows' Remarriage Act, 1856, had no particular effect on Badagas since there was never any interdict against remarriage of their widows. The Hindu Women's Right to Property Act, 1937, has always been ignored by Badagas, and the women have never challenged their traditional treatment: the property is only inherited by males. Nor does the Hindu Marriage Act, 1955, receive due recognition from Badagas: marriages are still not always monogamous and are sometimes contracted with grooms below eighteen or brides below fifteen. Kotas and lowland Harijans, although supposedly protected by the Untouchability (Offences) Act, 1955, are never allowed into Badaga temples and are normally served with separate 'untouchable' glasses when they drink at a village teashop. People in Nilgiri villages may not be ignorant of such legislation, but there certainly remains some resistance to the idea of integrating the official system of law and administration into Badaga culture. Even more resistance can be found among the Todas, Kotas and Kurumbas.

NOTES

1. Meaning, respectively, Toda division, Western division, Europeans' division (from *ferańgi*, 'Franks') and peak division (from Tamil *kuṉṟu*, 'mount'). Why one division should have been named after Europeans is not clear, unless it be a reference to seventeenth-century Jesuits who may have entered this area from Sattiyamańgaḷa and Me:ṭṭupa:ḷaya, where they were then active; Société des Missions-étrangères, 1933, vol. xii, 234–235. The name is certainly ancient. Grigg, 1880, 13, n. 1, and Macleane, 1893, 678, derive this name however from Tamil *periya Rańga*, 'great god Rańga,' who is worshipped in this area; see above, p. 127. Throughout the nineteenth century these territorial divisions were adopted by British administrators, but in 1882 they were superceded by the three *taluks* (Gudalur, Ootacamund, Coonoor) that are still recognized today.

2. A *commune* can be defined as the smallest administrative unit above the village, consisting of a number of contiguous villages under one headman and council; compare the definition in *The Oxford English Dictionary,* 1933, vol. II, 698. The commune used to be found in Serbia, and as the *tambon* it is a basic administrative unit in Thailand; there the headmen of the villages constituting a *tambon* elect one of their number to be commune chief.
3. *u:r gauda,* or *natame.* An exceptional area near De:na:ḍu, on the eastern rim of the plateau, was so isolated and broken in terrain that it was only around 1960 that the nine Torea villages there formed a commune and elected a man from Tumbimale as their *u:r gauda;* before that they had recognized as a higher authority the headman of De:na:ḍu, a Wodea who was also the *parpati* (see below, note 5) for Poranga:ḍu.
4. *haṭṭi gauda;* small villages may do without a headman for years.
5. *parpati,* or *si:me gauda;* Thurston, 1909, vol. I, 80–81.
6. *na:ku beṭṭa gauda,* often referred to as Tu:ne:ri *Manegar.* (See Plate 4.)
7. Much the same system of headmen has been noted in the South Canara, Coimbatore and Coorg Districts; see, respectively, Thurston, 1909, vol. II, 269–272; Nambiar & Bharathi, 1965, 10, 63; Srinivas, 1965, 57–59.
8. Until some thirty years ago wealthy Badaga households had Badaga serfs, mainly from the poverty-stricken area of Kundena:ḍu, who were children bound to serve for a period of from five years (in the case of pre-puberty girls) to a maximum of twenty-one years (in the case of some youths). In return they received food and housing, and their parents were paid a sum of money. Those in servitude were generally well treated, being like children of the households where they worked. Harkness, 1832, 115, notes they were paid two or three rupees *per annum.*
9. Such divine utterances have not been given credence in this century but oaths have. The scale of oaths, in order of increasing severity, is this: (1) to assert 'it is true!' (2) to pull up some grass with the finger-nails and throw it onto the meeting-ground; (3) to touch the ground with one hand; (4) to put a cloth one is wearing on the ground and step over it; (5) to lay one's child on the ground and step over him—if a false oath, the child will magically die; (6) if non-vegetarian, to sacrifice a goat at the temple; (7) to visit the temple at a set time and swear one's innocence before the god. Divine punishment will fall on whoever breaks such oaths.
10. If after disposal of a case further evidence came to hand the headman could reopen the discussion and perhaps reach a different decision; this might protect him from being fined for a faulty judgment by a higher headman.
11. Grigg, 1880, 366; Natesa Sastri, 1892, 831; Thurston, 1909, vol. I, 79–80. The Collector was always British.
12. These received the title of *sub-manegar* and a small salary from the British administration.
13. Officially these two roles entailed the following: 'The head of the village [*manegar*] is the representative of Government in the village. He is the village magistrate and head of the village police. He is the collector of the revenue of the village over which he presides, and has also to perform [miscellaneous small] duties . . . The karnam, who is entrusted with the keeping of village accounts, is subordinate to the head of the village. He should help and advise the head . . . in every way. He is the clerk of the head of the village in his

capacity as village munsif [*manegar*] and Magistrate. He has to prepare reports, accounts, statements, etc., which it is necessary to put in writing . . .'; Madras, 1958, 1.

14. Thurston 1909, vol. I, 80. This unusual treatment was not obligatory and was rarely possible because a *manegar's* rounds were short and could not have kept him away from home at night. A *manegar* with a penchant for girls would quickly have lost his reputation.
15. The India-wide term for a village council. The distinction between civil and criminal law is made explicit in the *Indian Penal Code,* which in this matter closely follows English common law.
16. The *panchayat* members are supposedly elected every four years; their position is prestigeful but unpaid. The chosen representatives tend to be relatively well-educated but rarely village headmen. The powers of this court, which is at the lowest level in the hierarchy of lawcourts, are: ' . . . to take cognizance of and try specified offences of a trivial nature and abetment of such offences committed within the local limits of their respective jurisdiction. Such offences are affray . . ., voluntarily causing hurt . . ., assault or using criminal force . . ., theft . . ., and mischief . . ., insult . . ., some nuisances . . ., and generally any other offence under the Indian Penal Code or any special or local law which is punishable with fine only or with imprisonment for a term not exceeding six months or with both.' Madras, 1958, 50.
17. It is supposedly the headman's duty to decide whether a case should be taken before a magistrate.
18. This case remained unsettled in 1975 (all names used are fictitious).
19. 'Satchit', 1940, 15; Dharmalingam, 1962; see Diagram 9. Just before his death H. B. Ari Gowder corrected what I have here written about his life.

9

A Period of Stress

Badaga social history since 1812 is recorded in sufficient detail for us to delimit confidently an especially stressful period in the last century and examine its relationship to the formation of factions and religious revitalization movements. We shall attempt to answer three questions: (1) What steps did Badagas take, in the face of stress-producing situations, to bring their society back to the previously existing stability? (2) Did these steps amount to what A.F.C. Wallace (1956, *passim;* 1966, 158–163) has called revitalization—a cult movement which reinvigorates, as it were, the society that has undergone too much stress? (3) If so, what new institutions arose from this cult behaviour, or if not, why did revitalization fail to occur?

The published sources portray some disaster confronting sections of the Badaga community almost yearly from 1845 to 1906—a period of unusual stress which threw more difficulties in the path of the Badagas than at any time since records began.

A succinct chronology of this time of troubles is presented below. Items concerning missionary endeavour have been included because their ideas were seen by the Badagas as strange and often upsetting, and proved to be a serious threat to the integrity of the Badaga community. It will be noticed that matters which can be viewed as the 'causes' as well as others which are clearly the 'effects' of stress, or its manifestations, have been included.

1845 Four Germans from the Basel Mission began preaching in

many Badaga villages; such itinerant preaching continued throughout the century.

1847 The mission took over a school established in the central village of Ke:ti and began persuading local parents to send more children there; parents objected to losing their children's labour and a salary had to be paid for school attendance. Other mission schools started in Ka:ṭe:ri and So:gatore. Epidemic among Badaga cattle; Toda sorcery held responsible. Badagas in fear of the magic of the Revd. Weigle, who was vaccinating them against smallpox.

1849 The mission schoolmaster and the son of a Badaga headman involved in (unspecified) 'misconduct'. The headman prevented children from attending the school or communicating with missionaries, and that school was closed for six months. Another school opened in Suḷḷigu:ḍu. Some smallpox prevalent.

1850 Ambivalent feelings towards missionaries expressed in the account of a village that begged the Revd. Metz to visit them, then vacillated and asked him not to as the village god might run away.

1853 Typhus epidemic killed over five hundred Badagas. Evangelists noted an increasing opposition to them.

1854 Cholera and typhus epidemics. Government made production and sale of opium illegal: this had been quite an important marketable item for Badagas; some of them were addicted.

1855 Smallpox epidemic killed over a thousand Badagas. Temple for Jesus Christ built. A Badaga presented himself for baptism but died before this could occur. Government prohibited the fire-walking ceremony.

1856 A missionary rest-house burnt down by Badagas. From this year until 1887 government continuously planting further tracts with eucalyptus trees.

1857 Mission school re-established in So:gatore and another in Ba:kola. Stories of the Indian Mutiny caused increased hostility among Badagas towards missionaries and indirectly prevented a conversion. Drought in the Nilgiris.

1858 The first Badaga convert to Christianity, Abraham Nerkambe (formerly Halaiya), was driven from his Kaṇakka village, which itself was ostracized; much opposition to his conversion, even from his wife. Large drop in school attendance coinciding with the conversion and the take-over of some government schools by the Basel Mission. Crops partially destroyed through drought; blamed by Badagas on a curse from the Christian preachers, and by the missionaries on Badaga idolatry.

1859 Continuing drought. By now, ten mission schools opened.

1863 Legislation to stop private parties clearing land to farm in reserved forests. Famine and some migration of Badagas away from their native villages; this was blamed on the missionaries, who were preaching that Christ was responsible for all that happens. The continuing conversions usually attributed by Badagas to sorcery; very low school attendance. Further government order prohibiting the annual fire-walking ceremony.

1864 A Badaga 'oracle' when questioned by villagers indicated the 'English god' was dangerous and evil-intentioned. Consecration of protestant chapel at Ne:rikambe.

1864-1884 Land Settlement; registration of all land holdings and the real end to swidden farming.

1865 Some headmen pulled down their temples and built new but bigger ones, for the first time in brick. Famine on the Nilgiris; drought blamed by Badagas on their gods losing power. A promise reportedly made by the god Irabattaraya to come to the plateau to cure the sick and destroy the missionaries; many disappointed that he did not come.

1873 A Badaga near Wellington became a deathbed convert to the Roman Catholic faith.

1875 Massacre of eighteen Kurumbas by Badagas armed with axes; this in retaliation for a fever among the Badagas.

1876 Monsoons failed; cholera epidemic among Badagas.

1877 Smallpox and cholera epidemics and dysentery on the Nilgiris and famine throughout South India; grain prices double the usual; heavy immigration of starving unemployed people from plains near the Nilgiris; among Badagas much loss of faith in the efficacy of Hindu rituals, and some conversions.

1880 By now 183 Badagas converted to Lutheranism since 1858, and the process continuing slowly; ostracism and physical fighting still associated with each conversion.

1882 Madras Forest Act: defined forest boundaries and further restricted the cutting of timber. Family of a Kurumba sorcerer killed by Badagas and Todas, after three sudden deaths in a Badaga headman's family.

1884 Conclusion of Final Land Settlement (1881–1884). Drought in Nilgiris, followed by crop failure.

1887 Some smallpox; school attendance decreased following a series of conversions. Kurumba shot by a Badaga whose wife he had bewitched.

1889 First mission school opened in Kundena:ḍu, at Bikkaṭṭi, by request of 'a friendly Badaga'.

1890–1910 'Bible women' (South Indian Christians) active in trying to convert Badaga women; very little success.

1891 Massacre of Kurumbas by Badagas.

1897 Opium-eating noted to be on the increase. Factions formed among Ha:ruvas over who should have precedence in walking over fire at their Mahaliṅga festival.

1900 Typhoid epidemic and famine among Badagas; earthquake in Nilgiris; massacre of Kurumbas by Badagas.

1901 Conversion of Kereha:da headman's daughter; attempt to isolate the Badagas of that area from the rest of their community.

1902–1903 Epidemic of plague among Badagas.

1904 Police used to suppress Badaga persecution of a new group of converts; after this date there was no further physical harrassment of Christians.

1904–1905 Plague among Badagas.

1906 Minor earthquake in the Nilgiris; houses shook. Much higher rate of intoxication than in previous years. By now about eight hundred protestant converts.

The cut-off date of 1906 in this skeleton history is somewhat arbitrary; nevertheless it is clear that the misfortunes that dogged the Badagas became considerably less frequent after this date. In 1907 the converts were having factional disputes amongst themselves.

FACTORS LEADING TO STRESS

Biographical material in publications of the Basel Evangelical Lutheran Mission and in the minutes of the Ke:ti parish for the latter part of the last century (Basel Mission, 1905, *passim*) leaves no doubt of a deep disturbance among Badagas during this period. Three distinct factors were responsible:

Land Legislation

The censuses for the last few decades of the nineteenth century record a steady increase in the Nilgiri population (both Badaga and other), implying a need for more farm-land. The British administrators responded, however, with several legislative moves to conserve land resources. They stopped the traditional Badaga practice of swidden farming, in which men cleared as much forest-land as they needed and farmed it for a few years before moving elsewhere. (To the British this practice was wasteful of land, and they believed it led to soil erosion.) As an additional check on the wasteful use of large tracts they compiled an exhaustive register of all land holdings in the district, the Final Land Settlement (1881–1884), and made this the basis for annual assessment of land revenues. Land holdings were restricted to a maximum of five hundred acres (202 ha.). Even the custom of cutting timber in nearby jungles was prohibited by the Madras Forest Act (1882). In the years 1863–1882 legislation thus changed the whole complexion of the Badaga farm economy and prompted doubts in many Badagas about the very survival of their community and culture. The situation was aggravated over this period by the continuing extension of eucalyptus, cinchona, tea and coffee plantations.

Missionary Activity

The sense of uncertainty was further aggravated by missionary attempts to convert Badagas to Christianity. This went on for many decades, and the extent of Badaga opposition to it was in a sense defined in 1856, when they burnt down the mission's rest-house at Kallaṭṭi (B.E.M.S., 1856, no. 16, 27, note). At about the same time the Revd. Metz (1864, 137) noted that 'some parties were so hostile to me that they intended bribing a Kurumba to kill me by sorcery . . . In one place the Badagas created a disturbance, and refused me admittance into their village . . .'. In 1858 the first

Protestant conversion occurred, and from then onward the ranks of Christians slowly increased, prompting a realistic fear among Badagas that their society would be split into two factions or parties each avoiding the other. Nothing comparable had ever occurred among the Todas or Kotas, nor had anyone in the Nilgiris been converted to Islam.[1] In the view of Badaga Hindus the techniques of proselytizing were as unsavoury as they were materialistic: the converts were told not to marry Hindus and were presented with comely Christian brides converted sometimes from communities other than the Badagas (or so it is claimed by present-day informants). Furthermore the missionaries occasionally arranged land grants for converts prevented from using their family's customary farming land; they often received loans from mission funds at the low interest rate of six percent; missionaries also helped converts obtain employment with European families and officials.[2] Though the Christians were always outcast, their existence still threatened to subvert the traditional values of Badaga culture and to some extent did so.

The Basel Mission established its first Nilgiri station at Ke:ti village in 1846, on a large property given them by George Casamajor, a retired judge.[3] In 1867 another station was opened in Kotagiri. In 1888 a Roman Catholic priest began proselytizing with scant success among some of the Protestant converts. In 1909 the Basel Mission opened a third outpost at Kallaṭṭi (Harvest Field, 1909, vol. XX, 477–478; Tignous, 1911, 156).

In the early years of the mission's work on the Nilgiris the Germans established a pattern of itinerant preaching that continued until they were expelled from India at the start of World War I. The ideal of their programme was for a missionary with a catechist to visit every Badaga village in turn. But there were some 370 villages and as missionaries were few, their health sometimes poor and travel by no means easy (journeys were mostly on foot), a village was usually visited only once a year for a few days at most. Sometimes the missionaries were welcome, sometimes not. Some of these men approached the villagers in an arrogant manner which did nothing to endear Badagas to Christianity. The Germans commonly turned up at ceremonies, especially funerals, to preach to the large crowds at these events (B.E.M.S., 1849, no. 9, 23; 1850, no. 10, 23; 1851, no. 11, 34; 1853, no. 13, 38; 1859, no. 19, 69; 1869, no. 30, 74; 1875, no. 36, 37; 1879, no. 40, 75). It was while preaching at a fire-walking ceremony that Metz, who had been nicknamed 'three-quarters God', lost face through declining an invitation to prove the superiority of his religion by walking across the fire.[4]

As another missionary recalled:

> The proclamation of the Gospel, which was repeated again and again in every village with scarcely any exception, met with an increasing opposition, till at last it became a great trial of faith and patience to go on preaching to the same well known and apparently hopeless generation. From the proverbially timid Badaga we even heard expressions like these:—'You have ruined our country, why do you come to us?—stay at home!' (Mörike, 1858, 96).

Apparently the missionaries capitalized on the misfortunes that struck at the Badaga community: on one occasion of drought (in 1859), the missionaries blamed the disaster on the continuing worship of idols; on another occasion Metz reported:

> The famine may have helped to awaken in many a fear of the wrath of God.... Especially one day, after four Badagas had been burned in one house... people were eager to hear the Word and ask questions about it, so that it was quite refreshing to me (B.E.M.S., 1866, no. 27, 78–79).

In 1855 missionaries prompted the government to issue a ban on Badaga fire-walking. The move back-fired, however, for a village had burnt down at about the same time, and this was considered a manifestation of the Badaga deity's wrath (B.E.M.S., 1855, no. 15, 39).

The mission schools were another important means of evangelizing. A school had been founded at Ke:ti in 1845, and by 1859 nine others were in operation. At first Badaga parents in the neighbouring villages were given one anna a day ($\frac{1}{2}$ cent U.S.) as inducement to send their unconverted children there rather than have them work in the fields. The schools were intended to create a favourable impression among the Hindus, but the missionaries recorded that the frequent changes of schoolmasters, their indifference to teaching, their loose morals and the periodic closure of the schools led to a halting literacy but scarcely any conversions.[5] A permanent day-school was established by the mission in 1871, yet the drawbacks remained.[6] No industrial training was given at these institutions. Only in the 1880s did the Badagas begin to appreciate the merit of schooling: the number of schools on the Nilgiri Plateau 'was only 3 in 1879, but 21 in 1889, and 36 in 1889'.[7]

Natural Calamities

A third class of stress-producing factors in the experience of nineteenth-century Badagas was one of natural disasters, sometimes drought, sometimes epidemics, sometimes earthquake, sometimes famine. Badagas were not slow to attribute these calamities to the mission.[8]

Yet on a few occasions the disasters were so intense that they prompted hundreds of people to turn to the German missionaries for sustenance. In 1877 especially the general famine and crop failure led to a steep rise in food prices in the Nilgiris and to a heavy immigration of indigents from the plains. Beggars came to Ke:ti in hundreds, and the missionaries had to restrict their alms-giving to the old and the sick. The mission established some relief-work for Christians and distributed rice to their congregation; and this clearly prompted many, especially the relatives of previous converts and people familiar with the Gospel, to forsake Hinduism. 'Their idols, some said, had been of no use to them in this calamity, they would now follow the God of the Christians.'[9] The missionaries were glad to enlarge their flock, but by the end of the century some of them became more realistic about the motives prompting Badagas to convert. Thus a Badaga pastor, Jacob Kanaka, noticed that 'The larger number of the famine-converts came from the village Tandanadu, the abode of a heart-hardened people and the seat of idol-worship in this district.'[10]

Indeed it would be no exaggeration to say that the Badagas came to the mission more often for temporal than for spiritual aid. In the 1870s mission staff felt many were willing to convert, yet seemed 'more concerned about their debts of money than those of sin; they promise to embrace Christianity if their debts will be paid by the Mission' (B.E.M.S., 1849, no. 9, 45; 1850, no. 10, 23; 1897, no. 58, 53–54). The missionary was commonly sought out in times of sickness when herbal therapy failed. Food was often begged from the mission people too. Thus, for example, a hungry Hindu

Badaga asked a Christian woman for food, and she remarked on the risk of her polluting him. The man answered: 'In your Bible it is written: If thine enemy hunger, feed him; if he thirst, give him drink. Therefore consider me as your enemy and act in accordance with your Bible.' The woman had to give the knowing heathen food (B.E.M.S., 1906, no. 67, 82).

Instances of spiritual aid being sought by Hindus from the missionary should also be noted, however; particularly at times of sickness and death: 'You are our Padre . . . if you only look at the sick or put your hand on their heads, they will feel relieved' (B.E.M.S., 1905, no. 66, 68).

REACTIONS OF THE BADAGAS TO EVANGELIZATION

Missionary activity and the other stress-producing factors we have mentioned led to a wide variety of reactions among nineteenth-century Badagas. Some attempted to incorporate Christianity into their own religion or to bolster their religion so that it might be as effective as Christianity; some attacked or intimidated the converts; some threatened the missionaries; some murdered Kurumba sorcerers; some took to opium or liquor; many became involved in factional disputes; while a few ignored the wishes of their relatives and were converted.

Conversion (1) was at one end of a spectrum of reactions that also included (2) quiet acceptance of much in Christian teaching, but without formal conversion; (3) ambivalent feelings leading a man to seek and appreciate temporal help from the missionaries, but only when he could not possibly do without it; (4) ignorance of Christianity and an uncomfortable avoidance of the missionaries; (5) ostracism and threats of violence directed against missionaries, converts and potential converts; (6) physical violence, using sticks, stones, fists and blunderbusses against converts.

Attempts to Syncretize Christianity and Hinduism

One reported pattern of behaviour among Hindu Badagas exposed to proselytization was the attempt to syncretize the two religions. As early as 1849 some people were praying to the 'God Jesus', and in 1850 a headman was heard to invoke Jesus among other gods as he knelt on the bank of a stream during a Hindu ceremony (B.E.M.S., 1850, no. 10, 23; compare B.E.M.S., 1854, no. 14, 41). Then, as later, Christ was considered *another* Hindu god, perhaps an *avata:r* of Vishnu.[11] Even the missionary could be incorporated into Hindu thinking. Metz, for example, once visited the village where a woman had just committed suicide by swallowing opium (the common method then among Badagas). As he had previously condemned her for leaving her husband and taking a lover he was now treated with great circumspection: the frightened villagers took him for either a sorcerer or a god (Metz, 1864, 71–76). Missionaries were sometimes called 'Shiva kandidhone Swami kandidhone', the man who has seen Shiva (B.E.M.S., 1849, no. 9, 45).

The 'Christian temple' was another case of syncretism. In one village Badagas claimed that a vision of Christ had appeared to them, telling them to believe the preachers. These people promised to build a Christian temple, which they did around 1855. In it they enshrined a New Testament in the Tamil language. A legend quickly developed that every night Jesus came to taste the milk and bananas offered on his altar. But when Metz visited that village in 1863 he found the temple fallen into disrepair and the village nearly deserted. He blamed this on the current famine; the Badagas tended to blame the famine on *him.* This was the occasion already alluded to, when the Badagas interpreted the preacher's explanation of Christ's authority as meaning that Christ was responsible for the death and starvation at that time (Metz, 1864, 69–70; Reclus, 1891, 239–240).

In the same year the Badagas of that particular village went to a temple for divination and asked: 'Is he who is called Jesus Christ a good Swami [lord]?' The response was negative (Metz, 1864, 71; Reclus, 1891, 238–240). Another instance of Hindu practices being directed towards the mission was cited by Wieland. A child in Ke:ti was sick; its Hindu father promised to give five rupees to the Christian God if He would cure the child. As the child subsequently recovered the missionary was given the coins (B.E.M.S., 1907, no. 58, 68). Such action is traditional and quite routine in Hindu temples all over India.

On one occasion the Badaga boys rushed from a school in consternation when a missionary asked them to repeat a prayer after him, for they feared that 'If we say the *mantroum* of the Christians, Christ will hear, Christ will come, Christ will carry us off!' (Reclus, 1891, 239–240).

In general we may say that Badagas found Christianity of some relevance to them only when they could treat it as an aspect of their own Hindu religion. The manner in which the spiritual message of Christianity was presented led to some wild misunderstandings of what Christianity stood for. Badagas could not comprehend why anyone should want to be converted. They asked Metz (1864, 138) if the new converts '... would soon mount horses and ride about like Europeans, and whether they had got plenty of money by the change?' Clearly some Badagas were viewing conversion as a process of social mobility whereby one should adopt the behaviour patterns of Europeans and abandon those of Badagas; and in this they were not altogether mistaken.

Hindu Reformers

The European missionaries were not the only ones to assume an aggressive posture in the conversion arena. The actions of these aliens prompted a counter-movement of Hindu proselytizing, using evangelistic methods to make the Badagas (and other communities) more orthodox Hindus. These Brahminic missionaries belonged to the Hindu Tractate Group of Madras City, and they visited a number of Badaga villages to distribute pamphlets and set up their own short-lived schools (B.E.M.S., 1854, no. 14, 41; Eppler, 1900, 306).

A Hindu reform movement that developed without any aid from outside emerged in the village of Eḍapaḷḷi in 1892. There the young Badaga men formed an organization called the Society of Virtuous People (or *Yedapullu Sajjana Sangha*; B.E.M.S., 1892, no. 53, 77–78). Among various proposals they advocated cleanliness of body and home, an end to tattooing, education for girls, cessation of lavish spending and of dancing to music at the funerals, stopping the use of drugs and intoxicants, and general adoption of monogamy (except that if one wife proved barren a second wife could be taken but the first should remain with the husband). The account of this society shows it aimed to put right the various 'evils' of Badaga life that Europeans had for so long been condemning. (One automatically thinks of the close parallel between this organization and the Arya Samaj in North India, also active in the last decades of the nineteenth century.) It is worth noting that, while nothing further is heard of the Society of

Virtuous People, the village of Eḍapaḷḷi became strongly Gandhian in the 1930s and today retains this idealism, has a well-balanced mixed farming economy and an optimistic outlook on the future—a combination of factors that is quite rare in Badaga villages. It was also the first village to send a Badaga to the United States for post-graduate training. Eḍapaḷḷi seems to have been a progressive community for some generations.

The Destruction of the Temples

Building and destroying temples were equated in Badaga thinking with establishing or destroying a religion. In one village, as we have seen, Badagas sympathetic to some aspects of Christianity built a temple to Jesus in which they placed the New Testament they had been given. In another village Metz knew some Badagas who were willing to pray with him but not openly to call themselves Christians. They even asked him to pull down their Hindu temple. Metz suggested it would be better if they showed their faith by doing this themselves. They refused but did remove the *pu:ja* offerings at the temple and kneel in front of it while the missionary prayed with them (Metz, 1864, 135–136).

In 1864 a Protestant chapel was consecrated in the Badaga village of Ne:rikambe, and in 1865 famine hit the Nilgiris. Some of the Badaga leaders felt this happened because their gods were not properly honoured, and during the next few months many villages went through the unprecedented steps of tearing down their temples and building new, bigger ones in their place. By this means the people hoped to regain the favour of the gods and counter the influence of the mission. It is noteworthy that brick, a European novelty which up until this time had rarely been used in Badaga building, was the material of these new temples; stone is the usual material even today. In one large village several temples were destroyed by the headman and four new ones built, two of them for gods not previously worshipped there.[12] The process of rebuilding temples continued for several decades and affected 'almost all the villages' (B.E.M.S., 1870, no. 31, 22–23; 1905, no. 66, 66).

Sanctions against Conversion

Social pressures were constantly being exerted on converts, their close relatives and any other Badagas who were receptive to the missionary message. Many cases could be cited from mission publications of Badagas who wavered in their attitude towards conversion. Metz for example commented that

> ... the people of a village can be really affected by the love of Christ, when it is preached to them ... But when I come again on my next tour ... I find that in the meantime they have been so frightened by Satan and his tools that they hide in their houses when they hear that I have come, or run away when I ask them to listen if only for $\frac{1}{4}$ hour. They fear to be convinced by my sermon and to have to suffer for it from their relations (B.E.M.S., 1870, no. 31, 22–23).

In some instances men waited till they were dying before openly requesting baptism (B.E.M.S., 1878, no. 39, 63). Individuals were always extremely reticent to become the first converts of their village. They often promised they would become Christians if their friends or relatives would lead the way. Thus Metz (1864, 135) remarked:

> ... there are Badagas who will readily kneel down with me and offer up a prayer in which their wants were often expressed more forcibly, than they probably would have been by many a nominal Christian, and who, for several years, have discontinued idol worship; but when I ask them to go one step further ... they immediately refer me to another, and say that if he will set the example, they will follow it; and if I appeal to him, he puts it off with a similar excuse.

Their immediate family problem was expressed by several to the preacher: 'What you say is true; but were we to follow your advice, we should have no hope of getting wives for our sons,' (B.E.M.S., 1853, no. 13, 39; 1856, no. 16, 34; 1858, no. 18, 92). Intermarriage between Hindus and Christians was unthinkable. Fear of ostracism was great, and held men back from the Christian fold.

The biographies of some converts vividly convey the extent to which the Hindus tried to force converts back into their old ways. The following slightly abbreviated quotations offer a representative pair of case histories.[13]

> (1) [Mada, baptized Mark] ... had a wife and a little

child ... The wife had promised to join him [in Christianity]. But on his return from Church the first Sunday, he found the door of his house locked, and his wife did not dare open it for him. Next day his father-in-law came, and took her and her child away to Adhikarhatti. His whole house was pillaged, and property to the value of several hundred rupees was taken away; even his potato field was dug up by his father-in-law. Shortly afterwards Mada's wife returned and was about to fulfil the promise she had made her husband before his conversion that she would also become a Christian. But next day her brother took her away by force, and after a few days she was sold [i.e., married after payment of bridewealth] to another husband. Only the little babe was left to Mada.

The bereaved husband then tried to get back his wife and his property by the help of the law ... But the [Moslem Police] Inspector treated the Christian witnesses with marked rudeness and would not listen to their evidence. Their depositions were sometimes taken down contrary to what was affirmed, in spite of [the missionary] Mr. Lütze's protests, while the witnesses of the opposite party were fully heard and recorded. Mada's wife was constantly surrounded by heathen Badagas, and when her husband asked her whether she had left him of her own free will or by compulsion ... she could only reply as she was told by the Badagas ... At last the police declared that the defendant [her father] had committed no unlawful action, and the case was dismissed ... Heathen neighbours and relations promised [Mada] their assistance to get back his wife and property, on condition that he returned to caste; Kalla especially pledged himself to that end. Mark [Mada] hesitated and wavered ... He stayed away from divine service, and when Kalla carried off Mark's wife by force from the neighbouring village and brought her back to him, when most of the plundered property also came back, he gave way ... (B.E.M.S., 1893, no. 54, 87–88; Harvest Field, 1894, ser. 3, vol. V, 546–551; Lütze, 1894, 22–23).

(2) About the beginning of 1893, several young men of Kerehada ... came repeatedly to Mr. Lütze, mostly at night, to express their willingness to become Christians. They were Kalla, ... Karcha, the son, and Konga, the nephew of the *headman* of the village. They broke caste and openly spoke against idolatry and heathenism ... After some time Karcha

and Konga asked [the missionary] to lend them some money to clear off their debts, which prevented their joining the Christians. Mr. Lütze had his suspicions, but Joseph, Kalla's cousin, said it would be wrong to hinder the victory of the gospel; he borrowed the money himself and lent it to the young men, getting a bond from them for the same. Then the three young men came to the mission-house at Kaity [i.e., Ke:ti] and openly joined the Christians ... The news spread like wild fire, and from the villages round to a distance of 15 miles people were flocking into Kaity sitting down inside and outside the mission-compound and trying to persuade the three young men to return to caste. For ten days the entreaties and tears of their female, and the promises and entreaties of their male, relations continued, and repeated endeavors were made to carry them off by force.

At last the young men could stand it no longer. On the 7th. April 1893 Karcha and Konga stole away, and four days afterwards Kalla followed them. By the intrigues of the headman they were after a month re-admitted into caste, and Kalla even succeeded in enticing back his son Madya (Immanuel). The poor boy is now a drunkard and totally ruined. 'It is better to be ruined body and soul than to be a Christian,' that is the opinion held and expressed by many of the heathen. But the heathen Badagas, especially the headman ..., were not satisfied with these successes. He induced the backsliders to deny the receipt of the money lent to them by Joseph and to force him to return the bonds. Joseph was threatened by them with a cudgelling and with death if he did not return the bonds. Moved by fear he at last returned them. But his tormentors were not satisfied; they refused acceptance of the bonds. Twice Kalla lay in wait for good-natured Joseph ..., dragged him to a safe place and beat him mercilessly, and Karcha lodged a complaint against Joseph accusing him of fraudulently eliciting a bond from him without paying him the money. He brought false witnesses, who swore to the truth of the complaint.... But the case was decided in favour of Joseph. Cheerfully Joseph and Isaiah returned that day from Coonoor to Kerehada. On the way they found Titus of Chogatorre [So:gatore] and invited him to spend the night with them. So the three men wended their way home, followed at a short distance by Isaiah's daughter and his brother-in-law. Just after they had crossed a deep

> [stream] . . . Karcha, armed with a cudgel, rushed forward from behind a rock and knocked the three men down. Kalla, Konga and Mark [Mada] also came forth from their hiding place, while the headman of the village with his servants was seen standing at a little distance encouraging the assailants. But as Isaiah's daughter and his brother-in-law called for help, they had to retire. Joseph and Titus were so injured, that they were unable to work for a whole month. Isaiah's arm had to be bandaged. When the assault was inquired into by the police, the assailants turned round and brought a complaint against their victims, whom they represented to have been the aggressors, and sued for Rs. 2,000 damages. This time, however, they were convicted and punished. Daniel also, the brother of Kalla, who had so greatly rejoiced at his brother joining the Christians, had to suffer from Kalla's spite. He drove him, his sick wife and his children out of their own house and locked it. After they got it back, he reaped Daniel's barley crop and filled his verandah with the straw. A few days afterwards the house was partially burned down. In consequence of this, Daniel's wife's illness was so aggravated that she died after long suffering . . . (B.E.M.S., 1893, no. 54, 88–90; my italics).

It is apparent from many such cases that the converts, their fellow villagers and even the missionaries were commonly undergoing stress during the latter part of the nineteenth century. Attempts to make the converts return were sometimes legalistic and sometimes not, sometimes violent and sometimes merely argumentative. Much of the behaviour that marked these feuds drew its form and inspiration from the old practice of ostracism. Even before the British came to the Nilgiris Badagas had been in the habit of banishing members of the community for certain categories of crime and anti-social behaviour. Such people would then have to clear a patch of land in the jungle and make a new home there or else find a distant village willing to house them. The attempts to exclude converts from their own villages fitted this pattern and obliged the mission to allocate land near its compound for some of the new converts. Male converts who later reverted to Hinduism were readmitted to the Badaga community by a ceremony which involved shaving the head, cutting the thread of the loincloth, and purifying the tongue by burning it with a golden wire or some charcoal ('Miles', 1951, 70).

Violent opposition to almost every conversion characterized relations between Hindu Badagas and the mission from the time of the first conversion in 1858 to 1904, the last year in which some conversions 'roused a storm of persecution which could only be suppressed by the help of the police' (B.E.M.S., 1904, no. 65, 68–69).

At about that time a story was circulating among Badagas and elsewhere in South India that just before Christmas the Christians sacrifice a human and offer the head on their altar; a Freemasons' Lodge in Wellington was said to preserve the skeletons.[14]

Personal Disorientation

There are a number of references in the Nilgiri literature to opium and intoxication. Opium had been produced and taken by the Badagas as early as 1812 at least, when there was an official reference to it (Keys, 1812, li; Macpherson, 1820, lix). But liquor was apparently unknown to them until three decades after their first contacts with the British (Marshall, 1873, 82). It was noted in 1820 (Macpherson, lix) that no intoxicant was distilled, drunkenness was unknown and opium chewed only in moderation. Though opium continued to be taken (Young, 1827, 42), locally made intoxicants were still unknown to the Badagas in 1834 (Ainslie, 1834, 36). By the time the mission was active among them, however, opium-eating was widespread (Metz, 1864, 132; Gover, 1871, 87), even though its manufacture was outlawed by the British in 1854 (Price, 1908, 224). Opium-eating was occasionally a problem in the Christian congregation and continued for long as a solace for the Hindus; it was stated to be on the increase at the turn of the century (B.E.M.S., 1897, no. 59, 64; Basel Mission, 1905, 119, 129–130). Drinking was also an increasing problem at that time: in 1892 the Society of Virtuous People at Eḍapaḷḷi tried to stop the use of liquor and drugs there (B.E.M.S., 1892, no. 53, 77–78; Basel Mission, 1905, 170–172, 179). In 1905, a year of plague, some Badagas near Kotagiri decided their whole community was being ruined by drinking, and '. . . pledged themselves to their goddess Hette to give it up and to excommunicate [i.e., ostracize] everyone who transgresses this convenant' (B.E.M.S., 1905, no. 66, 68). The next year in Ke:ti Wieland noted that drinking was increasing rapidly among Badagas (B.E.M.S., 1906, no. 67, 63). The anecdotes quoted above contain a specific instance (in 2) of acute stress leading to apparent alcoholism; the Ke:ti parish minutes contain other examples.

Although none of the mission sources has suggested the correlation, it can hardly be doubted that the increased use of opium and liquor in the latter half of the last century was generally related to the higher frequency of stressful situations in the lives of most Badagas during that period.

Massacring of Kurumbas

On several occasions (1824, 1836, 1875, 1882, 1887, 1891 and 1900) Kurumbas were massacred by parties of Badagas.[15] The techniques of killing varied from case to case but usually involved burning down a hut or even a whole hamlet to make the slaughter seem accidental. In 1875 a head Kurumba had bewitched a Badaga woman into loving him and had supposedly caused a fever among Badagas. He was killed in a gun duel, and altogether six households of Kurumbas were massacred with axes. The story was immortalized in the epic ballad of *Kadare Gauda*. In the gruesome case of 1882 the family of another sorcerer were impaled and burnt alive. Common to such killings was the fact that they followed closely on some catastrophe in the Badaga village responsible for the carnage, and also that one or two Todas were always involved. According to Badaga witnesses at the ensuing court trials Kurumba sorcerers had caused deaths or epidemics in the Badaga village, and this sorcery might be halted by the massacre only if a Toda, himself considered a sorcerer, were to strike the first blow against the unfortunate Kurumbas.

Thus, for example, a Badaga killed a Kurumba out of fear of his sorcery after epidemic disease had attacked both the villagers and their cattle and a great part of the murderer's family had died. The heavy sentence given that Badaga by a British magistrate was incomprehensible to the community and reportedly 'gave much encouragement to demonology, and tended greatly to increase the insecurity both of themselves and of their cattle' (Harkness, 1832, 83–84). Without questioning why the buffaloes should have been so perturbed at British justice, we cite this as an early example (*c*. 1828) of Badagas' insecurity being aggravated by British official practice.

Occasionally Todas were accused of witchcraft by Badagas. The relation between the accusation and feelings of stress is also dramatically shown in another incident:

> One day a respectable man interrupted Br. Metz by remarking that through his new doctrine their gods had lost much of the respect and reverence in which they were formerly held and this he said was the cause of the great drought and all their misfortunes.... Just at this time he was interrupted... by a body of people dragging a dead calf along with them and accusing a Toda boy of having killed it by witchcraft. (B.E.M.S., 1858, no. 18, 91–92; the Toda was rescued by Metz; see Metz, 1864, 22–24, 34).

The last known instance of Badagas killing a supposed Toda sorcerer, around 1895, was in retaliation for the death of a Badaga child (Rivers, 1906, 261; Francis, 1908, 144).

Factionalism

There is no published evidence of any kind of factional division among the Badagas until the late 1850s. The challenging question that this poses must therefore remain unanswered: was the emergence of factional disputes really a reaction to the stresses of crossing the threshold into the modern world, a world which introduced the Badagas to a cash economy with international markets, a code of law under which they were theoretically on an equal footing with everyone else, opportunities for schooling and literacy, obligations to pay taxes and obey strange foreign officials? Or was the periodic factional restructuring of the community an integral part of Badaga life, something which has occurred for as long as Badagas have existed? We have no means of knowing.

There are two different types, or rather different scales, of factions, but both are designated by the same word.[16] First, there are what might be called 'personal' factions or feuds, which stem from differences of opinion in a single village about someone's personal grievance. The second kind of faction embraces virtually all Badaga villages, each of them taking one side or the other in some dispute of general concern to everybody. Descriptions of Badaga reaction to the earliest religious conversions suggest that this type of faction grows out of what is initially a dispute confined to a single village (B.E.M.S., 1889, no. 50, 67–68; Anonymous, 1894, 547–551; Eppler, 1900, 153–155).

From these nineteenth-century descriptions several accounts

might be culled of the process by which factional behaviour starts. However, because of the partisan attitude in the early mission writings, a more recent example of faction formation is preferable. The following case is a summary of my informant's account (the name is fictitious). What happened prompted the formation of two factions, although the division was probably founded in part on earlier experiences and previous disputes.

> In 1963 when one village was preparing to stage a funeral the headman asked every household to donate three meals for the expected visitors. One man, Ajja, was requested to prepare four meals, perhaps by mistake; and he did as asked, only to find that nobody came to his house to eat them. Why this was so is not clear; but apparently Ajja was not a very pleasant person to get along with. He demanded a refund of the cost of the meals from the general village funds, but the headman decided to do nothing about it. This situation divided the village into two separate communities.
>
> At first only three households closely related to him supported Ajja; but after another funeral in the village, other people belonging to the same lineage as those three households found themselves drawn into Ajja's faction. At this point the village council led by the headman forbade any women to help members of Ajja's faction with such tasks as working in their fields. Because of this proscription a number of women were forced to join Ajja's faction: they perhaps had no strong feelings about the actual dispute, but were too poor to forego the Rs. $1\frac{1}{2}$ they were earning as daily labourers.

Thus within a few weeks from the start of the grievance typical factional behaviour was characterizing interaction in this village: no one was supposed to talk to members of the opposite faction or to visit their houses and eat with them. In effect, what had been a single village now took on the organization of two non-communicating but interdigitated villages. Within two months from the initial funeral there was a complete break-down in village cooperation at the celebration of festivals: each faction celebrated its own separately from the other.

Yet some ten weeks after the dispute began there were already signs that the factional structure was falling apart. No longer could a rigid separation be maintained between the two factions. Members of one were paying supposedly secret visits at the back doors of friends in the opposite faction; but everybody knew what was really going on. Already it was acceptable behaviour to talk to members of the other faction on the street, so long as no interdining occurred. The break-up of the factional organization was spear-headed by women from other villages who had married into this one. In a number of instances there were pairs of sisters from another village who were married to men of opposite factions. In such cases the sisters felt seriously inconvenienced in being separated by a dispute which did not really concern them; and they took every opportunity to meet secretly and interact with each other across the cleavage that was currently separating their husbands. Nobody in the village really expected the factions to become more rigid: slowly but surely these kinship ties were bringing the two sides together.

By comparison with such frequent and short-term factional disputes as this example, the all-Nilgiri factions are few but long-lived. Altogether only a half-dozen of these are known, only two of them antedating this century.

The first major factionalism we know of, and certainly the most important if judged by its effects, was that engendered by the conversions that split the community into Christians and Hindus. The second major dispute in Badaga history emerged in 1897 and, like the first, is still the basis for a factional cleavage today. Whether this dispute was triggered by the tensions which mission activity and other trials of that period generated is nowhere clearly indicated in our sources. Initially it was only a dispute over which Ha:ruvas should first walk on the fire during their annual festival for the god Mahaliṅga at Me:lu:ru—those of Maṇihaṭṭi or those of Taṅga:ḍu.[17] (By 1897 both these villages had mission schools, but Taṅga:du, though ritually inferior, was much wealthier than Maṇihaṭṭi). The dispute grew, and the entire Ha:ruva clan consolidated to claim superiority in status over the Wodeas and all other groups. The Ha:ruvas and certain other Badagas who support them—pre-eminently in Gauda villages of Kundena:ḍu division—believe the Ha:ruvas were of the high Brahmin *varna* before they left Mysore to settle in the Nilgiris. In support of this belief they cite the facts that they belong to the Brahma sept, they have always been priests for the non-vegetarian Badagas, they are strict vegetarians themselves and they wear a thread across the shoulder. Opponents of the Ha:ruva claim include the majority of Badagas. They perhaps recognize that the Ha:ruvas have no knowledge of Sanskrit or any other sacred literature—since until the present century they were all illiterate; furthermore there is no ceremony for investiture of the 'sacred' thread and no concept of being 'twice-born'. But the argument most generally used against the Ha:ruvas' claim is that they are only priests in Badaga temples (including the one at Me:lu:ru) because the various non-vegetarian phratries appointed them to act in this role; just as they appointed certain Todas, Kurumbas and Toreas to act in special economic and social roles for the benefit of the entire village. Gaudas commonly assert the Ha:ruvas are equal in status with the Gaudas, amongst whom they find spouses.

Although it is the Wodeas whom the Ha:ruvas contest for ritual superiority, there has been no open clash between Ha:ruvas and Wodeas. This is not too surprising, considering that Wodeas are Lingayat while Ha:ruvas are not; Wodeas never employ Ha:ruva priests; Wodeas do not intermarry with Ha:ruvas at all and do not live near those who triggered the dispute; and thus Wodea/Ha:ruva interaction has always been minimal.

The main clash in this dispute has been between Ha:ruvas and most of the lower-status Gauda phratry, who resent the Ha:ruvas' claim. Only a minority of Gaudas support the Ha:ruvas; the remaining villages have not only denounced Ha:ruva pretensions but some decades ago broke off their ceremonial relations with them. In most Gauda villages the Ha:ruva priests were supplanted in their duties by non-Ha:ruva members of the village; Gauda marriages with Ha:ruva men and women ceased, and already married couples were sometimes peremptorily divorced by the village headman; interdining with Ha:ruvas was stopped; and occasional fights would break out, particularly at festivals when the customary Ha:ruva priests tried to perform their ritual duties and members of the anti-Ha:ruva faction tried to stop them.

The Ha:ruva dispute has never been resolved. In the earlier decades of its history it was marked by the usual fights, lack of intermarriage or interdining between disputants and even by resort to the British Indian legal system. (A case against Ha:ruvas was carried, I am told, as far as the Privy Council.) Recently the dispute has cooled to the point where it only becomes relevant in the arrangement of marriages. This also seems to be the present case with the conflict between Hindu and Christian Badagas. In either instance marriages now sometimes occur across the cleavage.

In summary we can say that Badaga factions arise from and give expression to a situation of stress in the community. However, only one of the half-dozen important factional disputes arose directly from the stressful experience of evangelization.

The Cult of Irabattaraya

So far I have described many types of reaction to evangelization and certain calamities without encountering any movement that meets Wallace's (1966, 158–163) criteria for a successful revitalization of a culture. Let us now review what little is known about the cult of the Wodeas' god Irabattaraya (Virabadraya), since this was a kind of eschatological movement.

> A rumour was spread that the God Irabattaraya, born of a white elephant, would come up to the hills within some months bringing to each [Badaga] a true Linga, & consuming Mr. Metz with the breath of his mouth. Even the Todas, ignorant as they are of Vishnoo & Shiva, accepted the mark of Shiva on their foreheads, that they also might be acknowledged by the God as his followers when he would appear. This excited such a sensation among the people, that for some time the proscribed Missionary had the utmost difficulty to get a hearing. But the appointed term elapsed & the god did not make his appearance. At last the news was spread, that Irabattaraya was in Satyamangalam, a town at the bottom of the mountains, performing the same wonders, as Mr. Metz was in the habit of relating of Jesus Christ. Multitudes of sick people, dressed in white, descended the mountain, but came back uncured & disappointed; and after a few weeks the god had disappeared. The impostor appears to have been a Mohammedan juggler. But the people were not yet satisfied. An embassy consisting of 20 men was dispatched on a 5 days' journey into Mysore to ask the old god of the Badagas when he would come up? This frenzy has now passed away. . . .(B.E.M.S., 1865, no. 26, 70–71).

The cult, which flared up briefly in 1865, contains features of both the Christian and Hindu religions. In this regard it is worth recalling that by the early eighteenth century the Sattiyamaṅgaḷa population was largely Christian as a result of proselytization there by the Jesuit Fathers, notably Roberto de' Nobili, from 1643 onwards. Persecution by Tippu Sultan, a Moslem (1749–1799), forced the entire town population to revert to Islam or Hinduism (Société des missions-étrangères, 1933, vol. XII, 234–235; 1938, vol. XVII, 632–633). One is thus left in doubt whether the Irabattaraya cult drew some of its inspiration from this earlier contact with Christianity or whether missionaries in Sattiyamaṅgaḷa in the 1860s prompted this anti-missionary movement.[18]

CONCLUSION

In asking whether Badaga reaction to stress either restored an equilibrium or amounted to a revitalization movement, we must recall the features of revitalization outlined by Wallace and Fuchs.[19] Wallace's view of revitalization as a social process stems from the general hypothesis that under certain circumstances a particular sequence of events is likely to follow.

First, he says (Wallace, 1966, 158–163), a society is in a 'steady state' when disorganization and stress remain tolerable to most people. Certain social groups may find some stressful incident intolerable but their restricted 'correction' does not overthrow the entire social system. Then increasingly large numbers of people may encounter stress from climatic or biotic change, war and conquest, social subordination and acculturation. There follows a sharp rise in crime, illness, alcoholism and anti-social behaviour. A third phase occurs when some people attempt to restore an equilibrium by certain socially dysfunctional means, such as by attacks on 'scapegoat' groups. Individual aberrations become institutionalized efforts to eradicate The Evil.

Once such severe 'cultural distortion' has occurred the society can usually return to a 'steady state' only through a revitalization process. This involves the following recognizable characteristics, according to Wallace: (1) a code is formulated, transforming the stressful conditions into an ideal society; (2) the code is preached in an evangelistic spirit to attract converts; (3) the movement becomes organized with the formulator of the code, the disciples and the sympathetic followers; (4) the code is adapted to face outside threats and to clarify ambiguities; (5) a large part of the population is converted and control of the communication networks is won, thus achieving the goals of the movement and drastically reducing the symptoms of anomie; (6) the movement changes from being an innovative to being a routinization and maintenance force.

We recognize that Wallace's impressionistic concepts of steady state and social equilibrium leave the reader in serious doubt about how to identify these conditions. If, however, we assume Badaga society was in a 'steady state' prior to the impact of the British (an assumption predicated on our ignorance of the society before the early nineteenth century!); then a phase of cultural 'distortion' had arisen by the middle of the century as the Badagas became increasingly uncertain about their future. Ecological change induced by the new land laws, epidemic diseases, acculturation and some subordination to the ruling caste all produced stressful effects on the social system of the Badagas. Some alcoholism and opium addiction followed as well as the sporadic attacking of opposite factional groups, both Hindu and Christian, within the community.

The stage was thus set for a revitalization movement, but what came along?—the cult of Irabattaraya. This cult was formulated by someone, perhaps a Moslem non-Badaga, around 1865, and word of it was spread to many Badaga villages by disciples and gossips. Followers by the hundred made a pilgrimage to where the god was supposedly residing; and after this the cult collapsed in disillusionment. It appears that no one of sufficient charisma had arisen to fuse Badaga sentiments in this particular cult; nor had it proved possible to institute an on-going movement in support of the cult and its anti-European goals. This cult had all the makings of a revitalization movement but failed for want of leadership. It is nonetheless worth noting that the following ten years were marked by no disturbances of any kind among the Badagas.

If an inability to become routinized was a mark of the Irabattaraya cult it was even more true of the earlier syncretic cult of Jesus Christ, as well as of the temple rebuilding fervour. Indeed no Hindu religious activity in the nineteenth century successfully revitalized this community; the Badagas recall no great charismatic leaders from their recent past (except perhaps the late H.B. Ari Gowder).

Yet a new 'equilibrium' was achieved by the early years of the present century; or at least the stress became much less acute. The

Hindu Badaga community continued to exist as a distinct, mainly endogamous group, with its own characteristic language and culture, and beside it there emerged a Christian community. What had happened to relieve the tensions that we have documented? Several features of the changing social condition can be mentioned here as a partial answer.

Accommodation of the Christian Community

After the final outburst of protest in 1904 the Hindus were no longer openly antagonistic to every new conversion (B.E.M.S., 1904, no. 65, 68–69). The community of Christian Badagas was by then so large, so influential with the Europeans, so well schooled and thus so powerful that it could no longer be threatened and attacked with impunity. The Badaga Christians came to be regarded as a caste, separate and inferior to the Badaga Hindus. Having thus been assigned a position in the social organization of the Nilgiris the Christians no longer posed such a serious question about the continuance of Badaga society. After the expulsion of German missionaries in 1914, the Basel Mission on the Nilgiris passed into the hands of the less evangelistic Wesleyan Mission. A stable family and economy were so encouraged among the Christians that they became something of a reference model for the remainder of the Badaga community in these respects. The first schoolteachers, the first government clerks, the first college graduates, the first factory workers and even the first published writers among the Badagas were Christian.

Major Factions Became Permanent

Like the division between Christians and Hindus, and another between Lingayats approving of marriages with Kanarese girls and those opposed to it, the factional division between Ha:ruvas and those who did not acknowledge their claims to Brahminic status became a persistent feature of Badaga social organization. Even today every lineage belongs to one or the other of these factions. We might wonder whether the rapid increase in the Badaga population over the past century has led to a growing awareness of impersonality in the community, which this and later factional splits have counteracted by 'dismissing' large sectors of the society as unfit for interaction. If the population of the undivided Badaga community in 1871 was just under twenty thousand, then there has scarcely been any growth in *scale* when we consider that today this would still be about the order of people with whom a Badaga could potentially interact *within* one of the several factions which divide the current community of over a hundred thousand (cf. Appendix 2, p. 249).

Health Improvements and Economic Growth

The hazards of famine and epidemic disease which confronted Badagas in the nineteenth century have posed less of a problem in the twentieth. The young generation has never known starvation. Standards of health have much improved and public health facilities, especially mass inoculations, have decimated the earlier scourges. Even the modern practice of piping water into the villages has caused a vast improvement in health (Grigg, 1880, 185, n. 2; Hockings, 1979b, 10–15).

The development of a mixed cash-crop farming economy and slight industrialization from the time of the First World War have been crucial factors in the improvement of Badaga living conditions. While there are still many families that are landless or very poor, the opportunities for earning cash are so much wider than they were a century ago that general famine is not a severe or recurrent threat any more.

Education, too, has broadened the Badagas' view of society and is now very popular with them. As early as 1887 it was noted that they had themselves built six schools out of village funds.[20]

The community thus managed to overcome the social and economic difficulties which, if not ameliorated, have often triggered some kind of revitalization movement.[21] There was no successful revitalization among the Badagas even though several small and localized cults showed some potential. Instead the people were able to survive their period of frustration, accept the existence of a separate Christian community and shift from subsistence to a cash-crop economy that allowed them to improve their standard of living significantly even though the ratio of people to farm-land was rapidly increasing. Thus we can say that while the society is in no sense static today it has managed to reduce its tensions and achieve something like a 'steady state' based on a cash-crop economy and the institutionalization of certain social divisions which were the major cleavages during the time of troubles in the latter half of the nineteenth century.

NOTES

1. More recently one Badaga was converted to Islam and was being trained to proselytize that faith on the Nilgiris; B.E.M.S., 1901, no. 62, 96.
2. Thus two days after the first Badaga conversion, the missionary wrote: 'I went with Abraham into the coffee plantation yesterday in order to present him to his master as a Christian and to ensure his work as a plantation supervisor there'; trans. from Mörike, 1858, 93. Basel Mission (1905) contains full details of the frequent loans, made against pledges of land.
3. Grigg, 1880, 421–422: B.E.M.S., 1900, no. 61, 104. The old mission house, still in use, was built by Lord Elphinstone for his residence in 1840; Grigg, 1880, 458; Macleane, 1893, 403; Francis, 1908, 331.
4. Metz, 1864, 55, reflected; 'Challenged to perform a similar miracle . . . I replied that a much greater wonder than that, was, that I should not cease to love such squalied fellows as they were; and that too, in spite of all the abuse they daily heaped upon me'; compare B.E.M.S., 1849, no. 9, 45; 1853, no. 13, 39.
5. B.E.M.S., 1849, no. 9, 44; 1863, no. 23, 50–51; Metz, 1864, 8–9, 56; Grigg, 1880, 424–425; Stokes, 1882, 177; B.E.M.S., 1887, no. 48, 98. By 1864 boys could earn three to five rupees monthly on coffee plantations; this, and the usual parents' contention that 'they have become old without knowing [how] to read or to write and could do their work as well as their forefathers', explain the initial unpopularity of schools; Metz, 1864, 9, note; compare Grigg, 1880, 425.
6. Ke:ti was by no means the first Badaga village with a school. One had been established at De:na:ḍu in 1820 or 1821 and another at Ku:kalu around 1830; Ward, 1821, lxx; Harkness, 1832, 69–70; Hayavadana Rao, 1908, 113.
7. Eppler, 1900, 306–307; in these years there were respectively 69, 497 and 967 students. See B.E.M.S., 1886, no. 47, 88; 1887, no. 48, 98. In 1904–1905 there were 39 Badaga schools with 1222 pupils; Thurston, 1909, vol. I, 64.
8. The epidemic of 1863 was attributed to Jesus, 'because the missionary had but lately been preaching that not a hair, not a bird, can fall to the ground without his [Jesus'] express will and his sovereign command'; Reclus, 1891, 238.
9. B.E.M.S., 1877, no. 38, 15. At this same period, the Revd. Stokes claimed that most of the converts 'embraced the Christian religion from conviction and not from unworthy motives, as is very often the case in the plains where large numbers are gathered in'; B.E.M.S., 1873, no. 34, 32, and Grigg, 1880, 422.
10. B.E.M.S., 1900, no. 61, 110; such a shift in attitudes was not confined to one village.
11. B.E.M.S., 1883, no. 44, 80. It must be remembered the Badagas were then rather ignorant of Hindu scriptures; B.E.M.S., 1867, no. 28, 73.

12. B.E.M.S., 1865, no. 26, 70–71; Stokes, 1882, 174; Sawday, 1884, 12–13; Francis, 1908, 130; Tignous, 1911, 116. To meet the cost four rupees were levied from each household. Prior to this time Badaga temples had been round thatched structures; compare Breeks, 1873, pl. LXXV, and B.E.M.S., 1904, no. 65, 68, plate.
13. There are many comparable anecdotes in the presbytery minutes and the various mission periodicals.
14. Schad, 1908, 134; Butterworth, 1923, 208. Since fresh skeletons were supposedly collected each Christmas, Badagas would only walk around in groups after dusk during November and December, for fear of European headhunters.
15. Breeks, 1873, 65; Grigg, 1880, 299, 411; Stokes, 1883, *passim*; Francis, 1908, 155; Thurston, 1909, vol. I, 86; Tignous, 1911, 155; Belli Gowder, 1923–1941, 50. I have been told of a much more recent instance (not well substantiated, however) in which Badagas burnt down a Kurumba hamlet near Mañjakombe because of the excessive demands for food that a Kurumba watchman had been making.
16. *káči*, or in one dialect *kaci*; see Burrow & Emeneau, 1961, 79 for cognates.
17. Wieland, 1900, 86. The Maṇihaṭṭi priests thought themselves superior as their service was done inside the temple while the Taṅga:ḍu priests remained in the outer precincts. The Taṅga:ḍu Ha:ruvas, who by then included several contractors and were distinctly wealthier than Maṇihaṭṭi people, held that fire-walkers should proceed in order of seniority; and in 1897 the senior-most candidate was an old man from Taṅga:ḍu. After that the festival was celebrated by the two villages on alternate years; see Francis, 1908, 340, and Jogi Gowder, no date, 3–5. In a few years the rift had widened, apparently over a marriage quarrel. A Ha:ruva from Maṇihaṭṭi had asked for the sister's daughter of a Gauda headman. The latter arranged her divorce, and she married the Ha:ruva. He, however had, agreed to pay six rupees worth of finger millet for the divorce but never did, precipitating a long court case and a rift between Ha:ruvas and Gaudas. About 1940 the Gaudas of Me:lu:ru successfully wrested the fire-walking ceremony from the now reunited Ha:ruvas of Maṇihaṭṭi, Taṅga:ḍu and two other villages, causing the latter to celebrate the festival on alternating years at two of their villages, but never more at Me:lu:ru. In effect these Gaudas refuse to acknowledge the ritual superiority of the Ha:ruvas with whom they used to intermarry, and also have won themselves legal recognition as owners of a temple which had previously employed Ha:ruva priests.
18. The London Missionary Society maintained a catechist there in the late nineteenth century, yet by 1891 there were only twenty-eight Christians in a population of 3574; Nicholson, 1898, 424–425.
19. The process of revitalization, though of concern to Max Weber (1946, 1947), was first clarified and labelled by Wallace, 1956, *passim,* and 1966, 158–163; compare Fuchs, 1965, 1–20.
20. Anonymous, 1887, 122. 'The increasing prosperity of the Badagas is unquestionably inclining them to seek instruction for their children'; Grigg, 1880, 426.
21. Fuchs, 1965, 1. He presents many examples of such movements from all over India.

10

Religious and Social Change in the Twentieth Century

We have seen how some aspects of Badaga culture have undergone significant change, how the economy was monetized, how national systems of law and administration were adopted by Badagas and how a Christian community became a persisting feature of the social organization. We now examine what other religious changes have come about, what has happened to the Christians and how the society has adjusted to new patterns of communication, marriage and residence during the present century.

The process of modernization has brought about some changes in Badaga religion. Temples may nowadays have electric lighting, for example, although strictly electrical cable is a polluting material as it is covered with rubber, which conservative Badagas consider to be 'like leather'. Polluting anthropologists and other strangers, including government dignitaries, are now conducted into some of the temples. Another change has come with the new value placed on time: ceremonies that used to last for three days are now finished in one, those that ran for a week now last for only three days; and in general there is a short-cutting of the inessential elements of ritual. Some ceremonies show signs of dying out, so irrelevant have they become. The annual festival for Be:da Sa:mi ('Lord of the Hunt') is now rarely performed. The aid of this god was sought to protect the villagers and their fields from tigers and other wild animals (Metz, 1864, 67–68; Francis, 1908, 339–340; Emeneau, 1971, 5, 42, 564, 744); but today, with the increase in population, illegal hunting and poisoning of carnivors, and the great extension in the area of tea estates, predatory tigers and other large animals have become so rare on the plateau that there seems little need to propitiate Be:da Sa:mi.

Lingayats, over the past century at least, have taken up the worship of gods other than Shiva. The non-Lingayat Badagas have also adopted new gods, mostly Sanskritic deities related to Shiva, such as his sons Gaṇapati and Subramaṇia, and also Aiyappan. A parochialization of the great Hindu tradition is evinced in the temple established at Tu:raṭṭi for a stone brought there from Benares, or the silver image of Subramaṇia brought to a Ka:ṭe:ri temple from Benares, or the 'footprint of Ra:ma' on a rock at Mañjakombe.

BAJAN AND KRISHNA WORSHIP

These styles of worship are new to the Badagas, who are Shaivites (Krishna and Ra:ma are Vaishnavite deities) (Karl, 1945, 5). The performance of *bajan* (group hymns) began amongst them some thirty years ago, and so popular has it become that nearly every village has one or more sets of *bajan* instruments and holds a weekly performance of the sacred songs. These are hymns mostly in praise of the Lord Krishna; they are played on the instruments of Tamilnad, not of the Nilgiris, and the words are Tamil, not Badagu. Many villages have built a *bajan* house specifically for these devotional evenings; it is owned by the village in common and is considered a kind of temple. Inside are lithographic prints of Krishna and other gods and perhaps an image to which *pu:ja* is performed during the course of the devotions. Once a year donations are solicited from every household in the village for support of the *bajan* singing group. Not every villager is interested in this form of worship, but its popularity is clearly increasing, especially among the youths who regard it as a modern, urban form of worship. The rising interest in *bajan* has been noted elsewhere in South India (Singer, 1959, 148–149).

TAMILIAN AND KANARESE CELEBRATIONS

Heavy immigration to the hills, together with greatly improved communications with the plains to the north and east, especially the frequent and cheap bus services, explain in part the proliferation of alien religious practices among Badagas during this century. Among the Wainad Gaudas there has been a comparable influence from Malabar to the west, an effect of heavy immigration from that direction.

Over the past fifty years a variety of memorial ceremonies has been instituted for the anniversaries of individual deaths; previously there had no been no such commemoration. A few corpses or their ashes have been buried at places beyond the village burial grounds, and stones have been raised to mark such spots or memorial statues erected. Here the closer relatives may perform an annual *pu:ja*; or they may do *pu:ja* at home before a photograph of the deceased. Some families invite more distant relatives to the ceremony; others do not but may distribute food to the indigent. Some have the ceremony in the daytime, others at night. Some will go straight to work after the *pu:ja,* others never work on that solemn day. In short, the scale and form of a memorial ceremony vary from family to family, but the general pattern reflects Tamilian influence.

As well as the new death ceremonies, several annual festivals have been adopted from the neighbouring plains people with varying degrees of enthusiasm and support. Over the past forty to sixty years Di:pa:vali, Ka:rttige and Ma:rgaźi have come from Tamilnad into many villages (just as the Ma:ri festival did a century ago), and Dassara, long the biggest celebration in Mysore City, has also been adopted; all of them in very attenuated form.[1]

Dipa:vali, the day on which the mythical Ra:ma was crowned after his return from Ceylon, is given very little importance. A minority of Badagas wear new dresses for the occasion but otherwise do not have so much as a *pu:ja* in honour of Ra:ma or Krishna.

Kartige extends over three days in November or December, but only the first day, dedicated to Shiva, assumes any importance. All the houses display lights throughout the night, and the priest does a *pu:ja* at the village temple, attended by most villagers. On the third day, dedicated to Vishnu, very few lights remain burning.

Dassara is also celebrated on a small scale compared with the major Badaga festivals at sowing- and harvest-time. It is universally supposed to last for ten days at the end of September, but only on the evening of the ninth do Badagas hold any celebration, and this a simple *pu:ja* to images or lithographs of gods that are kept in the houses. On that occasion some Badagas also do *pu:ja* to bring blessings upon agricultural implements and even school books.

Ka:rttige is followed by the month of Ma:rgaźi (December–January), the most inauspicious month of the Dravidian calendar. Some Badagas have now adopted the Tamilian practice of daily *pu:ja* throughout the month. Early each morning a group of men goes along every village street singing *bajan* songs about Shiva and Vishnu. Before this daily tour the women clean the houses, put auspicious markings on the ground outside their doorways and leave the doors open with a lamp burning inside until the *bajan* group has passed by. The many villages which have adopted this ritual conclude the unlucky month with a big communal feast.

In short, we find that there is some local variation in the form taken by the borrowed memorial ceremonies and festivals. They are not celebrated by all Badagas and those who do so show less enthusiasm for them than for native Badaga festivals. Furthermore, Badagas are much less enthusiastic about them than are the Tamilians and Kanarese now living in the Nilgiris.

GROWTH OF LINGAYAT TIES WITH MYSORE

Before the twentieth century those Badagas who were Lingayats were mostly illiterate and knew little about their religion as it was practised in the Mysore homeland. Perhaps once or twice a year a Lingayat *guru* would wander up into the Nilgiris from nearby Aṅgala or Nanjangud, selling *liṅgas* and performing family ceremonies (Harkness, 1832, 137); whatever he taught about the Lingayat faith would have been transmitted by word of mouth. In this century, in contrast, Badaga Lingayats are literate, and some are avid readers of books on Lingayat philosophy. Cheap bus transport has also enabled them to visit the Nanjangud temple and other places of pilgrimage easily and so to meet well-informed monks and priests in the towns of Mysore State.

One significant fruit of this increased contact has been a number of marriages between Badaga Lingayat men and Kanarese Lingayat girls; even a few of the conservative Wodeas have taken this step. However, the move for marital ties with Mysore has not found ready acceptance among most Badaga Lingayats, even though Kanarese brides usually bring a substantial dowry with them. For several decades this matter has been the subject of a bitter factional dispute within the Lingayat segment of the community. Many Badagas argue that as people from even the lowest castes could be converted to Virashaivism (though they seldom are) there is a danger that the girls brought from Mysore are really descendants of Untouchables converted to the faith. For upwardly mobile Badagas that is no easy pill to swallow.

CHANGING PATTERNS OF MARRIAGE AND RESIDENCE

Since 1890 small minorities in nearly all phratries have contracted marriages beyond the boundaries of the community. A few Wodeas, Kaṇakkas and Adikiris have arranged marriages with Lingayat girls from Mysore, generally from Mysore City itself. The Be:das and Kumba:ras have sought brides from the Be:da and Kumba:ra castes of the plains, too. With improved transportation and literacy such marriages have become possible; and the Lingayat cases reflect a move towards closer ties with orthodox Lingayatism.

Since 1950 there have been occasional marriages between a Gauda boy and a Badaga Christian girl, provided that the girl's ancestry traced back to a clan other than the boy's. Such unions, which would earlier have been unthinkable, now occur among the more progressive who have had a college education.

These shifting patterns of alliance have altered the phratry system but little, though changing criteria in marriage arrangements have had a profound impact. The appearance of dowry-like transactions in a society which previously expected only a type of bridewealth is the most portentous of a whole complex of changing criteria. Before the wedding the boy's family always pays the *honnu* to the girl's family; *honnu* thus has the appearance of a bride-price, but this is not a good English translation of the term. It is money to be spent on the gold ornaments that bedeck the bride when she leaves her home to join her husband and without which the marriage would not be performed. By providing the cost of the ornaments the groom's family ensures that the ceremony will proceed. If a divorce later occurs the wife must return the ornaments or their cost, together with any other gifts of clothing or jewellery that her husband may have made (Harkness, 1832, 116–117; Metz, 1864, 86–87; Thurston, 1909, vol. I, 105–106; Tignous, 1911, 119). With rising gold prices the *honnu* has also increased steadily. Early in the last century it was generally '15 to

20 rupees' (Ward, 1821, lxxi); and then 'on an average between twenty and twenty-five rupees' (Harkness, 1832, 42); by 1867 it was Rs. 80;[2] early in this century it was about Rs. 100;[3] in the 1930s and 1940s it was more often Rs. 150 (Ranga, 1934, 3); today it is usually about Rs. 200 (Moses, 1964, 4) but may go as high as Rs. 500 among the wealthy or as low as Rs. 50 in a poor village.

Though *honnu* is still paid, a gift from the girl's family has become common in recent marriages. Some older men, especially those with marriageable daughters, attribute the expectation of such a present to the avarice of modern youth, but the general reason for the development is that young men show much greater variation both in their family's wealth and in their own potentiality to earn than was true of earlier generations. Previously the most affluent and prestigeful families were the gentry, and gentry boys normally married only the daughters of the gentry. Today a wealthy Badaga, whether of the gentry or not, may sometimes be willing to offer thousands of rupees if his daughter can marry into another affluent family. Such a gift is not a dowry, for it is not agreed to as a condition of marriage and is not handed over with any ceremony. It is, however, deemed appropriate when a boy's family has benefitted him with the prestigeful expense of a university education, which promises secure support and enhanced status for the girl. Several hundred Badaga men have now (1975) earned college degrees whereas few girls have. The preponderant choice of groom is thus between secondary-educated and tertiary-educated men, and one method of ensuring the girl's marriage with a college graduate is the payment of what one elder described as a 'bribe'. While not an old Badaga custom it is now becoming somewhat fashionable.[4]

The traditional preference is for marriage with a cross-cousin, whom a youth commonly finds in the same village into which his sister has married. This is still the normal choice: either he marries his sister's husband's sister (a cross-cousin) or else a related neighbour of that husband. The intrusion of a demand for a substantial present into this reciprocal exchange between two clans and two villages can be an unpleasant shift away from custom: two families, lineages or villages which have exchanged several daughters in marriage have established an alliance that proclaims their social equality. If one side seeks a financial settlement it may rupture this stability, as such a gift will imply social inequality between the contracting parties. Offering a financial inducement for a progressive, educated groom is like purchasing security for one's daughter.

No longer are the wealthiest families members of the gentry. The latter have recently been supplanted by *parvenus* with the ability to wield more influence and political power. These *nouveaux riches,* contractors, businessmen, dealers in illicit liquor[5] and plantation owners, have wherever possible reinvested their earnings in tea or coffee estates and private bus lines. Occasionally, too, this new-found capital has been invested in Badaga-owned businesses in the towns. Another popular type of investment is in sending sons to college, which can bring prestige to a family in a short space of time. Men who obtain degrees in law or medicine are assured a high social position in the Nilgiris, where they usually practise, but those who manage only a B.A. or B.Sc. find it brings some prestige but rarely a well-paying job. Nevertheless, upwardly mobile families wish their sons to take a bachelor's degree and then to settle down in their home villages and farm the land.

Among those wealthy enough to expect or to pay a substantial gift at marriage, fulfilment of their traditional roles in the society can become a problem-laden, anachronistic burden. Such men may command annual incomes a hundred times greater than the average for other men in their home village. As a consequence of this newly apparent inequality the wealthy are constantly plagued by importunate villagers and distant relations, as well as Toda and Kota friends, who try to activate traditional bonds of kinship or friendship so as to grasp their share in the power and influence of the *nouveaux riches.* It is therefore not surprising that the wealthiest Badagas have tended to leave their natal villages and build themselves comfortable houses in a town or in the middle of their tea estates. As the wealth of these families grows and as the possibility of their upward mobility, as modern Indian families rather than Badaga villagers, becomes a reality, their attitudes towards the traditional society and its marriage regulations change. No longer are the requirements of their old culture so demanding or so relevant, for these people are now oriented towards a larger South Indian society whose aims and ideals are for them represented in the morality and the cultural paraphernalia of modern romantic Indian films.

THE NEW FACTIONS

By the end of the nineteenth century there may have been several intra-commune or intra-village factional disputes of which no record exists; small inter-family feuds were undoubtedly common; but there were only two factional divisions of Nilgiri-wide scope, one separating Hindus from Christians, and one disputing the relative superiority of Wodeas and Ha:ruvas (see above, pp. 203–204). During the twentieth century these divisions have remained and others have developed alongside them.

The Wodea/Ha:ruva dispute was intensified by another conflict in 1930 which quickly assumed Nilgiri-wide proportions (Benbow, 1930, 11, 13). It concerned the question of whether it was dignified to dance around a corpse to Kota music during a Badaga funeral (see Plate 8; Mandelbaum, 1960, 302–303). Those who supported the Ha:ruva claim to superiority wanted to continue the use of Kota music; those opposed to the Ha:ruva faction and to the use of Ha:ruva priests were equally opposed to this music. The latter, who formed the majority faction, felt that such music was an indignity to both mourners and Kotas, and that dancing was an indignity to the dead since it was an expression of joy and therefore inappropriate, un-Hindu, and 'uncivilized' in this context. Those who wanted to continue the dancing, a conservative minority, stressed that it had been an integral and time-honoured element in Badaga culture and that to discontinue it would be to dishonour and even jeopardize the deceased with an incomplete funeral. The new-found opposition to what had always been an essential part of mortuary ritual arose indirectly from contact with Tamilian culture and a consequent shift in Badaga cultural orientations, and found its leaders in the first Badaga M.L.C. and his father. Today most Badagas no longer invite Kotas to play either at funerals or at weddings and festivals, and most of their economic connections have also been severed in an attempt to increase the social distance between themselves and their more backward and polluting Kota neighbours (Emeneau, 1938, 104–105; Mandelbaum, 1960, 302–303). In dropping the practice of dancing at funerals while adopting anniversary ceremonies for the dead and such festivals as Ma:rgaźi, Ka:rttige and Di:pa:vali, many Badagas are now striving for upward mobility by taking the model and assuming the conduct of orthodox Shaivite Hindus. The younger Kotas meanwhile show no interest in playing funeral music or otherwise underpinning the old Badaga culture. They, too, have their handful of graduates and well-to-do families who are looking for a better style of life than that they used to know.

Another factional dispute that lasted for nearly a quarter-century prior to Indian Independence was a political one: political behaviour during that time took the form of a factional division. Many villages were not at all concerned with political matters, but the more informed ones—with higher literacy and closer links to the towns or missions—tended to be aligned either with the Indian National Congress and the Independence movement or with the Justice Party and a reliance on the British administration of India. The most aggressive phase in this factional history, when most villages became involved, was from Gandhi's salt *satyagraha* in 1930 up to the outbreak of war in 1939. The two factions would not eat together or talk to each other, would sometimes maintain different headmen and celebrate separate festivals, forbade intermarriage across the cleavage, and occasionally gave vent to outbreaks of violent fighting.

Just as the dispute over use of Kota music reinforced an existing factional division over the status of Ha:ruvas, so this political dispute became yet another facet of the same old quarrel: those who supported the Ha:ruva claim also supported the Indian National Congress. The reason for this is quite clear: in Madras Presidency the Justice Party was an anti-Brahmin party; its support depended largely on opposition to the apparent preponderance of Brahmins in the Congress and to the ease with which the Brahmin minority was getting the lion's share of government employment, to the envy of many non-Brahmins.[6] In the Nilgiris the dispute over Ha:ruva superiority was thus able to assume a political colouring, those opposed to Brahmins in general and *ipso facto* to the Ha:ruvas' claim being in support of the Justice Party.

Before the Kota music factions and this political division arose, a factional feud had split the Lingayats but did not involve other Badagas at all. It was triggered by intermarriage with Kanarese Lingayat girls, the first case of which occurred in an Adikiri family around 1890. Those who favoured marriage with Mysorean girls felt that it might raise their status to have connexions with the City of Mysore and its *Umland,* particularly as this was an area with many monasteries and an orthodox interpretation of Virashaivism, where the Badaga bridegrooms would receive the blessing *(ubadeś)* of a high-status *guru*; a dowry could also be asked of a Mysorean family. Most of these Badagas knew that the Lord Basava himself had taught that all men and women are equal, that caste distinctions and endogamy are social evils and not divine prescripts. Badaga Lingayats who have opposed these marriages since about 1925 contend that because Lingayat philosophy countenances conversion from any caste the girls' families might originally have been in low or even polluting castes; yet once converted there is no means of checking their ancestry. Although these marriages are rare occurrences, the factional split they engendered has been marked by more violence than most: its culmination came one day in 1944 when a thousand or more Lingayat men waged battle with sticks and rocks until restrained by the police. For many years the two groups had not intermarried or dined together and had litigated against each other; after this fight the temples in the feuding village were sealed and festivals were only permitted under police surveillance, separate times being allotted for each side to use the temples. For over a decade this village maintained such a heated division that each faction had its own headman and council. The entire dispute was resolved around 1959, and members of the two factions now dine together and support a single headman and council. [7]

A factional dispute over unconventional marriages, which only concerns Lingayats, or a dispute over political affiliations, which concerns primarily the more well-informed villages, are two examples of a faction type that is neither community-wide nor confined to a single village: it is an intermediate type concerning particular interest groups. The Christians are another interest group providing more recent examples.

In 1955 a Badaga Christian studying at Madras University wanted to join the Badaga Students' Association there; and shortly afterwards another Christian posed the same problem. Since this Association had always tacitly been a Hindu organization two factions emerged, one accepting Christian members, the other not. They celebrated their annual Day on separate occasions for as long as the Christian Badaga remained in the University.

Another case concerned Christians alone. Two decades ago a majority of the Badagas and some Tamilians in a Christian village decided it was disrespectful for the minister to wear shoes while conducting a church service: they apparently reasoned from the fact that it would be grossly improper for a Hindu priest to wear shoes in a temple. For some time the congregation was divided, and those opposed to shoes in church would neither wear them there nor attend the service of a minister who wore shoes. The dispute later subsided and the two sides now interdine and talk together. People wear shoes to church if they want to, while some ministers have judiciously refrained from doing so despite the cold stone floors.

In another Christian village an unusual three-way split developed between converts coming from the Gauda, Kumba:ra and Be:da phratries. Each claimed they were socially superior to the other two categories. In this village little intermarriage now occurs across the boundaries between ex-Gaudas, ex-Be:das and ex-Kumba:ras. They normally interdine but refuse to do so during holy festivals. They have no objection however to attending the same church service together. Somewhat similar retrospective factions appeared in the past between ex-Hindus and ex-Protestants in the Roman Catholic community of Badagas, and in the Protestant community, around 1918, between Wesleyans and ex-Basel Mission converts (Société des missions-étrangères, 1928, vol. VII, 573; Périé, 1933, 100).

We thus find that factional divisions are a deep-seated feature of Badaga social organization. Even when people are converted to Christianity or go off to a distant university cleavages still occur among them which are marked by a rigid pattern of antagonistic interaction. One is tempted to see in this an urge for a periodic reorganization of the society.

THE CHRISTIAN COMMUNITY

From the start of the century, the Christian community has been recognized by Badagas as a distinct caste inferior to Hindu Badagas but superior to Kotas, and rigid patterns of interaction have been formalized. During the period 1900–1947 the Hindus, like the Christians before them, became increasingly dependent on an economy and a labour market that ultimately was controlled by the British. As a result partly of this, partly of assigning the Christians to a separate caste status, the acts of violence towards Badaga Christians came to an end. As many Hindu Badagas now found it lucrative to maintain outwardly friendly attitudes towards the British they could not at the same time be openly hostile to the religion of the British.

After the Christians became a separate phratry (made up of twelve clans; see Diagram 7, p. 76), and the moment the German Lutheran missionaries were expelled from India in 1914. French

Catholic priests became very active—mainly in converting Protestant Badagas—and thereby split the Christians into two culturally similar but structurally opposed groups, each maintaining a self-righteous and antagonistic stance not only towards the other Christian Church but also towards all Hindus.[8] By 1924 there were about a thousand Protestants and a hundred Roman Catholics (Société des missions-étrangères, 1924, vol. III, 466).

Since around 1935 an American couple, Pastor and Mrs. E.D. Willmott, succeeded in converting a few dozen Badagas—again mainly from the Protestants—to the Seventh Day Adventist Church; today some two hundred Badagas are members. Otherwise there has been little change in the balance between Catholics and Protestants, who were almost equal in number by 1947. After national Independence, although Badagas continued to become Adventists, the conversion of Hindus to the two major Christian sects virtually ceased, as did most conversion of Protestants to Roman Catholicism. Some recent conversions were engineered by a Catholic priest (a European) who was able to provide imported clothing, houses, CARE food packets and some land to new converts.

A recent count found 2093 Badaga Christians, of all denominations (Moses, 1964, 35). While there are still points of disagreement between members of the two main sects (pre-eminently in ecclesiastical matters), as there are between Hindus and Christians in general, these are being obfuscated as other cultural orientations become more relevant to the changing living conditions. There are now indications in casual conversation that Badagas are adapting their orientations to a newly emerging pattern of social solidarity, one linking all Badagas, whether Christian or Hindu, in the face of competition with other Indians. Some Hindu Badagas, for instance, are willing to admit that the Christians set them a good example—an allusion to the standards of honesty, hard work, education, and 'progressive' treatment of their womenfolk that are admired in some Christians and that make them a westernizing model for other Badagas (Ranga, 1934, 5–6). The Badaga community is now usually called a caste, and its members are more strongly aware of their identity as Badagas, a group for which the state government shows particular concern and beneficence by treating as a 'Backward Class'.[9] Thus the chances of material betterment through wider employment opportunities which a century ago prompted a few Badagas to change their attitudes sufficiently to become Christians now prompt people to alter other orientations not allied to religious values but rather to a secular government and its new ranking of employment and educational priorities. Such a change in orientation holds out the chance of upward mobility, but in that process conversion to Christianity has become an anachronistic mechanism.

NEW PATTERNS OF COMMUNICATION

The idea of communication embraces the physical facilities of road and rail transport, postal and telegraph services, as well as the mass media of radio, film and newspaper, and the channels for communication between individuals within a local setting. We shall review briefly how these have changed in recent decades.

Transportation

Steady improvements in transport have helped the production and sale of cash crops. In the last century all goods had to be carried up or down the Nilgiri escarpment by coolies, on horseback or in bullock carts.[10] Faced with such restrictions Badagas were unable to export produce to other parts of India (Grigg, 1880, 480). Then in 1899 a railway was completed from Coimbatore to Coonoor (a remarkable engineering achievement), and by 1908 it reached to Ootacamund. Its construction involved Badaga contractors and labourers, giving some their first experience of earning regular wages. When the 1914–1918 War began there was thus a quick means of exporting vegetables to all parts of India and even beyond.

During the years between the two wars trucks became common in the district, and roads were improved to accommodate them. A few Badagas who became middlemen bought lorries to improve their business. At the same time a bus service began, and in the years since World War II the network of bus routes has become so complex that there is now scarcely any Badaga village more than five kilometres from a bus route leading to a town. Seventy routes are travelled within the district, some by several competing companies.[11]

The Impact of Towns

The availability of such a profusion of buses has helped the

Badagas in more matters than marketing. They are now able to go to town frequently—typically once a week—and their children can attend high school or even college without losing much contact with the home. (Ootacamund has two colleges and Coonoor another, all three affiliated with Madras University.) Literacy and newspapers in Tamil have spread, too, in part because of the easy transportation system. The literacy rate is now seemingly higher in the rural Nilgiri Plateau than in Madras City: in 1963, 78% of adult Badaga males and 52% of females were literate, while in 1961 70% of Madras City males and 48% of females were literate.[12] Even old Badagas are often quite familiar with daily news stories, weather forecasts and even some political predictions (cf. Hockings, 1965 a, *passim*).

The cheap railway and bus services have made visits to the great pilgrimage centres of South India possible for thousands: the famous temples at Cape Comorin, Madụrai, Palni, Tirupati and Tanjore now receive Badagas almost daily. Nor must we overlook the business trip: increasingly farmers as well as traders find it worth visiting cities when they have a harvest to sell or bulk supplies to purchase.

The modern cities and great pilgrimage centres can have two different types of psychological effect: a city shows the Badaga visitor profusions of consumer goods, among them new household devices, radios, watches, bicycles and cameras, as well as interesting foods, cloths and ornaments; the pilgrimage centre, on the other hand, stresses ties with the mythical past of South India, with the gods represented in the temples, with priestly authority and with the grand history of the temples themselves. It is an important distinction: the man who goes to a distant temple may come home with his attention focussed on the past and on separation of the self from worldly matters, whereas the man coming from a business trip may be full of a desire to buy some implement he has seen or try out a new skill or save money so that his son may attend college in the city.[13] This distinction between the conservative and the modernizing effects of travel is to some extent paralleled in the choice between mythical and modern film themes or between religious and secular magazines. Not all contact with the cities necessarily introduces people to modern ways of life; not all who patronize radio, films or periodicals are drinking at a source of non-traditional knowledge, for though the media may be modern the villager discriminates in what he derives from them.

Film-Going Habits

In the eyes of many Badagas one of the greatest benefits of the bus system is that it permits frequent trips to cinemas in the towns. Most families now see films often, and what they see has a great impact on them. Some of the most popular films are dramatizations of Indian history or of epic stories which reinforce traditional ideas about Hinduism and the nature of the universe. But equally popular are the films about modern life, about social problems like divorce, widow remarriage, 'love' marriages and intercasts marriage; dramas which are presented against a background of affluence that is unfamiliar yet fascinating to the villager. These modern themes extol city life, non-traditional marriage practices and luxury goods such as cameras, watches, radios, mechanical toys and sports cars. The impact of these films is already clear: younger Badagas yearn for watches, motorcycles, and all the other paraphernalia they have come to associate with modern urban life.

Radio

Among the most commonly desired gadgets are transistor radios, which are appreciated partly as a source of light music and partly as a prestige symbol. Only the weathier Badagas own radios, but every village has at least one set, either owned privately or provided by the government; many teashops also have radios. All-India Radio presents much government propaganda, especially talks directed towards improvement of farming and village co-operatives. These broadcasts—in the Tamil language—are not very much listened to, because the vast majority of village radios are constantly tuned to light music coming from the commercial Radio Ceylon. In a sample of 420 Badaga men and women in 1963, 17% said they never listened, 16% only heard music, 38% heard news as well as music, 14% listened specifically for news broadcasts and only 2% mentioned informative talks as being of interest to them.[14] The higher the incidence of *regular* listening, the higher the popularity of news broadcasts, two variables correlated no doubt with the length of time a village has been electrified.

Newspapers

My survey on the use of the media in 1963 showed that radio is much less effective as a source of news than is the press. It was also found that the farther away from towns respondents live, the less information they get from friends and the more from newspapers: only for items of local news are friends everywhere more effective than newspapers as channels of communication. When a Tamil newspaper reaches a village it commonly circulates and is read aloud to a much larger number of people than one copy could reach in a town. The wide circulation of papers and the presence of well-educated men even in out-of-the-way villages helps explain the unusually high levels of knowledge about the world beyond the Nilgiris that Badagas now command.

NETWORKS OF COMMUNICATION

Beside the traditional marriage and exchange networks which supplied Badagas with their basic needs, there have always been social networks through which important information has passed by word of mouth. These have been modified and amplified in the present century and have become linked to some extent with the mass media (on networks, see Hockings, 1977, *passim*).

In Hulla:da, a typical Badaga village, there are now four types of network: intra-village, inter-village, inter-tribal and a new type, village-and-town. Each of these categories can be subdivided according to the following outline.

Intra-Village Networks

There were in 1963 several different adult male *loci* for decision making and opinion formation. The most important here, as in nearly every village, were these:

(1) the traditional council, and especially the village headman;
(2) the festival committee;
(3) elders of the four indigenous lineages and of a fifth composite group of more recently settled families;
(4) three middle-aged, influential men;
(5) the local Swatantra Party organizer;
(6) the educated young men.

Two or three of these groupings may operate together in popularizing an idea or solving a problem that faces the village. In a class by themselves are the women's work-groups, small cliques of village wives who work together in the fields and elsewhere, exchanging gossip and favours in the process. These female networks link up with the male ones through the wives of influential men (cf. Plate 10).

The sequence of contacts that have to be made if someone in the village is to influence or be influenced by people in the above list constitutes an intra-village network.

Inter-Village Networks

Two kinds of network fall under this heading, one linking agnates, the second affines. The first are ritual and juridical networks, linking up with distantly related men in other villages of the commune. This commune was first settled, it is claimed, by a man who founded the maximal lineage to which nearly all of the inhabitants belong. Hulla:ḍa people mostly belong to one of the three major lineages, this one established by Koṅga Hetappa, one of the commune founder's three sons. Within Hulla:ḍa and a nearby village (Ke:ti) the lineage is further divided into four minimal lineages, each descended from one of Koṅga Etappa's four sons. The more important festivals are celebrated in common by all sixteen villages in the commune, using ritual personnel from any of these villages. Serious problems are discussed by all the village headmen at the commune council. Hulla:ḍa villagers can establish contact with the wealthiest and most influential men in the commune by activating these two networks, either through a village headman or through a friend who has helped in the rituals.

Secondly, the marriage and visiting networks link Hulla:ḍa with villages beyond this commune. Marriages account for a network of social contacts with nearly two dozen other villages, and these are frequently activated by informal visits and by attendance at the festivals, weddings and funerals of affines. Small loans may be sought along these networks (Hockings, in press).

Inter-Tribal Networks

The Badagas of Hulla:ḍa were linked for certain economic and ritual purposes with particular Kotas, Todas, Kurumbas and Chettis. For the most part these associations have fallen into abeyance, but until about 1930 they did follow the pattern detailed in Chapters 4 and 5.

Village-and-Town Networks

These more modern networks may roughly be classed as either formal or informal. Formal ties are those that use the recognized channels of local government. Information about personal or legal problems may sometimes be obtained from the *panchayat* office in the next village. A clerk in that office, which is an organ of the state government, will either supply information himself or direct the enquirer to a government office in town (where he will possibly be sent to yet other offices!).

The informal ties between town and village make use of Badaga friends and relatives who work, study or live in the towns, or connect with non-Badagas living in the towns who know where to get information or how to solve a problem. Informal networks are often used by villagers when the formal ones do not resolve a difficulty: this is probably true of many communication systems (Frank, 1958–1959, *passim*).

THE POSITION OF BADAGAS IN NILGIRI SOCIETY

The customary interdependence between the Badagas and other groups is so complex and yet so loose that it has changed to varying extents in different parts of the plateau during this century. Some Badagas are much more dependent than others on the cash economy and usually try to avoid the burden of old obligations. The potentialities of a labour market, nearness of bus routes to town, aboriginal residence patterns and the relative proximity of tribal settlements have all been important in determining the extent to which the Badagas of each village have dropped their traditional ties with the indigenous tribes.

Thus, to cite one example, Badagas of the Kundena:ḍu region tend to be more conservative in outlook than other Badagas: they still invite a Kota band to play at their ceremonies and in other ways keep up their ties with the nearby Kota village. Elsewhere in the Nilgiris the great majority of Badagas eschew contact with Kotas as they now consider it demeaning. A modern Badaga who wants to be regarded as an orthodox Shaivite would not wish to attend a funeral where Kotas play dance-music beside the corpse: not only have the (once) carrion-eating Kotas (Breeks, 1873, 42; Grigg, 1880, 205, 479; Mandelbaum, 1960, 274) become 'Untouchables' in the new terminology, but Hindu orthodoxy frowns upon the idea of dancing at a funeral. The new orientation—for a man who is now more a Hindu citizen and less a Nilgiri peasant—seems appropriate to a Badaga who finds himself competing for jobs or official favours with people from all over southern India. The relatively conservative Badagas of Kundena:ḍu, on the other hand, are among the wealthiest villagers in the district, as nearly all of their land is given over to flourishing tea and coffee plantations. This source of profit and employment is apparently so secure that these people do not feel themselves in serious competition for positions with men from elsewhere. Their confidence in the future allows them to continue at least their ceremonial links with the local Kotas. Few tools are now made by those Kotas, however, for the great quantity of specialized metal items including machinery needed on a plantation has necessarily to be sought in towns, and furthermore these particular Kotas are preoccupied with their own tea estates. Both Kotas and Badagas here activate their traditional relationship only so far as economic expediency permits: where the required tool is too complicated for a blacksmith to make, where the market has the same item at a lower price or where one's labour can be more profitably spent on plantation work than on some customary obligation, the traditional links fall into abeyance (Mandelbaum, 1955, 240).

Similar adaptations to the expanding cash economy may be seen in other aspects of the traditional intercommunity relations. Few Todas, to mention another example, now take the trouble to make their annual rounds of Badaga villages in search of their customary dues: Todas feel this smacks of beggary, while most Badagas would find reasons for not giving anything. Badagas for their part never request the Todas to come and take their gifts and only rarely may seek out a Toda friend when a special requirement can be obtained only from him.

In a survey made in 1963 it was found that 33% of Badaga respondents no longer had any contact with or attitude towards the Todas, Kotas and Kurumbas; and the younger they were, the more alienated they felt from these tribes. Nevertheless many more respondents in all age groups disliked the Kurumbas than disliked

Todas or Kotas: the old fear of witchcraft lingers on. In the middle age-group of the sample (35 to 54 years) there was a significant correlation[15] between dislike of Kurumbas and a feeling that the world in general is a dangerous and evil place—an interesting confirmation of our earlier assertion that witchcraft accusations against Kurumbas have in the past been associated with general feelings of insecurity and stress (see above, pp. 200–201).

In general Badagas feel little compunction to maintain an association that is clearly not economically feasible. Among the indigenous peoples they are taking the lead in finding and internalizing new orientations, which help them secure a place in the national economy and society at the expense of their traditional position in Nilgiri society. While Kotas, Kurumbas and even some Todas are adopting the Badagas as a model, Badagas are following urban Tamilians and Christians in valuing the products of modern technology, seeking monetary profit, good education and a westernizing life-style they think acceptable in a modern urban context.

CHANGING SOCIAL STRUCTURE

We have already commented on changing patterns of marriage and residence and will now examine how the position of the gentry and the roles of the individual have altered with recent changes in the social structure. The central idea in this discussion is that social structure can usefully be defined as a system of linked network-clusters and that the status of a villager is determined by his position in these clusters.

The distinction between gentry[16] and non-gentry is sufficiently precise that all families can be assigned to one category or the other by those who know them. Perhaps five per cent of the community is now considered as gentry. Until the mid-nineteenth century the most prestigious family of gentry was the largest family possible. This was often achieved through polygynous marriages; in one case in the 1950s, probably a record for Badagas, a wealthy but infertile man had five wives simultaneously. In these families men were often several decades older than their wives; I know of a case where the husband was over 90 when the youngest of his three wives was 26. Polygyny, however, is no longer common.

During the latter part of the last century there was a transitional phase when neither the size of the gentry family nor its wealth determined its status: its influence derived mainly from its reputation or strength of character, we are told. In this century all Badaga families, whether gentry or not, have a prestige commensurate with their wealth: the unusually affluent family now receives the respect and wields the power of a gentry family even though it is not one.

Generally all the headmen and their key assistants belong to the gentry; and during the nineteenth century the British appointed *manegars* and *karnams* from among the gentry, too.[17] In the twentieth century, as we have seen, literacy was considered more important than birth in these appointments. In fact this century has witnessed a shift away from ascribed status towards achieved status. It is now becoming less relevant whether a man was born to the gentry or is a Ha:ruva or Torea than whether he has acquired college education and a good job. However, even though there are now signs of socio-economic classes emerging, rural Badagas do not yet discuss their social life in terms of such distinctions as landed/landless, wealthy/poor or educated/uneducated. Individuals are known to vary in these qualities but so far the variation is a matter of degree and has not been schematized in Badaga thinking into a series of neat dyadic contrasts.

In the operation of their social system today the Badagas recognize a dozen major criteria for social differentiation,[18] which they do conceive as the following dyadic contrasts:

(1) Man/woman
(2) Adult/child
(3) Nilgiri/non-Nilgiri
(4) Badaga/non-Badaga
(5) Gentry/non-gentry
(6) Lingayat/non-Lingayat
(7) Vegetarian/meat-eater
(8) Our phratry/other phratries
(9) Agnates/affines (or our clan/other clans)
(10) Our village/other villages
(11) Factional divisions
(12) Hindu/Christian.

This classification is one of cross-cutting categories: each person can place himself and everyone he normally interacts with on one side or the other of each category. These are at different levels of generality and have different relevance depending upon circumstances. An individual's position on each of these contrasts constitutes a role, entailing certain well-recognized expectations of behaviour on appropriate occasions.

How does a social system fragmented by cross-cutting divisions keep from falling apart into small splinter groups? The answer lies with the interaction patterns which are indicative of social cohesion, which mark out the clusters of networks and which counteract the long-standing factional disputes. Four major types of public reciprocity, of which the first is the most widespread, hold together the people separated by these cleavages: (1) public discussions; (2) the exchange of women in marriage; (3) joint participation in ceremonial meals; and (4) the exchange of goods and services. All four are types of communication, and to operate as such they must depend on network clusters; in other words, reciprocity can only be maintained on a continuing basis when it activates a persisting social structure. Badagas do not offer their goods, their meals, their daughters or even their conversation in a haphazard way to *anybody*: the social structure, analysed by Badagas in terms of these dyadic contrasts, determines quite clearly who shall receive certain goods and services, who shall marry the daughters and so on. Not only is the pattern of reciprocity dictated by the social structure—by the positioning of network clusters—but it in turn gives coherence to that structure: there is a dialectical process in the integration of the society. If Badagas were to recognize the emergent socio-economic classes as a new criterion of social differentiation their communication networks, patterns of reciprocity and system of role allocation would all have to be drastically revised. At present they prefer to think somewhat anachronistically in terms of their old social organization, for it provides a reassuring stability to present-day social relations.

Although the social system assigns an individual to certain positions from birth, however, he continuously adapts himself to what he perceives of the shifting organization of network-clusters. In these adaptations the individual has a certain amount of choice. It is clearly limited by what he considers to be the relevant expectations of his fellows; but cultural norms do not dictate role change so absolutely that a man is unable to exercise his personal preferences. Cultural orientations are used by a Badaga to bolster or direct his motivations in the pursuit of the valued ends of his life. While he is busily making a living, gaining respect and maintaining status he apparently goes through a continuing process of re-evaluating these activities in the light of changing conditions and new information. Such re-evaluation takes the dual form of private thought or meditation and of informal public discussions about his clique, their friends, and their various attitudes to life. So important is this re-evaluation process that many men can be seen devoting a major part of their waking time to it. The womenfolk are equally concerned with re-evaluation through conversations, but are obliged to work physically at the same time (Harkness, 1832, 114; Metz, 1864, 98–99; Benbow, 1930, 3–5; Vivekanandam Pillai, 1937, 247; Subrahmanyam, 1962, 5–6; see Plate 10). In such discussions Badagas experience the need to make manifest from time to time the norms by which their behaviour is guided. This process not only makes the norms explicit but reinforces their validity in most cases, too. At the same time ambiguous or anachronistic norms are subject to scrutiny and then modification or total rejection. In view of this re-evaluation process it is no longer enough to know that a modern Badaga is a male of a certain age, from a certain village and phratry or of one particular category in their social system in order to predict how he will conduct himself in any given situation. We also need to understand the more transient social formations and networks with which he is associated, the social functions of these formations and networks, and also the manner in which their members are recruited. As I have observed on many occasions, the play of elementary logic, of conflicting orientations, personalities and proverbs, the relevance of everything said to everyone within earshot are all factors making for fascinating and valuable conversation among Badagas. Slowly yet dynamically their culture is changing, not simply through external programmes devised for the modernization of India, but consciously, indeed conscientiously, through this tedious and time-consuming procedure. Faced with the need to vote for a variety of parliamentary candidates, confronted with propaganda on the value of family planning or with another current topic, individuals discuss the issues, try to reach a consensus and then act accordingly.

Those cleavages in the social system across which conversation is not permissible are barriers to the free flow of communication, and on either side of these barriers variant orientations develop. To understand cultural change we should pay some attention to this mechanism, for it is illuminating. The crucial factor here is the re-evaluation process, for conversations contributing to it take place separately for the different phratries and factions and for males and females. Children furthermore are intellectually equipped for only a very peripheral part in adult discussion. Over a period of years rather different adaptations to living conditions therefore tend to be worked out by each phratry or faction, by men and by women, by the successive generations This accounts for the most obvious subcultural variations within the community; and because children naturally grow into adults and replace the older generation in most roles, an on-going process of changing cultural adaptations is in evidence even though the model for thinking about social relations has remained remarkably stable for some generations.

NOTES

1. Benbow, 1930, 39–42. Other Tamilian festivals now celebrated by some Badagas are Pongal, Ma:ri Habba, Rangana:tan car festival, and the birthdays of various gods; Stokes, 1882, 173.
2. B.E.M.S., 1867, no. 28, 70. It did range as high as Rs. 150 or 200; see Metz, 1864, 99, and Grigg, 1880, 222.
3. But 'varying from Rs. 10 to Rs. 200 . . .'; Natesa Sastri, 1892, 763; compare Tignous, 1911, 119, and Vivekanandam Pillai, 1937, 250.
4. Dowry may once have been a Badaga custom; Harkness, 1832, 41–42; Metz, 1864, 87. Even today Badagas should give their daughters upon marriage a present *(ado:li)* of at least one milking buffalo, one cow and one trained ploughing ox. If she is later divorced the gift is returned to her father.
5. The official claims that 'The vigilant working of the Prohibition department has made Prohibition a success in this district,' is farcical and is belied by lawcourt statistics; Madras, 1965, 23. It has merely provided a further concern for a burgeoning bureaucracy and another cottage industry for the landless. Most villages had at least one still in full-time production during the 1960s.
6. The great majority of people in the Presidency were not Brahmins and looked upon them as incursors from the north; yet 'In Madras the civil service and the professions were dominated almost completely by Brahmins . . . '; Béteille, 1969, 35, also 50–52, 164–168, 173–179.
7. Another village had three headmen recently when its anti-music faction divided into two groups over another matter; these two and the music faction each had a headman.
8. Tignous, 1911, 156; Illustrated Catholic Missions, 1916, vol. II, 8; Périé, 1933, *passim.* There had been some earlier Catholic conversions, the first in 1873 when Father J.M.J. Pottier had baptised a dying Badaga man in a village near Wellington. During the period 1892–1916 about a dozen families had been baptised by Fathers E.J.B. Foubert, M.-L. Robin, F.-F. Deniau, and J.-T. Gudin. Thereafter the pace of conversion increased.

9. See above, pp. 166, 168. On the designation of Badagas as a caste, see Hockings, 1968 b, *passim*.
10. Ward, 1821, lxv; see above, p. 142. Until 1878 the mails were carried by teams of runners; Grigg, 1880, 408.
11. The district is unusually well endowed in this respect, for it is only the size of Warwickshire or Luxemburg and slightly smaller than Rhode Island State. From Ootacamund some of the major cities of South India are also served: Madurai, Salem, Mysore, Bangalore, Coimbatore, Palghat and Calicut (Kozhikode).
12. India, 1962, 133; Moses, 1964, 33, found 73% of Badaga males and 50% of females literate ($N = 200$). My sample in 1963 was 420.
13. There are a few who combine the business trip with a pilgrimage, but this is not usual.
14. This purposive sample was drawn from 656 interviews in the district.
15. $Chi^2 = 5.18$, $P < 0.03$. This middle-aged group had grown up during the slump which spanned the 1930s and which is reflected in the low food-grain prices of those years; see Madras, 1965, 37.
16. *manetana,* literally 'house-stage' or 'house-level'; compare Kannada *mane-tana,* translated as 'household,' 'race, family' by Kittel, 1894, 1207, the connotation being a family of worthy people.
17. Grigg, 1880, 366. These were village magistrates and clerks; see above, p. 172.
18. These social distinctions have over a century of history. They are crystallized in various proverbs as well as being universally recognized normative concepts. One proverb, for example, runs: 'Though it is hot water it will extinguish fire.' This refers to group loyalties: though we may have a friendship with a man of another lineage, village, faction, phratry or community, we will take the side of our own group against his when the need arises. Other proverbs relate to particular social distinctions, e.g., between one village and another:

    'Even if he is headman of his own village, he is not superior to the son of the widow of the last house in another village.'

    'If you are not cunning, do not go to Jakkatala; if you are poor, do not go to Ke:ti.'

    E.g., between phratries.

    'If a crow makes a dropping on you it is a bad sign; if a Ha:ruva shouts at you it is a bad sign.'

    E.g., between affines and agnates:

    'If brothers curse each other, one can still build his house on his brother's threshold; if in-laws curse, leave and run away.'

    'Though she is our sister, is her husband ours?' (In a later work I plan to analyse some 1300 Badaga proverbs).

11

Summary and Conclusion

The Badagas migrated to the Nilgiris from southern Mysore in small bands between the sixteenth and eighteenth centuries. Some came out of fear of the Moslems, some because of famine and some were brought to the plateau by the chieftains of Ummattu:r. They cleared land, scattered their hamlets across the rolling hills and took to a mixed farming economy that was augmented by some hunting and swidden cultivation. What they needed but did not themselves produce was either obtained from the neighbouring Todas, Kotas, Kurumbas and Chettis or was bought in market towns near the foot of the Nilgiris, usually by bartering homegrown millets.

Up to the beginning of the nineteenth century coinage hardly circulated on the plateau; for the most part it only changed hands during family ceremonies. The levying of tribute under the rule of Haidar Ali and Tippu Sultan, and the subsequent demand for land revenue at the British outpost of Dannaika Ko:ṭe, put some pressure on Badaga farmers to sell more in the lowland markets in order to get sufficient coinage to pay their assessments. At about this time, if not before, some differentiation based on wealth was apparent within the community: certain men, descended from the village founders, became more affluent and were treated as gentry, while at the other extreme were people so poverty-stricken that they had to contract their children into servitude with well-to-do families.

Though the British had acquired the Nilgiri Plateau by the

Treaty of Seringapatam in 1799, they were slow to appreciate their prize. It was only after twenty years and several preliminary explorations that a British official, John Sullivan, had serious thoughts of settling on the plateau. In this he was prompted by his own romantic inclinations after hearing the reports of others and making a tour of the area himself; but he was also invited to come there by the Badagas, as they wanted someone to survey their lands and determine if they were being assessed for too much revenue.[1]

As soon as Sullivan had taken up residence in what later became Kotagiri he began experimenting with several European crops, also giving seeds to some interested Badagas. Even after his arrival, while the new township of Ootacamund was becoming established, the British continued for a decade to collect the land revenue in the plains. They had adopted a policy of fixing grain prices, which gave some encouragement to the Badagas who sold their grain surplus in the lowland towns; and this indirectly fostered the practice of storing credit gained there by selling the food-grains for coinage.

After 1823 roads were developed and a market established at Ootacamund. Thereafter the Badaga economy became monetized, with Ootacamund as the new centre for their trade. By 1840 they were making most of their bazaar purchases with coinage.

The first estimate of the Badaga population (in 1812) was only 2207, and by 1821—perhaps a better census—it had reached 3778. The British population increased rapidly too, offering Badagas who lived near the towns an opportunity to labour for a cash wage or to grow European vegetables for the market that was suddenly on their doorstep. While their tradition of intensive farming in small fields was well suited to the new crops, and the Nilgiri climate by chance blessed their endeavours, learning to compete in a labour market was another matter: it was only because some feared the government might otherwise increase the land tax out of revenge that Badagas let themselves be persuaded to work for Europeans.

The early British influences on Badaga culture were thus the introduction of a local market, a cash economy and a demand for labour and vegetables. But this was enough to trigger a rise in the fortunes of the community and also to prompt a remarkable increase in the size of the Badaga population. Another significant British novelty was education. Within a year of Sullivan's arrival a school had been opened in De:na:ḍu; yet it was only after 1856 that Badagas perceived some value in schooling. This value lay in Tamil literacy, which was slowly becoming the one sure passport to such coveted official positions as *karnam* and *manegar*.

During the 1860s and 1870s legislation put an end to shifting cultivation, cutting timber in the jungle and paying a light tax on undemarcated land holdings. No longer was there land available for everyone to clear and farm: those who could not pay the government land-tax became tenant small-holders, landless labourers or plantation workers. These successive blows to the customary farming practice, following hard upon the first Christian conversion (1858), fostered a half-century of mistrust of Europeans which the numerous epidemics, droughts, conversions, temple rebuildings and surveys of field ownership did nothing to dispel. Over this period land erosion became a serious problem, fields were inadequately manured and rarely terraced, much Badaġa land was sold to European planters, and indebtedness became widespread. Only some villages near the towns achieved a measure of prosperity. Jakkatala, a prime case, sold much of its land to the government for the Wellington Barracks and then profitted further from contracts for gangs of labourers to build the barracks and some other public structures. By the turn of the century a few families had become very wealthy as contractors, some of them in building the railway to Ootacamund.

At the start of the twentieth century the Badaga population had climbed to 34,000 (having increased fifteen-fold in the preceding century), and the density of the rural labour force had also increased appreciably through continued immigration. Alongside this growth Grigg (1880, 321) had observed: '. . . each year has the area of cultivation and permanent occupation been extending with the growth in numbers of the hill-tribes [Badagas], the increase of wealth among them, and the great extension of plantations.'[2]

Although tea, coffee and potato had been grown in the district for over half a century, it was only with the onset of World War 1 and the completion of the Nilgiri railway that Badagas shifted the emphasis in their farming from millets to potato and in the 1920s to tea as well. This made many of them cash-crop farmers, since they did not eat much potato and had to buy their food-grains in the bazaar. Their initial interest in tea cultivation was merely as a method of increasing the value of land before selling it to European planters.

By now the Badaga Christians were viewed as a separate caste, and the old antagonism over Christian conversion had given place to a new realism which accepted the British, tolerated their religion and sought to collaborate with them in the realms of commerce and administration. The periodic massacres of Kurumbas had also come to an end.

Land fragmentation and indebtedness continued to be problems for the twentieth-century farmer, but new techniques of commercial cultivation raised the per capita income appreciably. Chemical fertilizers and insecticides were now used, along with good seed and reputable tea cuttings. Money-lenders, middlemen and truckers all appeared on the scene to answer local needs. Most of the hillsides were terraced to permit efficient farming, and the emergence of co-operative societies from 1911 helped with this as well as with the more general problem of rural credit.

These new directions in the farm economy were fully in evidence by 1930, at which time most Badagas broke off their time-honoured exchange relationship with the Kotas, Todas and Kurumbas and began to seek the artifacts these tribesmen had made in town markets instead. The ostensible reasons for this break are several. Badagas usually mention the increasing cost of having a Kota band at their ceremonies; while Kotas mention an insulting article in a national newspaper of 1928, 'The Hindu', which implied that Kotas were descended from the unions of Todas with Badagas.[3] A glance at the population graph in Appendix 2, however, will make it clear that the over-riding reason for the break must have been the disproportionately large number of Badagas. By 1931 there were 42,500 of them, too many to be adequately supplied in the customary way by a few hundred Todas and Kotas.

The Second World War brought a further surge in the demand for potatoes to feed the European troops stationed throughout south and southeast Asia; at the same time government financing helped the growers, with the result that this new capital and the high prices potatoes were fetching greatly alleviated the former indebtedness of Badagas. After 1957 potato production fell sharply with a series of disease-ridden crops, and tea, first planted by Badagas some thirty years before, now became a popular cash-crop too. By 1970 cabbage had also become an important crop.

Modern Badagas enjoy a high standard of living, occupy comfortable tiled houses, send their sons to college, make frequent trips to various South Indian cities, see numerous films and delight in mechanical devices. The minority who now live in the Nilgiri towns, among them numerous Christians, have taken on a variety of new urban jobs and are found in most of the professions. Few were involved in the Independence movement, fewer are under the influence of Gandhi's philosophy and fewer still understand or care for Marxism. The Communist vote is negligible, and the idea of revolutionary communism unappealing. For Badagas change means securing profit in a capitalist economy, adopting a westernized style of individualism and thus shifting away from ascribed status towards that which is achieved.

This transformation has come about while physical communications have been improving steadily. All the more populous villages are linked with the towns by regular bus services. Since the beginning of the century there has been a railway to the plains. Many of the middlemen who sell fertilizer or buy potatoes have their own trucks; some large-scale tea planters have cars or jeeps. Radios are widely accessible now that the villages are electrified; yet radio is mainly a channel for light music and is not as important as the 'social' films in introducing new, primarily urban, values and wants to the Badagas. Newspapers have a broad circulation in the villages and are much more effective than radios in transmitting news. Today, therefore, every Badaga village has easy access to information about the world beyond the Nilgiris, through seeing films, reading the papers or talking with friends and relatives who work in the towns.

SOME CONCLUSIONS ON MODERNIZATION

There is a multi-causal type of linkage in socio-cultural hanges like those documented in this study: one single factor does not by itself cause a new situation, but several discernible factors combine to cause variant patterns of a new situation. We may state this process in another way. When a community moves from subsistence cultivation to rational participation (i.e., maximization of gains) in a cash economy, certain changes come about in the culture and the social organization. These are conditioned by a combination of local ecological factors, outside governmental activity, the availability of certain goods, services and entrepreneurial personnel, adequate flow of information, and the play of chance events or 'historical accidents'. Because the combination of all these conditions will vary from one region to another, the manner of the economic transition will also vary. We should therefore not expect a replication of the successive phases of the Badagas' development elsewhere in India, even though such people as the Coorgs may suggest a superficial parallel (see Muthanna, 1953, *passim*; Srinivas, 1965, *passim*).

The Badagas' transition to a cash economy depended in part on very favourable ecological conditions. Their land and the climate were well suited to the new crops, and for some decades it was even possible to extend the area of cultivation. A protectionist government fixed grain prices, provided roads and encouraged railway construction and even supplied Badagas with technical information and improved seeds. No external pressure was placed upon them to make the transition; yet some of the more affluent farmers living near towns took the chance with initial crops of marketable vegetables or grain to sell to the two breweries. Their decision found some reward and incentive in the profits from the local market; and with the advent of the railway and the First World War this expanded dramatically. Once some success in the market had brought these profits into the community, reinvestment and spending took a variety of forms. The Badaga economy became increasingly differentiated, there was considerable variation in wealth from one family to another, a class structure based on affluence began to emerge and most families sought to maximize their gains, even at the expense of their customary relations with the neighbouring tribes.

Though the details of their history are unique, there are some regularities that tie the Badaga case in with others; in particular, the modern stress on education, the desire for non-essential consumer goods, reinvestment of profits in land (Epstein, 1962, 326–328), the role of mass media in popularizing urban tastes (Rao, 1966), the replacement of traditional co-operative associations by market relations and co-operative societies, and the periodic restructuring of society through factional disputes.

NOTES

1. A survey was actually made in 1820; see above, p. 166, n. 2, and Hockings 1973, 869.
2. So also the Sanitary Commissioner, Dr. Cornish: 'I have no doubt the native

population is increasing, and that the position of the Badaga has materially improved. I notice especially the facts that they are now tiling their houses, that their women and children earn money on the tea and coffee estates, and that they buy rági and grain from the low country, and get a better market for their straw and cattle. They wear jewels of gold and silver, saved from their earnings'; quoted by Grigg, 1880, 34. This contrasts with the situation at the start of the British occupation of the hills, when the Badagas were so few in proportion to the land available that there was no need for crop rotation, as fields could be left fallow for years at a time; Mackworth, 1823, 124–126.

3. Emeneau, 1946, 265. Ranga, 1934, 4, reports that around 1930, 'In addition to this heavy expenditure upon funerals, more than three hundred Badagas cease work for more than two days and live at the expense of the relatives of the deceased or the people of the village. The expenses of a funeral incurred by all the Badagas in a hamlet come to more than Rs. 600. To add to this, their European employers lose their confidence in the ability of these people for regular service, since they cease work without giving any notice whatever . . .'; similarly Metz, 1864, 89–90.

APPENDIX 1

Population of the Main Nilgiri Communities, 1961

Indigenous Groups

Badagas (including Christians)	84,823[1]
Panias (including Christians)	5139
Irulas and Kasuvas	3958
Kurumbas	2600
Mauntadan Chettis	1650
Nayakas	1168
Kotas	956
Todas (including Christians)	759[2]
Wainad Chettis	711
Uralis	33[3]
Total:	101,797

Immigrant Groups

Tamil-speaking	158,057
Malayalam-speaking	64,622
Kannada-speaking	37,690
Telugu-speaking	30,118
North Indians, etc.	17,024
Total:	307,511

NOTES

1. The district total at time of census; there were then an additional 640 Badagas beyond the district boundaries, and thus the real total was 85,463. By 1971 it had become 104, 919.
2. Another six Todas, indigenous to the Nilgiris, were outside the district at time of census. By 1971 there were 930 Todas.
3. Though a few live within the district, they are not primarily a Nilgiri tribe: their national total was 1,078. In 1971 their Nilgiri total was only 46.

Pl. 1

3

Pl. 4

Pl. 5

Pl. 6

Pl. 7

Pl. 8

Pl. 9

Pl. 10

l. 11

Pl. 12

'l. 13

Pl. 14

l. 15

Pl. 16

APPENDIX 2

Badaga Population Growth Compared with that of Todas and Kotas

	1812	1821	1825	1847*	1856	1866	1871	1881
BADAGAS	2207	3778	5147	6569	13352	17778	19476	24398
TODAS	179	222	326	337	316	704	693	689
KOTAS	130	317		307	484	802	1112	1067

	1891	1901	1911	1921	1931	1951	1961	1971
BADAGAS	29613	34178	38180	40329	42526	67251	85463	104392
TODAS	739	807	748	640	597	879	765	812
KOTAS	1201	1267	1163	1204	1123	1200	956	1269

* THE 1847 CENSUS UNDER-ENUMERATED; MARSHALL (1873), P. 102; GRIGG (1880), P.30.

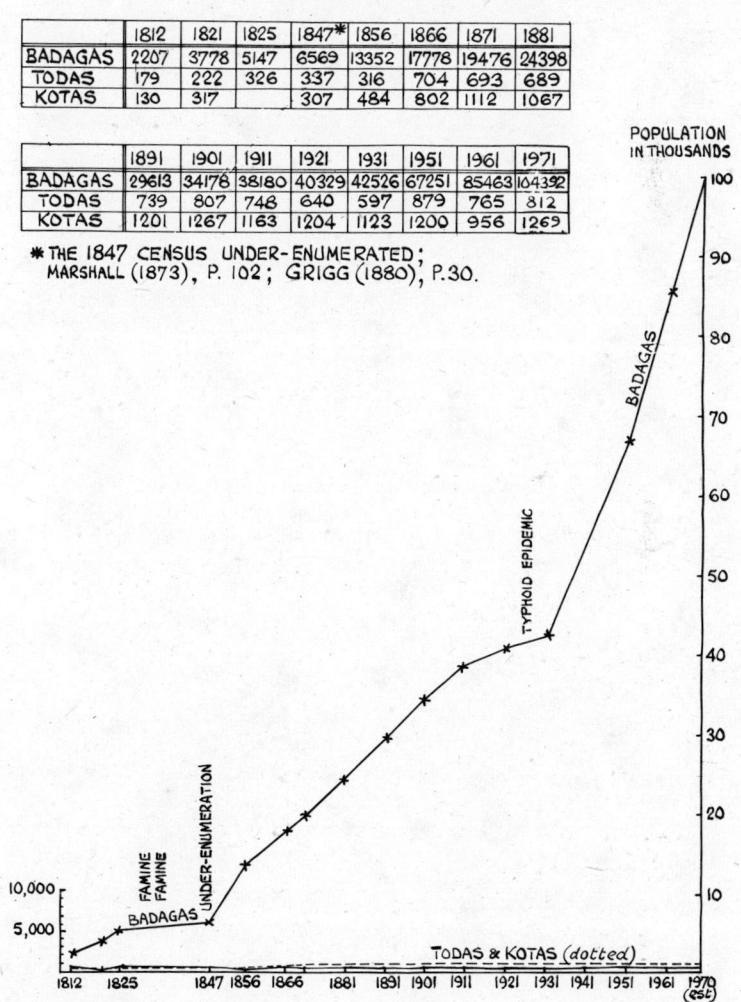

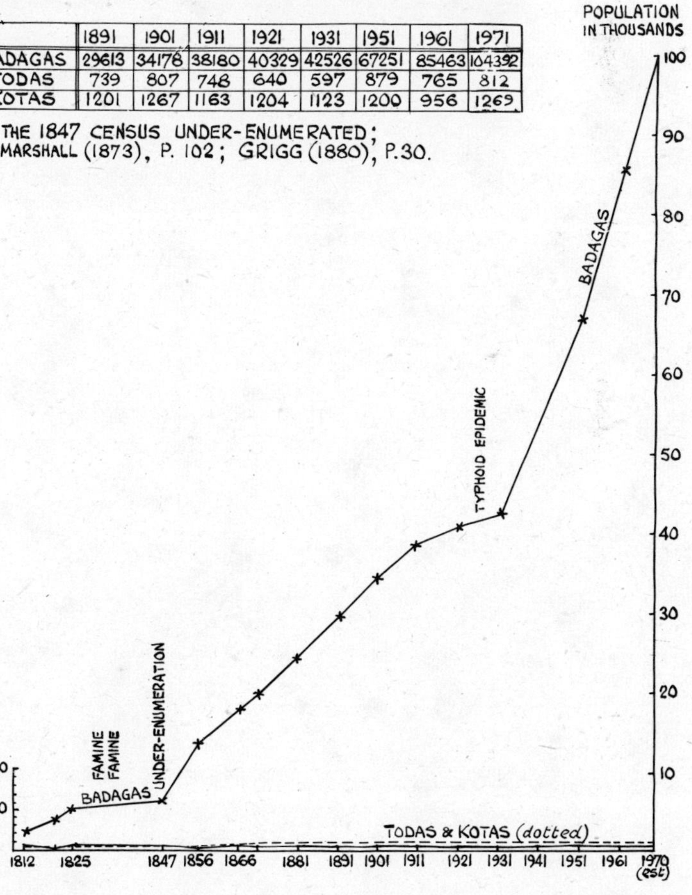

Plate Section

Plate 1 A typical Badaga hamlet (Dimbaṭṭi), above the valley floor but sheltered by a hill from the south-west monsoons. Note the strips of land running downhill. The well in the foreground is new.

Plate 2 Typical work-space (ke:ri) in front of houses in Ka:ṭe:ri. The two-story house is a twentieth-century innovation. The poles carry electricity to most houses.

Plate 3 A Toda couple, both wearing embroidered shawls (pu:txuḷy).

Plate 4 Pāda Rāja Gowder, paramount chief of the Badagas since 1956, and headman of Tu:ne:ri. His gold earrings are of a traditional design.

Plate 5 Two schoolgirls carrying their lunch, O:ranaṟi hamlet. Both have an auspicious mark on the brow.

Plate 6 Sithamma, grandmother of the girls in Plate 5; she lived in O:ranayi, was a traditional Lingayat, and a noted herbal therapist. Her gold ornaments are traditional.

Plate 7 Kumba:ras in Kempola hamlet, here enshrouded in mist.

Plate 8 Kotas from Kolmel playing for Lingayats dancing during a funeral at the neighbouring hamlet of O:ranayi, 1963. Women do not dance in public.

Plate 9 Cattle threshing grain on a work-space in O:ranayi. The hired labourers are non-Badagas.

Plate 10 Women's work-group outside a house in Ki:ṛkunda village. All wear sarees in place of the traditional dress.

Plate 11 The Goddess Hette with bell, a wreathed *linga,* and a tray with plantain and half-coconut offerings, decorating a Lingayat temple in Ka:ṭe:ri.

Plate 12 Council of elders at Ke:ti village. The commune headman is on the extreme left, in white.

Plates 13 and 14 The *manevale* (memorial ceremony) at Ittala:r in 1905. (Courtesy Basel Mission.)

Plate 15 A funeral in Hulla:ḍa hamlet, 1963. The widower leads a procession of men, in order of their generation level and absolute age, three times around the corpse, upon which they deposit the grain held in their hands. Unrelated men and women sit on either side of the grassy space.

Plate 16 Medieval carved orthostat, now a shrine, at Be:ṭḷa:ḍa.

References*

Ainslie, W., (1834) 'Observations on atmospheric influence, chiefly in reference to the climate and diseases of eastern regions, in five parts. Part I', *Journal of the Royal Asiatic Society of Bengal,* II (1835), 13–42.

Anonymous, (1887) [Note on the Nilgiri mission.] *Evangeslisches Missions-Magazin,* XXXI, 122.

—(1894) 'Success and persecution on the Nilgiris', *Harvest Field* (Ser. 3), V, 546–551.

Arputhanathan, J. I., (1953) *1951 census handbook: The Nilgiris District.* Madras: Government Press.

Baber, Thomas Hervey, (1830) 'Journal of a route to the Neelghurries from Calicut', *Asiatic Journal* (new ser.), III, 310–316.

Baikie, Robert, (1857) *The Neilgherries: Including an account of their topography, climate, soil and production; and of the effects of the climate on the European constitution,* 2nd ed. Calcutta: J. Thomas.

Balfour, Edward Green, (1885) 'Nilgiris'. In *The cyclopaedia of India and of eastern and southern Asia, commercial, industrial and scientific; products of the mineral, vegetable, and animal kingdoms, useful arts and manufactures,* 3rd ed., Vol. II, 1098–1099, London: Bernard Quaritch.

Balu (pseud. 'Hilpaks'). (1960) *Ni:lakiri carittiram. Mutal pakippu* [History of the Nilgiris, Third part]· Ootacamund: Saint Regina Press.

Basel German Evangelical Missionary Society, (1846–1913) *Report of the Basel German Evangelical Missionary Society . . . Report of the Basel German Evangelical Mission in south-western India.* Mangalore. [Here referred to as B.E.M.S.]

Basel Mission, (1905) *Presbytery minutes of the Basel Mission, Ketti,* 1887–1905, Ms.

Beidelman, Thomas O., (1959) *A comparative analysis of the Jajmani system.* (Association for Asian studies Monograph, no. 8). Locust Valley: Augustin.

Belli Gowder, M.K., (1923–1941) *A historical research on the hill tribes of the Nilgiris.* Ms.

*Full bibliographic details on the Nilgiris can be found in my *Bibliography for the Nilgiri Hills of southern India* (1978).

—(1938–1941) *Origin of the Badagas.* Ms.

B.E.M.S. See Base German Evangelical Missionary Society.

Benbow, J., (1930) *The Badagas—Beliefs and customs.* Ms.

Benson, Ralph Sillery, (1881) *Descriptive memoir . . . [and] survey and settlement register of the village of Kethi in the Merkunad division of the Nilgiri District.* Ootacamund: Revenue Settlement Office.

—(1884) *Descriptive memoir . . . [and] survey and settlement register of the village of Sholur in the Toda-nad division of the Nilgiri District.* Ootacamund.

—(1895) *A statistical atlas of the Madras presidency; Compiled from existing records . . .* Madras: Department of Land Records and Agriculture.

Bertrand, Joseph, (1848) *La Mission du Maduré d'après des documents inédits,* vol. II. Paris: Poussielgue-Rusand.

Béteille, André, (1969) *Castes: Old and new; Essays in social structure and social stratification.* Bombay: Asia Publishing House.

Blasco, François, (1971) 'Montagnes du sud de l'Inde: Forêts, savanes, écologie'. *Institut français de Pondichéry, Travaux de la section scientifique et technique,* 10, fasc. 1.

Breeks, James Wilkinson, (1873) *An account of the primitive tribes and monuments of the Nīlagiris.* London: India Museum.

Buchanan, Francis (afterwards, Hamilton), (1807) *A journey from Madras through the countries of Mysore, Canara, and Malabar, performed under the orders of the most noble the Marquis Wellesley, Governor General of India, for the express purpose of investigating the state of agriculture, arts, and commerce; the religion, manners, and customs; the history natural and civil, and antiquities, in the dominions of the Rajah of Mysore, and the countries acquired by the honourable East India Company, in the late and former wars, from Tippoo Sultaun,* vol. II. London: W. Bulmer and Co.

Burrow, Thomas, and Murray Barnson Emeneau, (1961) *A Dravidian etymological dictionary.* Oxford: Clarendon Press.

Burton, Richard Francis, (1851) *Goa, and the Blue Mountains; or, six months of sick leave.* London: Richard Bentley.

Butterworth, Alan, (1923) *The southlands of Siva: Some Reminiscences of Life in Southern India.* London: John Lane, the Bodley Head Ltd.

Coleridge, Henry James, (1872) *The life and letters of St. Francis Xavier,* vol. I. London: Burns and Oates.

Congreve, Harry, (1847) 'The antiquities of the Neilgherry Hills, including an inquiry into the descent of the Thautawars or Todars', *Madras Journal of Literature and Science,* XIV, i, 77–146.

Das, Gopi Nath, (1957) 'The funerary monuments of the Nilgiris', *Bulletin of the Deccan College Research Institute,* XVIII, IX–X & 140–158.

Dharmalingam, Ari, (1962) 'Voters in Nilgiris: Apathy towards elections', *Hindu,* 16 Feb.

Dubois, Jean-Antoine, (1906) *Hindu manners, customs and ceremonies.* Trans. by H.K. Beauchamp. Oxford: Clarendon Press.

Dulles, John Welsh, (1855) *Life in India; or, Madras, the Neilgherries, and Calcutta. Written for the American Sunday School Union.* Philadelphia: American Sunday-School Union.

Emeneau, Murray Barnson, (1938) 'Toda culture thirty-five years after: An acculturation study', *Annals of the Bhandarkar Oriental Research Institute,* XIX, 101–121.

—(1939) 'The Christian Todas', *Proceedings of the American Philosophical Society,* LXXXI, 93–106.

—(1946) 'Kota texts. Part four', *University of California Publications in Linguistics.* 111, 191–335.

—(1971) *Toda songs.* Oxford: Clarendon Press.

Eppler, P., (1900) *Geschichte der Basler Mission 1815–1899.* Basel: Verlag der Missionsbuchhandlung.

Epstein, Scarlet Trent, (1962) *Economic development and social change in South India.* Bombay: Oxford University Press.

Finicio, Jacome, (1603) 'Two Portuguese Mss. on the mission of Todamalâ'. In *A collection of annual reports relative to the state of the Portuguese Jesuit Missions in the East Indies; of various dates, from 1601 to 1659.* British Museum Additional Ms. 9853, 464–465, Ms. 25–26 vol.; and 479, Ms. 40 vol. Trans. by A. de Alberti in Rivers, 1906, 719–730 [whence my pagination].

Firth, Raymond, (1951) *Elements of social organization.* London: Watts & Co.

Francis, Walter, (1908) *The Nilgiris.* Superintendent, Government Press.

Frank, Andrew Gunther, (1958–1959) 'Goal ambiguity and conflicting standards: An approach to the study of organization', *Human Organization,* XVII, 4, 8–13.

Fuchs, Stephen, (1965) *Rebellious prophets: A study of messianic movements in Indian religions.* London: Asia Publishing House.

Fürer-Haimendorf, Christoph von, (1954) 'Hereditary friendship and inter-tribal sex relations between Todas and Mudugas', *Man,* LIV, 24, 28–29.

Gaymard, Felix-Adolphe, (1924) *Les Badagas, tribus des Montagnes Bleues de 1 Hindoustan.* Coonoor: New Albion Press.

'Geofry', (1881) *Ooty and her sisters, or our hill stations in South India; with sketches of hill tribes, their customs, caste, religion, &c., also, tea, coffee and cinchona cultivation, &c., and appendix of routes; distances and fares.* Madras: Higginbotham and Co.

Gillin, John, (1948) *The ways of men: An introduction to anthropology.* New York: Appleton-Century-Crofts Inc.

Gover, Charles, E., (1871) *The folk-songs of southern India.* Madras: Higginbotham and Co.

Grigg, Henry Bidewell, (1880) *A manual of the Nīlagiri District in the Madras Presidency.* Compiled and edited by H.B. Grigg. Madras: E. Keys, Government Press.

Hanumantha Rao, K. and M.D. Azariah, (1953) 'Potato on the Nilgiris'. In *Horticultural and Economic Plants of the Nilgiris* (S. Krishnamurthi, Ed.) pp. 67–79. Coimbatore: Coimbatore Co-operative Printing Works Ltd.

Harkness, Henry, (1832) *A description of a singular aboriginal race inhabiting the summit of the Neilgherry Hills, or Blue Mountains of Coimbatoor in the southern peninsula of India.* London: Smith, Elder, and Co.

Harvest Field, (1880–1924) *The harvest field: A missionary magazine.* Bangalore.

Hayavadana Rao, C., (1908) 'Political History'. In Francis, 1908, 90–122.

—(1930) *Mysore gazetteer compiled for government,* vol. V. Bangalore: Government Press.

Hockings, Paul Edward, (1965a) Communication and cultural change in an emergent region of south India. Mimeo. Stanford: Stanford University.

—(1965b) Cultural change among the Badagas, a community of southern India. Ph. D. thesis Berkeley.

—(1968a) 'A bibliography of studies on the Nilgiri Hills of Madras', *Bulletin of the Deccan College Research Institute,* XXVI, pts. I and II.

—(1968b) 'Identity in complex societies: Are the Badagas caste or tribe?', *Journal of African and Asian Studies* (Delhi), II, 29–35.

—(1968c) 'On giving salt to buffaloes: Ritual as communication', *Ethnology,* VII, 411–426.

—(1973) 'John Sullivan of Ootacamund', *Journal of Indian History,* Golden Jubilee Volome, 863–871.

—(1976) 'Paikara: An iron-age burial in south India', *Asian Perspectives,* 18, 26–50.

—(1977) 'Communication networks'. In *Dimensions of Social Change in India* (M.N. Srinivas *et al.,* Eds.) New Delhi: Allied Publishers Ltd.

—(1978) *A bibliography for the Nilgiri Hills of southern India,* Revised ed. 2 vols. New Haven: HRAF Press.

—(1979b) Sex and disease in a mountain community. New Delhi: Vikas Publishing House; Columbia, Mo: South Asian Books.(Forthcoming)

Hodgson, Brian Houghton, (1856) 'Aborigines of the Nilgiris, with remarks on their affinities', *Journal of the Royal Asiatic Society of Bengal,* 25, 31–38, 498–522.

Hough, James, (1829) *Letters on the climate, inhabitants, productions, &c.&c. of the Neilgherries, or Blue Mountains of Coimbatoor, South India.* London: John Hatchard & Son.

Illustrated Catholic Missions, (1886) *Illustrated Catholic Missions: an illustrated monthly record in connection with the Society for the Propagation of the Faith.* London, New York.

India, Government of, (1962) *Census of India, Paper No. 1 of 1962. 1961 Census, Final Population Totals.* Delhi: Government of India Press.

Jagor, Andreas Fedor, (1876) 'Die Badagas in Nilgiri-Gebirge', *Verhandlungen der Berliner Gesellschaft für Anthropologie, Ethnologie und Urgeschichte,* 1876, 190–204.

Jogi Gowder, B.K., *et al,* (no date) *The origin of the Badiga Brahmins of Nilgiris, and the temple of "Mahalinga" at Melur village in Merkunaad division in the district of Nilgiris.* Ootacamund.

Kariabettan, N., (1958a) 'Kallaṭṭi ko:ṭṭai' [Kallaṭṭi fortress], *Malai Na:ṭṭu Kural,* (Ketti), Sept., 14.

—(1958b) 'Ni:la malai va:cikaḷ' [The inhabitants of the Nilgiri Hills], *Malai Na:ṭṭu Kural,* (Ketti), July, 2–4.

Karl, William Victor, (1945) The religion of the Badagas. B.D. thesis, Serampore.

Keys, William, (1812) 'A topographical description of the Neelaghery Mountains. From a letter by William Keys, Assistant Revenue Surveyor, to W. Garrows, Collector of Coimbatore.' In Grigg, 1880, xlviii–li [whence my pagination].

Kittel, Georg Ferdinand, (1894) *A Kannaḍa-English dictionary.* Mangalore: Basel Mission Press.

Krishnamurthi, S., (1953) *Horticultural and economic plants of the Nilgiris.* Coimbatore: Coimbatore Co-operative Printing Works, Limited.

Krishnaswami, S.Y., (1947) *Rural problems in Madras: Monograph.* Madras: Superintendent, Government Press.

Lawley, A.A.C. and F.E.F. Penny, (1914) *Southern India.* London: A. & C. Black.

Lévi-Strauss, Claude, (1968) *Les structures élémentaires de la parenté,* 2nd ed., Paris, The Hague: Mouton & Co.

Ling, Catharine Frances, (1892) 'Mission work on the Nilgiris', *Harvest Field* (ser. 3), III, 74–77.

Lowie, Robert Harry, (1948) *Social organization.* New York: Rinehart & Co., Inc.

Lütze, Christoph Wilhelm, (1887) 'Auf den blauen Bergen. Einige Beobachtungen über den Einfluss der Missionsschulen', *Evangelische Heidenbote,* 1887, 13–14.

—(1894) 'Verfolgung auf den Blauen Bergen', *Evangelische Heidenbote,* 1894, 19–23.

McIver, Lewis and Gabriel Stokes, (1883) *Imperial census of 1881. Operations and results in the Presidency of Madras,* 5 vols. Madras: E. Keys, Government Press.

Mackworth, Digby, (1823) *Diary of a tour through southern India, Egypt, and Palestine in the years 1821 and 1822. By a Field-Officer of Cavalry.* London: J. Hatchard and Son.

Macleane, Charles Donald, (1893) *Manual of the administration of the Madras Presidency, in illustration of the records of government and the yearly administration reports. In three volumes,* Vol III. Madras: Superintendent, Government Press.

Macpherson, Evans, (1820) 'Letter to John Sullivan Esq. Dated June 12, 1820'. In Grigg, 1880, lv-lx [whence my pagination].

McPherson, James, (1870) *The Neilgherry tea planter.* Madras: Higginbotham & Co.

Madras, Government of, (1928) *Statistical appendix for the Nilgiri District. (The Nilgiris,* Vol. II) Madras. Superintendent, Government Press.

—(1949) *A statistical atlas of the Madras Province revised and brought up to date to the end of Fasli 1350 (1940–41).* Madras: Superintendent, Government Press.

—(1958) *Village officers' and ryots' manual.* Madras: Government Press.

—(1965) *A statistical atlas of the Nilgiris District.* Madras: Government Press.

Maffei, Giovanni Pietro, (1589) *Ioan. Petri Maffeii, Bergomatis, è Societate Iesv, Historiarvm indicarvm libri XVI. Selectarvm, item, ex India epistolarum, eodem interprete, libri IV. Accessit Ignatii Loiolae vita. Omnia ab auctore recognita, & nunc primum in Germania excusa. Item, in singula opera copiosus index.* Coloniae Agrippinae, in officina Birckmannica, sumptibus Arnoldi Mylij, Rome.

Malinowski, Bronislaw, (1926) 'Anthropology'. *Encyclopaedia Britannica,* 13th ed., 1st supp. vol. p. 132.

Mandelbaum, David Goodman (1955) 'The world and the world view of the *Kota.*' In *Village India* (McK. Marriott, Ed.) pp. 223–254, Chicago: University of Chicago Press.

—(1960) 'Social trends and personal pressures'. In *Anthropology of Folk Religion* (C.M. Leslie, Ed.) pp. 221–55, New York: Vintage Books.

—(1970) *Society in India,* 2 vols, Berkeley, Los angeles, London University of California Press.

Markham, Clements Robert, (1862) *Travels in Peru and India while superintending the collection of Chinchona plants and seeds in South America, and their introduction into India.* London: John Murray.

Marshall, William Elliot, (1873) *A phrenologist amongst the Todas or the study of a primitive tribe in South India: History, character, customs, religion, infanticide, polyandry, language.* London: Longmans, Green and Co.

Metz Johann Friedrich, (1864) *The tribes inhabiting the neilgherry Hills: Their social customs and religious rites,* 2nd ed. Mangalore: Basel Mission Press.

'Miles, Arthur' (pseud. of GERVEE Baront, afterwards Breckenridge). (1951) *Le culte de Civa,* 2nd ed. Paris: Payot.

Miller, E. Joan. W., (1969) 'The naming of the land in the Arkansas Ozarks: A study in cultural processes', *Annals of the Association of American Geographers,* 59, 240–251.

Mörike, C.E.G., (1858) 'Mission of the Basel Society on the Neilgherries'. In *Proceedings of the South India Missionary Conference, Held at Ootacamund, April 19th–May 5th, 1858* (M. Winslow, J. Sewell, A.B. Campbell, P.S. Royston, Eds.) pp. 94–96, Madras: Society for Promoting Christian Knowledge.

Moses, William, (1964) Tribal awakening in the Nilgiri Hills: The church's responsibility. B. D. thesis, Serampore.

Mueller, Herbert (1909) Untersuchungen über die Geschichte polyandrischen Eheformen in Südindien. Ll.D. diss., Bonn.

Murdock, George Peter, (1949) *Social structure.* New York: Macmillan Co.

Muthanna, I.M., (1953) *A tiny model state of South India.* Mysore: Usha Press.

Naik, Iqbal Abdul Razak. (Mrs. N.K. Wagle), (1966) The culture of the Nilgiri Hills with its catalogue collection at the British Museum. Ph. D. diss., London.

Nambiar, P.K., (1965) *Census of India 1961,* vol. IX, *Madras, Part* X-x, *District Census Handbook, Nilgiris,* vols. I and II. Madras: Huxley Press.

Nambiar, P.K. and T.B. Bharathi, (1965), *Census of India, 1961,* vol. IX, Madras, Part VI, *Village Survey Monographs,* 23. *Nellithorai.* Delhi: Manager of Publications.

Nanjundayya, H.V. and L.K.A. Iyer, (1931) *The Mysore tribes and castes,* Mysore: The Mysore University.

Natesa Sastri, Sangendi Mahalinga, (1892) 'The Baḍagas of the Nīlagiri District', *Madras Christian College Magazine,* IX, 753–764, 830–843.

Nicholson, Frederick Augustus, (1898) *Coimbatore.* Madras: Superintendent, Government Press.

Noble, William Allister, (1967) 'The shifting balance of grasslands, shola forests, and planted trees on the Upper Nilgiris, southern India', *Indian Forester,* 93, 691–693.

—(1968) Cultural contrasts and similarities among five ethnic groups in the Nilgiri District, Madras State, India 1800–1963. Ph.D. diss., Baton Rouge.

—(1976) 'Nilgiri Dolmens (South India)', *Anthropos,* 71, 90–128.

O'Malley, Lewis Sydney Steward, (1941) *Modern India and the West: A study of the interaction of their civilizations.* London: Oxford University Press.

Orans, Martin, (1965) *The Santal: A tribe in search of a great tradition.* Detroit: Wayne State University Press.

Ouchterlony, John, (1848) 'Geographical and statistical memoir of a survey of the Neilgherry Mountains, under the superintendence of Captain J. Ouchterlony. 1847'. *Madras Journal of Literature and Science,* XV, 1–138 [1849].

Périé, Edmond, (1933) 'Mission de Coimbatore. Résumé historique de l'évangélisation des Badagas et bénédiction d'église à Ketti (Nilgiris)', *Bulletin de la Société des Missions-étrangères de Paris,* XII, 96–103, 159–167.

Phythian-Adams, Edward Gwynne Phythian, (1958) *The Madras Regiment 1758–1958.* Wellington: The Defence Services Staff College Press.

Price, John Frederick, (1908) *Ootacamund: A history. Compiled for the Government of Madras.* Madras: Superintendent, Government Press.

Ranga, Nagayya Gogineni, (1934) *The tribes of the Nilgiris (their social and economic conditions).* [Andhra Economic Series, No. 5.] Bezwada: Vani Press.

Rao, Y.V. Lakshmana, (1966) *Communication and development: A study of two*

Indian villages. Minneapolis: University of Minnesota Press.

Réclus, Élie, (1891) *Primitive folk: Studies in comparative ethnology.* New York: Scribner & Welford; London: Walter Scott.

Rhiem, Hanna, (1900) 'Die Badagas', *Allgemeine Missions-Zeitschrift,* XXVII, 497-509.

Rice, Benjamin Lewis, (1894) *Epigraphia Carnatica,* vol. III: *Inscriptions in the Mysore District (Part I); published for Government.* Bangalore: Government Central Press.

—(1897) *Mysore, a gazetteer compiled for Government,* rev. ed., 2 vols. London: Archibald Constable & Co.

'Rifle', (1872) 'The hill tribes of the Neilgherries', *Indian Antiquary,* II, 32 [1873].

Rivers, William Halse Rivers, (1906) *The Todas.* London: Macmillan and Co.

Sarada Raju, A., (1941) *Economic conditions in the Madras Presidency 1800–1850.* Madras: University of Madras.

'Satchit, T.M.', Ed. (pseud. of T.M. Satchidanandam Pillai), (1940) *Who's who in Madras, 1940.* Cochin: The Pearl Press.

Sawday, George W., (1884) 'A visit to Kaity', *Harvest Field,* V, 8–15.

Schad, Friedrick, (1908) 'Arbeit unter den Badaga', *Jahresberichte der evangelischen Missionsgesellschaft zu Basel,* 1908, 132–136.

Schusky, E.L., (1965) *Manual for kinship analysis.* New York: Holt, Rinehart and Winston.

Sewell, R., (1882) *Lists of the antiquarian remains in the Presidency of Madras. Archaeological survey of southern India. Reports. Old Series,* vol. I. Madras: Government Press.

Shaposhnikova, L.V., (1969) *Taĭna plemeni Golubykh gor.* Moscow: Akademia Nauk S.S.S.R.

Shortt, J. and J. Ouchterlony, (1868) *An account of the tribes on the Neilgherries, by J. Shortt . . .and a geographical and statistical memoir of the Neilgherry Mountains, by the late Colonel Ouchterlony.* Madras: Higginbotham & Co.

Simmel, G., (1923) *Soziologie, Untersuchungen über die Formen der Vergesellschaftung.* 3rd ed. Munich & Leipzig: Duncker & Humbolt.

Singer, Milton, (1959) 'The great tradition in a metropolitan center'. In his *Traditional India: Structure and change.* American Folklore Society, Bibliographical and Special Series, X, 141–82.

Sociéte des Missions-Éntrangeres, (1922+) *Bulletin de la Société des Missionsétrangères de Paris.* Hong Kong: Société des Missions-etrangères.

Srinivas, M. N., (1942) *Marriage and family in Mysore.* Bombay: New Book Co.

—(1965) *Religion and society among the Coorgs of South India.* Bombay: Asia Publishing House.

Strokes, William, (1882) 'Mission work amongst the Badagas and other hill tribes on the Nilgiris', *Harvest Field,* III, 169–170.

—(1883a) 'Ein dunkles Bild des Heidenthums', *Evangelische Heidenbote,* 1883, 6–7, 11–12.

—(1883b) 'Mission work on the Nilgiri Hills'. In *Report of the Second Decennial Missionary Conference held at Calcutta, 1882–1883* (J.M. Mitchell and G.H. Rouse, Eds.). Calcutta: J.W. Thomas, Baptist Mission Press.

Stuart, H.A., (1893) *Census of India, 1891,* vol. XIII, *Madras. The report on the census.* Madras: Superintendent, Government Press.

—(1901) *Report on the administration of the police of the Madras Presidency, 1900.*

Madras: Superintendent, Government Press.
Subrahmanyam, C.V., (1962) Socio economic survey, with special reference to the assessment of the effects of plan projects and savings patterns. Mimeo. Ootacamund: Government Arts College.
Sullivan, J., (1819) 'To the editor of the *Government Gazette*'. Copy of an anonymous letter dated 30 Jan., reprinted in Grigg, 1880, lii-lv [whence my pagination].
Tanna, K.J., (1970) *Plantations in the Nilgiris—A synoptic history.* Wellington: C.D. Dhody & Sons.
Thorner, D., (1964) *Agricultural cooperatives in India: A field report.* Bombay: Asia Publishing House.
Thruston, E., (1906) *Ethnographic notes in Southern India.* Madras: Government Press.
—(1909) *Castes and tribes of Southern India,* 7 vols., Madras: Government Press.
—(1912) *Omens and superstitions of Southern India. London,* Leipzig: T. Fisher Unwin.
Tignous, H.P.J.A., (1911) 'In the Nilgherries', *Illustrated Catholic Missions,* XXVI, 99–102, 116–119, 154–157.
Vivekanandam Pillai, T.H., (1937) 'The Badagas', *Journal of the Madras Geographical Association,* XII, 246–250.
Wainwright, F.T., (1962) *Archaeology and place-names and history: An essay on problems of co-ordination.* London: Routledge & Kegan Paul.
Walker, A.R., (1965) Toda social organization and the role of cattle. B. Litt. diss., Oxford.
Wallace, A.F.C., (1956) 'Revitalization movements', *American Anthropologist,* LVIII, 264–287.
—(1966) *Religion: An anthropological view.* New York: Random House.
Ward, B.S., (1821) 'Geographical and statistical memoir of a survey of the Neelgherry Mountains in the province of Coimbatore made in 1821 under the superintendence of Captain B.S. Ward, Deputy Surveyor-General'. In Grigg, 1880, lx-lxxviii [whence my pagination].
Watt. G., (1889) 'Coffea arabica'. In his *A dictionary of the economic products of India.* Vol. II, 460–491. Calcutta; Superintendent of Government Printing, India; London: W.H. Allen & Co.
Weber, M., (1946) *From Max Weber: Essays in sociology.* Trans. by H.H. Gerth and C.W. Mills. New York: Oxford University Press.
—(1947)*The theory of social and economic organization.* Trans. by A.M. Henderson and T. Parsons. New York. Oxford University Press.
Wieland, G., (1900) 'Aus der Nachthütte in Woderu', *Evangelische Heidenbote,* 1900, 85–86.
Wilks, Mark, (1930) *Historical sketches of the South of India, in an attempt to trace the history of Mysoor; from the origin of the Hindoo government of that state, to the extinction of the Mohammedan Dynasty in 1799. Founded chiefly of Indian authorities collected by the author while officiating for several years as political agent at the court of Mysoor, 1810.* Edited with notes by M. Hammick.

2 vols. Mysore: Government Branch Press.

Wiser, W.H., (1936) *The Hindu jajmani system: a socio-economic system inter-relating members of a Hindu village community in service.* Lucknow: Lucknow Publishing House.

Wood, R.C., (1927) *A notebook of agricultural facts and figures.* Madras.

Young, D.S., (1827) 'An account of the general and medical topography of the Neelgerries', *Transactions of the Medical and Physical Society of Calcutta,* IV, 36–78 [1829].

Zvelebil, K., (1955) 'Hospodářské a Společenské Vztahy Nīlagirskych Kmenů'. Československá *Ethnografie,* III, 236–248.

*General Index**

*Phonetic spellings of names have been used except where other spellings are already established in English.

Basin, 103
Basket, 117–118, 124, 130–131, 171
Bazaar, 25–26, 63, 102, 105, 114, 116, 121, 138–146, 152, 156, 160–161, 239–242, 244–245
Bean, 137
Bed, 96, 108, 117, 131
Be:da phratry, 11–12, 15, 17, 19, 27, 33–35, 37, 40–41, 76, 79, 88, 92–93, 97, 217, 223
Be:da Sa:mi (god), 119, 213–214
Beekeeping, 163
Beer, 150, 244
Bees-wax, 124, 128, 136–137, 151
Bell, 122, 261, Plate 11
Belli sept/clan, 30–31, 33, 76, 79–80, 85
Betting, 119
Bezoar, 104
Bhima (god), 42
Bible women, 186
Bibliography, 251–259
Bicycle, 226
Blacksmith, 103, 137, 168, 231
Boat, *see* Coracle
Book, 150, 216
Botanical Gardens, 146
Boundary, 35, 59–60
Bow and arrow, 93, 103, 107, 119
Boycott, 102, 113
Brahma sept, 17, 20, 79, 97, 203
Brahmins, 5, 17, 20, 41, 82, 86, 95, 97, 178, 203, 221, 236
Brewery, 244
Bribery, 160, 173–176, 187, 218
Brick, 105, 168, 185, 194
Bride, 72, 83–84, 217–219, 236
Bridewealth, 133, 140, 196, 217–218, 236
Bridle, 103
British, 7, 21, 45–47, 130, 136, 140, 147, 149, 151–152, 155, 169, 172–173, 180–181, 199–200, 207, 221, 223, 239–240, 242
Broker, 161–163, 225, 242–243
Broom, 171
Buddhists, 43
Buffalo, 46, 58, 73, 77, 90, 100, 105, 109–110, 113, 115, 118, 120, 123, 125, 128–133, 135–139, 150, 169, 184, 200–201, 236, 245
Builder, 104, 119, 130, 152, 163–164, 166, 168, 241
Bullock-cart, 142, 225
Bureaucracy, *see* Official
Burial, 14, 215
Bus, 164, 215–216, 219, 225–227, 230, 237, 243
Businessman, 219, 226, 237
Butter, 116–117, 119, 121, 127–128, 131, 133, 136–137, 139, 143, 150

Cabbage, 149–150, 163, 242
Camera, 226–227
Canarese, *see* Kanarese, Kannada
Candle, 150
Cane, 117, 120, 124, 131, 137, 146
Cannon, 38
Capital, 156–160, 162–163, 219, 242
Car, 227, 243
CARE, 224
Carpenter, 104, 131, 168
Carrion, 105, 131
Carrot, 149–150
Cash, *see* Coinage & Cash
Cash economy, 100, 102–103, 105–106, 114, 116, 118, 136–137, 147–168, 201, 209–210, 223, 230, 240–244
Caste, 5–6, 8, 27, 30, 71, 77–78, 81–82, 96, 165, 208, 217, 221, 223–224, 237, 242
Castration, 103, 108
Catafalque, 94, 107–109, 120, 125, Plates 13 and 14
Cattle, *see* Buffalo, Cow, Ox
Cattleshed, 104
Census, 8, 27, 45, 97, 165–166, 168, 187, 240, 247–249
Central Co-operative Bank, 158–160, 163
Ceremony, 73, 93, 104, 108, 119, 131; *see also* Festival, Fire-walking, Funeral, Marriage, Memorial etc.
Chandra sept, 79
Chariot-dragging, 31, 138, 145–146
Charismatic leader, 207
Chattram, *see* Rest-house
Cheras, 14
Chettiars, 157
Chettis, 7, 32, 100, 116, 121, 126, 129, 138, 142–145, 161, 229, 239

Name Index

*Place-name Index**

*All Nilgiri place-names are rendered according to their Badagu pronunciation, and are expressed phonetically except where other spellings are already well established in English. Diacritical marks follow the usual conventions for Dravidian phonology except that a colon after a vowel (a: & c.) makes it long.